Green Finance and Investment

Promoting Clean Urban Public Transportation and Green Investment in Kyrgyzstan

OECD
BETTER POLICIES FOR BETTER LIVES

Please cite this publication as:
OECD (2019), *Promoting Clean Urban Public Transportation and Green Investment in Kyrgyzstan*, Green Finance and Investment, OECD Publishing, Paris, *https://doi.org/10.1787/b6b91b9a-en*.

ISBN 978-92-64-39276-2 (print)
ISBN 978-92-64-34551-5 (pdf)

Green Finance and Investment
ISSN 2409-0336 (print)
ISSN 2409-0344 (online)

Photo credits: Cover © mika48/Shutterstock.com.

Corrigenda to OECD publications may be found on line at: *www.oecd.org/about/publishing/corrigenda.htm*.

Foreword

This report presents the main findings and conclusions from the project on "Low-Carbon Public Spending at the National Level in Kyrgyzstan: Designing a Green Public Investment Programme", implemented within the framework of co-operation between the Organisation for Economic Co-operation and Development (OECD) and the Kyrgyz Republic (henceforth, also Kyrgyzstan), as well as the GREEN Action Task Force, for which the OECD provides a secretariat.

The main objective of the OECD-Kyrgyzstan co-operation was to assist the partner country in setting out on a greener development path, in particular by reducing the energy and carbon intensity of its economy. Its approach involved assisting the Ministry of Economy to design a green public investment programme in line with good international practices. It aims to demonstrate in practice how to use scarce public funds to encourage the private sector to invest in clean and socially important projects.

The specific focus of the Clean Public Transport (CPT) Programme is on reducing air pollution and greenhouse gas (GHG) emissions from the public transport sector. Two cities were identified to participate in the first pilot phase of the investment programme: Bishkek and Osh. In its second phase, the programme is designed to be extended to cover the suburban areas of the two pilot cities and some key inter-city connections in Kyrgyzstan.

The programme contained four main activity areas and outputs: 1) an initial scoping and analytical stage; 2) a costing methodology; 3) a programme design aligned with international good practice; and 4) an analytical report and training. This report summarises the results.

The report provides an extensive review of environmental legislation – reflecting standards in Kyrgyzstan and the European Union – and technical regulations regarding public transport. It also offers an extensive collection of primary and secondary data on the environment, transport and public services. The stocktaking analysis took into account the country's national green growth and climate change commitments and budgetary requirements. The report also draws on several visits by the project team to Kyrgyzstan in 2018, where they discussed various elements of the investment programme with a number of experts from government offices and local public administrations in Bishkek and Osh, as well as with experts from various international and non-government organisations active in the country.

This project builds on previous work carried out by the OECD in the areas of public environmental expenditure management, integrating the environmental sector into medium-term budgetary processes and on climate change economics. More specifically, it uses a programme costing methodology (called OPTIC) that was developed by the OECD, with support by Germany, and tested previously in Kazakhstan. The methodology is focused on climate-related investment programmes.

The project in Kyrgyzstan was financially supported by Germany's Federal Ministry for the Environment, Nature Conservation and Nuclear Safety (BMU), through its 2014 International Climate Initiative (IKI). It is part of a regional programme – "Strengthening public finance capacity for green investments in the countries of Eastern Europe, Caucasus and Central Asia (EECCA)" – that included two other country case studies: Kazakhstan (completed in 2017) and Moldova (completed in 2019).

Acknowledgements

The project was managed by David Simek (OECD). The costing model and methodology were prepared by Rafal Stanek and the market and programme analysis was co-ordinated by David Toft (both Kommunalkredit Public Consulting/SST Consult). The final version of this study benefited from attentive guidance and constructive comments by Krzysztof Michalak and Nelly Petkova (both OECD).

Substantial input into on-site data collection and support for project in-country co-ordination were provided by Dastan Asylbekov and Nurgul Akimova (independent consultants).

We are also very grateful to Biljana Spasojevic (Kommunalkredit Public Consulting) for sharing with us and our partners their personal and company's experience and expertise – both reflected within this report and in the comprehensive presentations delivered during several country visits.

We also highly appreciate the supportive role of the Kyrgyz Republic's Ministry of Economy; Ministry of Finance; Ministry of Transport and Roads; State Agency for Environmental Protection and Forestry; National Statistical Committee; Investment Promotion and Protection Agency; State Agency for Regulation of the Fuel and Energy Complex; State Committee for Industry, Energy and Subsoil Use; National Energy Holding Company; and, very importantly, the municipalities of Bishkek (including Bishkek City Development Agency) and Osh and their public transport operators.

Appreciation is also extended to colleagues from the UN Partnership for Action on Green Economy (PAGE), the United Nations Development Programme (UNDP) and its Biodiversity Finance Initiative (BIOFIN), German Development Cooperation through GIZ, and the Czech Republic Consulate.

We also express gratitude for co-operation with the European Bank for Reconstruction and Development, Asian Development Bank, Eurasian Development Bank, Russian Kyrgyz Development Fund, Association of Microfinance Institutions, Union of Banks of Kyrgyzstan, and the Kompanion Bank.

The team would also like to thank the Center for Renewable Energy and Energy Efficiency Development, Climate Change Centre of the Kyrgyz Republic, Kyrgyzhydromet, MoveGreen, Bicycle Kyrgyzstan, Public Foundation "Fluid", BizExpert, American University of Central Asia and the "*Achyk Asman*" (Clean Air) Initiative.

We are grateful to all government and non-government experts (practitioners and academics) for their active participation in the stakeholders' meetings and training workshops held as part of the project.

Fiona Hinchcliffe is due a special thanks for her helpful, comprehensive and detailed editorial feedback on the draft report.

Oleg Surduleac professionally translated the report into Russian.

Janine Treves (OECD) attentively assisted with processing the publication. Peter Carlson and Lupita Johanson (OECD) expertly guided the editorial process as well as outreach and communications for the project and disseminating the work.

Irina Belkahia and Aleksandra Bogusz (both OECD) provided excellent administrative support to the project.

All these contributions are gratefully acknowledged. Without the personal and institutional commitment of all these individuals, the project would not have been possible.

The report draws on multiple sources of information, including unpublished material such as documentation from government and state agencies, personal communication with experts and policy makers and questionnaires distributed to the stakeholders during the main project events.

The views expressed in this report are those of the authors and do not necessarily reflect those of the OECD or its member countries.

Table of Contents

Foreword **3**

Acknowledgements **5**

Abbreviations and acronyms **11**

Executive summary **17**

What will the Clean Public Transport Programme involve? 17
What does it aim to achieve? 18
How will it be run and financed? 18
Creating the policy framework for green investment 19

1. Setting the scene for a green public investment programme **21**

1.1. What are the main air pollution and climate change challenges? 22
1.2. What steps have already been taken? 23
1.3. What is this report about? 25
Notes 26
Bibliography 27
Laws and regulations 28

2. Main elements of the Clean Public Transport Programme **29**

2.1. What are the objectives of the Clean Public Transport Programme? 30
2.2. What will the programme involve? 31
2.3. What will the costs and benefits be? 37
2.4. What is thc optimal co-financing level? 45
2.5. What will the implementation set-up be? 47
2.6. What will the timeframe look like? 48
2.7. Conclusions 49
Notes 49
Bibliography 51

3. Economic analysis of the Clean Public Transport Programme **53**

3.1. Overview of clean technologies and fuels in the bus transport sector 54
3.2. Main economic variables of Kyrgyzstan's public transport 57
3.3. Sources and types of financing for investment projects 63
3.4. Conclusions for the CPT Programme 64
Notes 65
Bibliography 66

4. Institutional arrangements and policy framework **67**

4.1. Institutional arrangements for managing public investment programmes 68
4.2. A proposed institutional set-up for the CPT Programme 70
4.3. Fundamental operating regulations 72
4.4. Promoting the programme 73

4.5. Eliminating policy distortions 74
4.6. Conclusions for the CPT Programme 77
Notes 79
Bibliography 80

5. Proposed procedures for project cycle management 81

5.1. Identifying and assessing projects 82
5.2. Preparing programmes 85
5.3. Financing projects 86
5.4. Controlling and monitoring project impacts 88
5.5. Conclusions for the CPT Programme 89
Note 90

6. Macro-economic and environmental overview 91

6.1. Demographic and macro-economic situation 92
6.2. Transport infrastructure in the Kyrgyz Republic 107
6.3. Greenhouse gas emissions and air pollution in the Kyrgyz Republic 123
6.4. Conclusions for the CPT Programme 128
Notes 129
Bibliography 134
Laws and regulations 137

7. Policy and regulatory framework for the transport sector 139

7.1. Regulatory framework affecting urban public transport 140
7.2. Regulatory framework for energy efficiency and fuel standards 148
7.3. Regulatory framework for environmental protection 149
7.4. Regulatory framework for air pollution 150
7.5. International agreements on climate change 150
7.6. Conclusions for the CPT Programme 151
Notes 152
Bibliography 153
Laws and regulations 153

Annex A. Overview of clean technologies and fuels in the transport sector 157

Compressed natural gas vehicles 157
Liquified petroleum gas vehicles 160
Diesel vehicles with Euro VI engines 161
Electricity-powered public transport 163
Notes 166
References 167

Annex B. Explanatory guide for using the OPTIC Model 168

Purpose of the OPTIC Model 168
Preparations for using the OPTIC Model 168
Programme costing for Phase 1 (pilot phase) and Phase 2 (scaling-up phase) 181
Sources of information used in the assumptions 181
Notes 186

Annex C. Example of a project application form 188

Annex D. Example of a project pre-appraisal form 189

Annex E. Example of a project appraisal form **190**

Annex F. List of public transport routes in Bishkek (in Russian) **191**

Tables

Table 2.1. Key costs and benefits of the pilot phase of the CPT Programme in Bishkek 34
Table 2.2. Key costs and benefits of the CPT Programme's pilot phase in Osh 35
Table 2.3. Key costs and benefits of the CPT Programme's pilot phase 36
Table 2.4. Key input and output parameters of the assessed CPT Programme phases 37
Table 2.5. Estimated key costs and benefits of the entire CPT Programme 39
Table 2.6. Summary of CPT Programme costs, Phases 1 and 2 44
Table 2.7. Summary of CPT Programme costs, Phases 1 and 2 44
Table 2.8. Summary of public support for the CPT Programme 46
Table 3.1. Consumption, export and losses of petroleum products, 2011-16 57
Table 3.2. Consumption, export and losses of natural gas, 2011-16 58
Table 3.3. Retail prices for fuel in the Kyrgyz Republic, 2018* 60
Table 3.4. Share of average per capita expenditure on natural gas in the Kyrgyz Republic, 2012-16.. 61
Table 3.5. Production of industrial goods in the Kyrgyz Republic, 2013-18 61
Table 6.1. Population density by region, 2013-17 93
Table 6.3. Distribution of fuel and energy sources, 2011-16 99
Table 6.4. Production of electric power in Kyrgyzstan, 2011-16 100
Table 6.5. Distribution of electric power in Kyrgyzstan 101
Table 6.6. Passengers carried by type of transport in Kyrgyzstan, 2012-18 109
Table 6.7. Freight by type of transport, 2012-18 111
Table 6.13. Overview of national GHG emissions, 1990/2000/2010 112
Table 6.14. Total GHG emissions in EECCA countries, 1990 and 2012 113
Table 6.15. Kyrgyzstan's major GHG emission trends, 2000-14 113
Table 6.16. Sectoral shares in CO_2 emissions in Kyrgyzstan, 1990 and 2018 116
Table 6.8. Passengers on non-electric public transport in Bishkek, 2016 119
Table 6.9. Ownership and age of Bishkek's urban public transport fleet, 2016 119
Table 6.10. Age of urban public transport fleet in Bishkek 120
Table 6.11. Non-electric passenger transport in Osh, 2016 122
Table 6.12. Ownership and age of urban public transport fleet, Osh, 2016 122
Table 6.17. Emissions of air pollutants in Bishkek, Osh and surrounding regions 124
Table 7.1. Ambient air quality standards (mg/m^3) 150

Figures

Figure 0.1. Official exchange rate (LCU per USD, period average) 15
Figure 2.1. Transport's share of GHG emissions in Kyrgyzstan, 1990 and 2010 30
Figure 2.2. Emissions of air pollutants from mobile and stationary sources in Kyrgyzstan, 1990 and 2010 31
Figure 2.3. Aggregate annual emission reductions resulting from the CPT Programme in Kyrgyzstan, 2021-26 39
Figure 2.4. Difference between old and new fleet in Bishkek – carbon dioxide and air pollutant emissions, 2020-26 40
Figure 2.5. Difference between old and new fleet in Osh – carbon dioxide and air pollutants emissions, 2020-23 40

Figure 2.6. Potential carbon dioxide reductions resulting from the CPT Programme 41
Figure 2.7. Potential carbon monoxide and nitrogen oxides reductions resulting from the CPT Programme 42
Figure 2.8. Potential particulates and sulphur dioxide reductions resulting from the CPT Programme 42
Figure 2.9. Total investment costs of the CPT Programme in Bishkek, Osh and other cities............... 43
Figure 2.10. Financing from own sources and public grant 45
Figure 2.11. Relationship between purchase price and fuel costs for diesel and cleaner buses 46
Figure 2.12. Relationship between consumption and fuel price for diesel and cleaner buses............... 47
Figure 2.13. Proposed timeline.. 48
Figure 3.1. The impact of Euro standards on air pollution from light commercial diesel vehicles....... 56
Figure 3.2. Retail sales of automotive fuel, 2018* (by region).. 58
Figure 3.3. Retail sales of automotive fuel in pilot cities and neighbouring oblasts, 2006-18*............ 59
Figure 3.4. Consumption of LPG in Kyrgyzstan, 1992-2012 59
Figure 4.1. Management scheme for the Austrian JI/CDM programme 70
Figure 5.1. Payment scheme 1: beneficiary receives public funds.. 87
Figure 5.2. Payment scheme 2: contractor is paid directly.. 87
Figure 6.1. Natural increase of population in selected EECCA countries, 2000-13 93
Figure 6.2. GDP and inflation growth rates, 2007-17 95
Figure 6.3. Gross regional product per capita, 2017 96
Figure 6.4. Unemployment rate in pilot cities and surrounding regions, 2006-17................................ 97
Figure 6.5. Fossil fuels in Kyrgyzstan – volumes of production, 2006-18 98
Figure 6.6. Average weighted interest rates for newly issued credits, 1996-2018 (by maturity)........ 105
Figure 6.7. Total volume of credits, 2019* (by sector) 106
Figure 6.8. Passenger transportation by transport enterprises in selected EECCA countries, 2000-13108
Figure 6.9. Passenger turnover in pilot cities and surrounding *oblasts* (all transport)........................ 109
Figure 6.10. Share of transport means in Kyrgyzstan, 2017 110
Figure 6.11. GHG emissions per capita in EECCA countries, 1990 and 2012 112
Figure 6.12. GHG emissions from transport in Kyrgyzstan, 1990 and 2010 114
Figure 6.13. CO_2 emissions by sector in Kyrgyzstan, 1990-2018.. 115
Figure 6.14. CO_2 emissions from liquid and gaseous fuel consumption in Kyrgyzstan, 1992-2014.. 116
Figure 6.15. Emission of air pollutants from stationary sources in Bishkek, Osh and surrounding regions, 2011-15 123
Figure 6.16. Assumed amount of health-damaging substances emitted per distance travelled (normative)* 126
Figure 6.17. Assumed amount of health-damaging substances emitted per distance travelled (real)* 127
Figure 6.18. Incidence of respiratory diseases Bishkek, Osh and surrounding regions, 2011-15 127

Boxes

Box 2.1. The OPTIC model.. 38
Box 4.1. Proposing a sensitivity analysis 76
Box 6.1. The impact of diesel exhaust emissions.. 125

Abbreviations and acronyms

ADB	Asian Development Bank
ATM	Automated teller machine
BAU	Business as usual (scenario)
BMNT	(Austrian) Federal Ministry for Sustainability and Tourism *(Bundesministerium für Nachhaltigkeit und Tourismus)*
BMU	(German) Federal Ministry for the Environment, Nature Conservation and Nuclear Safety *(Bundesministerium für Umwelt, Naturschutz und nukleare Sicherheit)*
BRT	Bus rapid transit (system)
CAREC	Central Asia Regional Economic Cooperation (Program)
CAREC	Regional Environmental Centre for Central Asia
CDM	Clean development mechanism
CHP	Combined heat and power (plant)
CI	Compression ignition
CIS	Commonwealth of Independent States
CNG	Compressed natural gas
COP	Conference of the Parties (to the UNFCCC)
CPT	Clean Public Transport (OECD Programme)
CRI	Climate risk index
EAEU	Eurasian Economic Union
EBRD	European Bank for Reconstruction and Development
EC	European Commission
EC	European Community
EECCA	Eastern Europe, Caucasus and Central Asia
EEA	European Economic Area
EEA	European Environment Agency
EEC	Eurasian Economic Commission
EEC	European Economic Community
EECCA	Eastern Europe, Caucasus and Central Asia
EEV	Enhanced environmentally friendly vehicle
EIB	European Investment Bank
EMEP	European Monitoring and Evaluation Programme
EU	European Union
EUR	Euro (Eurozone currency)

GCF	Green Climate Fund
GDP	Gross domestic product
GEF	Global Environment Facility
GGE	Gasoline gallon equivalent
GHG	Greenhouse gas (emissions)
GIZ	German Development Cooperation *(Deutsche Gesellschaft für Internationale Zusammenarbeit)*
GNI	Gross national income
GoK	Government of Kyrgyzstan
GOST	State/national *(Gosudarstvennyj)* (standard)
GWP	Global warming potential
HPP	Hydroelectric power plant
ICCT	International Council on Clean Transportation
IFC	International Finance Corporation
IFI	International financial institution
IKI	International Climate Initiative *(Internationale Klimaschutzinitiative)* of Germany
IMF	International Monetary Fund
INDC	Intended nationally determined contribution
IPCC	Intergovernmental Panel on Climate Change
IPPA	Investment Promotion and Protection Agency of the Kyrgyz Republic
IU	Implementation unit
JI	Joint implementation
JSC	Joint stock company
KGS	Kyrgyzstani som (national currency of Kyrgyzstan)
KPC	Kommunalkredit Public Consulting
LNG	Liquefied natural gas
LPG	Liquefied petroleum gas
LRTAP	Long-range Transboundary Air Pollution (Convention)
LULUCF	Land use, land-use change and forestry
MAC	Maximum allowable concentration
MTEF	Medium-term expenditure framework
NAMA	Nationally appropriate mitigations action
NCF	Net cash flow
NGO	Non-governmental organisation
NMVOC	Non-methane volatile organic compound
NPV	Net present value

NSC	National Statistical Committee of the Kyrgyz Republic
OECD	Organisation for Economic Co-operation and Development
OJSC	Open joint stock company
OPTIC	Optimising Public Transport Investment Costs (OECD Model)
PAGE	Partnership for Action on Green Economy
PCM	Project cycle management
PE	Programming entity
PI	Positive ignition
PM	Particulate matter
PPP	Public-private partnership
PPP	Purchasing power parity
PTO	Public transport operator
SAEPF	State Agency on Environmental Protection and Forestry (of Kyrgyzstan)
SME	Small and medium-sized enterprise
TLV	Threshold limit value
TSU	Technical support unit
UN	United Nations
UNDP	United Nations Development Programme
UNFCCC	United Nations Framework Convention on Climate Change
US	United States
USAID	United States Agency for International Development
USD	United States dollar
VAT	Value added tax
WB	World Bank
WHO	World Health Organization

Units, quantities and compounds

cm	Centimetre
cm^2	Square centimetre
CH_4	Methane
CH_2O	Formaldehyde
CO	Carbon monoxide
CO_2	Carbon dioxide
g	Gram
Gg	Gigagram
GWh	Gigawatt hour

H_2O	Water
kcal	Kilocalorie
kg	Kilogramme
km	Kilometre
km^2	Square kilometre
km/h	Kilometres per hour
koe	Kilogram of oil equivalent
kpvpd	Kilometre per vehicle per day
kt	Kilotonne
kWh	Kilowatt hour
l	Litre
m	Metre
mg	Milligram
MJ	Megajoule
mln	Million
MPa	Megapascal
MW	Megawatt
MWh	Megawatt hour
m^3	Cubic metre
NH_3	Ammonia
NO	Nitric oxide
NO_x	Nitrogen oxides
N_2O	Nitrous oxide
ppm	Parts per million
p-km	Passenger-kilometre
SO_2	Sulphur dioxide
t	Tonne
tCO_2	Tonne of CO_2
tCO_2e	Tonne of CO_2 equivalent
tNO_x	Tonne of NO_x
tPM2.5	Tonne of PM2.5
tSO_2	Tonne of SO_2
TJ	Terajoule
TWh	Terawatt hour
t-km	Tonne-kilometre
µg	Microgram

Figure 0.1. Official exchange rate (LCU per USD, period average)

KGS/USD

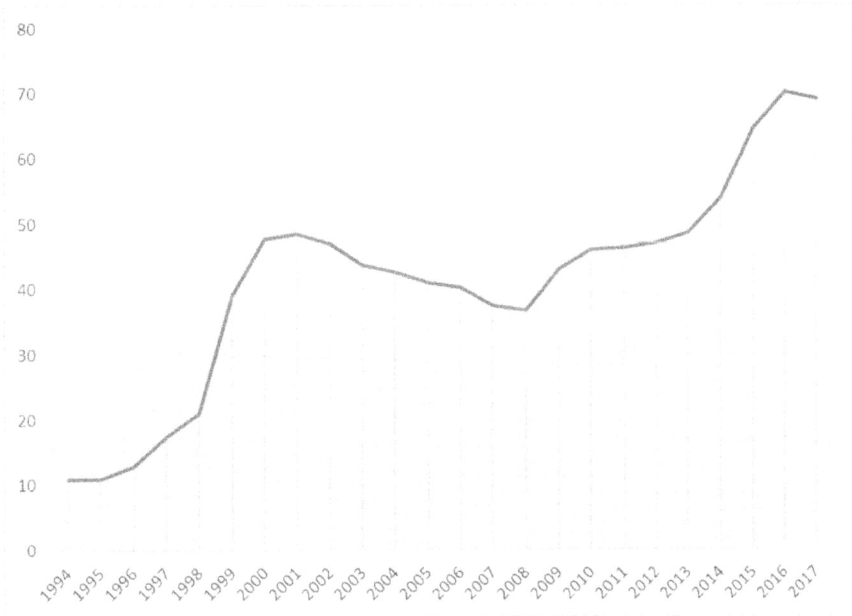

Note: As a reference exchange rate, the report takes the 2017 average of KGS 68.867 per USD (and EUR 0.877 per USD).
Source: World Bank (https://data.worldbank.org).

Executive summary

The transport sector is responsible for 28% of Kyrgyzstan's greenhouse gas (GHG) emissions, and in cities like Bishkek, for 75% of air pollutants. Within the transport sector, almost all GHG and air pollutants emissions can be attributed to road transport – 99% and 100%, respectively. Most public transport vehicles are old and in need of replacement.

The volume of air pollution emissions in Bishkek is also almost three times as high as the surrounding Chui Region, despite being over 100 times smaller in surface area. The topography of cities like Bishkek – which are situated between mountains – contributes to inversions that trap pollutants in the ambient air. From 2011 to 2015, Bishkek experienced a 20% increase in the incidence of respiratory diseases; Osh – the second largest city saw a 14% increase. World Health Organization statistics show that diseases of the circulatory system are the main cause of death in Kyrgyzstan (50% of early deaths in 2018). Pollution from urban transport is seen as an (increasingly) important contributor to these health problems.

In 2016, the Organisation for Economic Co-operation and Development (OECD) and the Kyrgyz Republic joined forces to analyse how a public investment programme could spur the development of cleaner public transport, and reduce air pollution and greenhouse gas (GHG) emissions from the public transport sector in the country's large urban centres. It was agreed that the main focus of the Clean Public Transport (CPT) Programme would be on supporting the shift to modern buses powered by cleaner fuels, such as compressed natural gas and liquefied petroleum gas.

The preparation for the programme involved four main activity areas and outputs: 1) an initial scoping and analytical stage; 2) development of a programme costing methodology; 3) design of a programme in line with international good practices; and 4) preparation of an analytical report and training. This report is the culmination of the preparation process and presents the results of the four main activity areas.

What will the Clean Public Transport Programme involve?

The CPT Programme is designed to be implemented in two phases:

- Phase 1, the pilot phase, covering the cities of Bishkek and Osh. This will run for a period of 1-2 years and aims to replace diesel-powered buses and minibuses, as well as outdated trolleybuses in Bishkek, with 98 **trolleybuses** and 118 compressed natural gas **(CNG) buses**. In Osh, 17 trolleybuses and 170 new CNG buses would replace outdated stock. In both cases, these purchases would also enable the expansion of services. Total investments for the pilot phase are estimated at **KGS 4 088 million (USD 59.36 million)**, of which KGS 2 037 (USD 29.58 million) in public financing will be required.
- Phase 2, the scaling-up phase, will extend the programme to the suburban areas of Bishkek and Osh (over 40 new settlements) as well as inter-city transport routes. It will last up to 5 years. It foresees the purchase of 730 additional new **CNG buses**

in Bishkek, 80 in Osh and 60 for the inter-city transport routes (i.e. a total of 870). Inter-city transport will also be strengthened with 90 **new diesel** buses. The total estimated investments for this phase would amount to **KGS 9 603 million (USD 139.43 million)**, of which KGS 3 762 million (USD 54.63 million) in public financing will be required.

In total, both phases of the CPT Programme would result in 1 363 new urban, suburban and inter-city public transport vehicles – 1 158 CNG buses, 115 trolleybuses and 90 modern diesel buses. Total investment costs for the entire programme are estimated at **KGS 13 691 million (USD 198.8 million)**, including KGS 5 799 million (USD 84.21 million) of public support.

What does it aim to achieve?

The CPT Programme is primarily designed to reduce the high levels of air pollution in urban centres. This includes **reducing emissions** of pollutants that form smog, such as carbon monoxide (CO), sulphur dioxide (SO_2), nitrogen oxides (NO_x) and particulate matter (PM). The programme also aims to reduce GHG emissions, in particular carbon dioxide (CO_2), in line with Kyrgyzstan's national and international commitments. In terms of emission reductions, the most significant improvements are expected to be in NO_x emissions, which would decline by about 1 236 tonnes a year following the two phases. Carbon dioxide emissions are estimated to decline by between 68 506 and 124 542 tonnes a year after the two phases. Particulate emissions – a significant air quality and public health problem in Bishkek – would be expected to decrease by a total of 29 tonnes a year under both phases.

The environmental objectives of the CPT Programme are expected to be accomplished by using state budget support (subsidies in the form of grants) to invest in replacing the outdated public transport fleet with modern vehicles powered by cleaner fuels or technologies, including compressed natural gas (CNG)/liquefied natural gas (LNG), liquefied petroleum gas (LPG), Euro 5/6 diesel and electricity.

The **public service** impacts will include greater transport reliability and comfort, and an extended and better service outside cities. By modernising the urban transport fleet, the CPT Programme will also contribute to municipalities' **socio-economic development** and, ultimately, that of the country. This will be achieved for instance by increasing the efficiency, reliability and reach of public transport networks. Improved mobility not only fosters productivity (access to jobs, markets) but also social inclusion (access to hospitals, schools), especially for low-income groups of society. The programme could also stimulate the domestic market to produce, or at least assemble, modern buses and trolleybuses through supporting the purchase of new buses, rather than the modernisation of engines. This could also generate new employment opportunities.

How will it be run and financed?

Implementing the CPT Programme will require **institutional arrangements** that ensure transparent and cost-effective decision making. The report suggests a three-level institutional structure comprising: 1) a programming entity; 2) an implementation unit; and 3) a technical support unit. It also lays out clear project cycle management procedures.

Although the CPT Programme is expected to be **financially supported** by a mix of public funds (national and international), the main source of financing will in most cases come from transport operators themselves, including their revenue, profits or commercial loans (in the future). Calculating the optimal level of public support to co-finance the purchase of cleaner vehicles was an important element of the analysis – financing should be designed to increase investment. As new vehicles are less polluting but also more expensive, state support will allow private operators to choose this option. It is proposed that the programme proceed without the involvement of the commercial banking sector.

The analysis showed that the average local price of CNG and LPG fuels is much lower than world prices, and much lower than petrol and diesel prices (which are also subject to an additional excise tax). Given the significant efficiency gains to be realised from replacing ageing and inefficient diesel-powered vehicles, the programme is expected to be financially attractive to investors.

The proposed investment "pipelines" under the CPT Programme will also need to be accompanied by **supporting investments**, either from public or private sources. These will be needed in infrastructure, such as new trolleybus lines, refuelling and charging stations, maintenance workshops; and other investment to improve the transport system in urban centres, such as creating separate bus lanes, improving bus stops and smart traffic control.

Creating the policy framework for green investment

The research and discussions in Kyrgyzstan revealed some obstacles to the implementation of the programme. These (and other) shortcomings should be addressed as complementary policy actions during programme preparation, as a prerequisite for its successful launch and implementation:

- **Inadequate resources for programme preparation and management.** The CPT Programme requires significant preparatory work, including fundraising, and building the capacity for project selection, implementation and monitoring (project cycle management).
- **Limited creditworthiness of private operators in public transport.** Regardless of how the CPT Programme is co-financed, bus owners will need to use loans or leasing for their share of the investment. Their limited creditworthiness could be overcome – besides using public subsidies in the form of grants – if the CPT Programme was to provide bank guarantees. Commercial loans to purchase modern buses are uncommon, however.
- **Inadequate passenger fares and collection system.** Fares for public transport are low in Kyrgyzstan – USD 0.12 for a single ride ticket in Bishkek and USD 0.09 in Osh. The manual fare collection system is also inefficient. This is undermining the profitability of public transport. Fare rates and collection methods must therefore be improved so that passenger fares alone, or in combination with a subsidy, can ensure the viability of private bus operators (who unlike municipal operators, are not subsidised).
- **Insufficient co-ordination and communication.** Public transport is provided by city-owned and private operators under short-term contracts (up to three years). Most private operators use minibuses. The goal to replace many minibuses by larger buses in the urban centres needs to be better communicated to all stakeholders (as well as details on future routes, the transport means to be used, how many buses will be needed and who will operate them).

- **Low emission norms and technical inspection standards.** Current emission norms are based on old diesel emission standards (Euro IV and lower) and the system of technical inspections of vehicles does not function properly. While Europe instituted the Euro 6/VI standard back in 2014, Euro 5 standards will only come into effect in Kyrgyzstan in 2019, and only for fuel, not engines. At the moment, the available diesel fuel in the country mostly only meets Euro 3 standards.
- **Weak pricing signals for the use of CNG and LPG-fuelled buses versus diesel.** Although CNG and LPG are cheaper than diesel, there are no other price incentives, such as VAT or duty tax exemption, for clean(er) transport or infrastructure. As the initial investment in alternatively fuelled/powered buses is higher, the decision to invest can be influenced by financial stimulus. Until critical mass is achieved (i.e. a sufficient market share and revenues), tax incentives could complement state support mechanisms such as grants, loans and loan guarantees.
- **Lack of proper financial products tailored to the needs of the sector**. The financial sector in Kyrgyzstan is relatively small and dominated by banks. High interest rates and collateral on loans limit their function as financial intermediaries. Banks are also constrained by limited trust from potential depositors, a lack of good bankable projects and a low rate of loan recovery.
- **Weak governance of the power sector.** Although energy companies were privatised in 2001, electricity prices are still regulated. Recent reforms have introduced a fixed progressive electricity tariff system divided into six groups of final consumers. The higher tariffs for trolleybus networks and budget institutions compensate for the lower tariffs for some users (including residential and pumping stations) that do not cover the energy producer's operating costs. The result has been deteriorating infrastructure due to deferred maintenance and chronic underspending on capital expenditures (despite direct and indirect subsidies).
- **Lack of interest in purchasing more fuel-efficient vehicles.** Apart from setting the right incentives at the policy level, the government also needs to provide correct, sufficient and timely information to eliminate consumer uncertainty about new technologies (e.g. their useful life) and fuels (e.g. future fuel prices). This could be one role for the government implementation unit of the CPT Programme.

1. Setting the scene for a green public investment programme

This chapter provides a brief overview of the main environmental issues facing Kyrgyzstan's energy and transport sectors, to set the scene for the proposed Clean Public Transport Programme. It reviews the key policy documents and international environmental agreements to which the country is committed in order to adopt a greener development path, and outlines the structure of this report.

1.1. What are the main air pollution and climate change challenges?[1]

Kyrgyzstan's greenhouse gas (GHG) emissions are relatively low. This can largely be explained by the prevalence of hydroelectric power plants (HPPs), which provide about 90% of the country's total electricity generation. However, climate change impacts are expected to decrease water flows from the 2030s onwards, consequently reducing the potential of hydroelectric power. As a result, given an annual gross domestic product (GDP) growth of 4%, the electricity demand of Kyrgyzstan's economy will be much higher than can be met by hydropower.

Around 95% of Kyrgyzstan's carbon dioxide (CO_2) emissions stem from the energy sector, while 63% of methane emissions are attributed largely to agriculture. Nevertheless, Kyrgyzstan has significant potential for unconventional and renewable energy sources – especially solar, hydropower and geothermal energy and biogas (though conditions are inadequate for expanding wind power[2]) (GoK, 2016[1]). However, since the late 1990s the shares of energy generated by hydropower stations and by burning of fossil fuels have hardly changed (90% vs. 10%, +/-5 percentage points, see Section 6.1.4).

In 2012, Kyrgyzstan's GHG emissions equalled 13.8 million tCO_2e (tonnes of carbon dioxide equivalent), amounting to 0.026% of global GHG emissions (whereas the country accounted for 0.079% of the world population in 2012). Between 1990 and 2012, Kyrgyzstan's GHG emissions fell by 58.6% in total (67.5% per capita), energy use per capita declined by 56.8%, and renewable electricity output (as a share of total output) increased by 30 percentage points. Despite this progress, CO_2 intensity (CO_2 emitted per energy use) slightly increased (by 8.7%) in the same period, and the energy intensity of the economy (GDP per energy use) was only 51.7% of the world average in 2012 (3.89 – constant 2011 purchasing power parity international dollar per kg of oil equivalent – compared to the world average of 7.53).[3]

Kyrgyzstan is one of the most vulnerable countries to climate change, especially in terms of water resources, health, agriculture, and climate emergency situations. In 2017, Kyrgyzstan ranked 52nd overall on the Germanwatch Global Climate Risk Index (CRI), but came 11th for the number of fatalities per 100 000 inhabitants (Eckstein and et al., 2019[2]). Climate change also negatively influences human health through the increase in number of days with abnormally high temperatures (which will mainly affect elderly people, those suffering from cardiovascular diseases, as well as the poorest part of population – 70% of whom are women in Kyrgyzstan). Preventive adaptation measures are outlined in Priorities for Adaptation to Climate Change in the Kyrgyz Republic till 2017 (updated to 2020), and aim to minimise threats to ecosystems, human health, economic development, property and infrastructure (GoK, 2013[3]).

The transport sector is responsible for 28% of Kyrgyzstan's GHG emissions, and in cities like Bishkek, for 75% of air pollutants. Most public transport vehicles are old and in need of replacement: of the country's entire public transport fleet (about 6 240 vehicles in 2017), about 54% are 15 years or older. Therefore, more than half the fleet is beyond its useful life. In the minibus fleet (5 370 vehicles), the situation is even worse – around 89% of the fleet is over 10 years old. Buses and minibuses mostly run on diesel, while diesel engines typically meet only Euro IV/4 standards or lower. Structural and technical features – i.e. the importance of road transport for the country combined with an inadequate network of technical inspection centres – also make vehicle transport an important contributor to air pollution in Kyrgyzstan.

Kyrgyzstan continues to lag behind advanced countries in the development of modern emission norms for both passenger cars as well as heavy-duty truck and bus engines. Since 2013, post-Soviet GOST[4] standards have been applicable to member states of the Eurasian Economic Union (EAEU). In 2014, the Eurasian Economic Commission (EEC) increased standards to Euro 5. These are set to come into effect in Kyrgyzstan in 2019, but only for fuels – not vehicle engines (vehicle emission requirements and the associated fuels do not necessarily align).[5]

1.2. What steps have already been taken?

To date, the Kyrgyz Republic has signed and ratified 13 international environmental conventions. It ratified the United Nations Framework Convention on Climate Change (UNFCCC) in January 2000 and the Kyoto Protocol in January 2003. In November 2006, Kyrgyzstan signed – together with Tajikistan and Turkmenistan – the Framework Convention on Environmental Protection for Sustainable Development in Central Asia. Most recently, in September 2016, Kyrgyzstan signed the Paris Agreement on Climate Change which was adopted at the 21st Conference of the Parties (COP21) in Paris in December 2015 (Box 1.1).

Box 1.1. Kyrgyzstan's greenhouse gas emissions targets

The Paris Agreement requires all Parties to put forward their best efforts to reduce greenhouse gas emissions through their nationally determined contributions (NDCs), and to strengthen these efforts in the years ahead. Kyrgyzstan's NDC identifies both "conditional" (those that depend on sufficient international support) and "unconditional" targets for mitigation and adaptation.

The country's unconditional mitigation target is to reduce GHG emissions in the range of 11.5-13.8% compared to business as usual (BAU) by 2030, and 12.7-15.7% below BAU by 2050. The conditional target is to reduce GHG emissions in the range of 29.0-30.9% below BAU by 2030, and from 35.1-36.8% below BAU by 2050, subject to international support available to the country (including low-cost financial resources, technology transfer and technical co-operation). See Section 7.5 for more details.

Source: (GoK, 2015[4]) *Intended Nationally Determined Contribution – Submission of the Kyrgyz Republic*, Government of Kyrgyzstan, Bishkek, https://www4.unfccc.int/sites/submissions/INDC/Published%20Documents/Kyrgyzstan/1/Kyrgyzstan%20INDC%20_ENG_%20final.pdf.

The Climate Change Co-ordination Commission, headed by the First Vice Prime Minister of the Kyrgyz Republic, co-ordinates all the activities in Kyrgyzstan related to climate change to meet the country's commitments under the UNFCCC. The commission is composed of all the heads of key ministries and divisions, and representatives of the civil, academic and business sectors.

Although Kyrgyzstan accessed the 1979 Convention on Long-range Transboundary Air Pollution (LRTAP Convention) in May 2000, until recently, air pollution in the country had received much less attention than other environmental issues, including climate.

According to data from the National Statistical Committee of the Kyrgyz Republic (NSC), stationary sources alone are responsible for releasing around 50 000 tonnes of harmful substances into the air annually (NSC, 2016[5]). Urban transport, however, outweighs stationary sources – based on data from the State Agency for Environmental Protection and Forestry (SAEPF), the annual total pollutant emissions into the atmosphere from Bishkek amount to 240 000 tonnes, of which 180 000 tonnes are from motor vehicles (Levina, 2018[6]). More importantly, over half of all air pollutants fall (literally) on the city of Bishkek (situated between mountains).

To address these challenges, national legislation and strategic documents on environmental policy and climate change have been improved. Amendments have been introduced to the Kyrgyz Republic's laws on environmental protection, atmospheric air (both adopted 1999 and last amended 2016), renewable energy sources (adopted 2008, last amended 2012), public health (adopted 2009, amended 2014), the forest code (adopted 1999, last amended 2014) and the water code (adopted 2005). Networks have also been established to bring together groups working on climate change (e.g. the Climate Network of the Kyrgyz Republic, set up in 2009).

Prior to participating in the United Nations Conference on Sustainable Development (or RIO+20) in 2012, Kyrgyzstan developed Priorities of the Green Economy in the Kyrgyz Republic. These were to be facilitated by attracting foreign and domestic "green" investments aimed at promoting new technologies to improve the energy and resource efficiencies of both production and consumption and to reduce emissions and pollution. This led to the establishment of the National Council for Sustainable Development under the President of the Kyrgyz Republic.

Since 2013, priorities for an effective energy policy had been reflected in the National Sustainable Development Strategy 2013-2017. The strategy also focused on energy efficiency and introducing renewable energy sources – including solar energy, wind, water, geothermal sources and biofuel – as key environmental priorities. Green technologies were to be promoted through the introduction of new financial tools such as green taxes, customs duties, green procurement and green investments (GoK, 2013[7]). To implement the strategy, Kyrgyzstan adopted the Programme on Transition to Sustainable Development 2013-2017 and its associated Five-Year Plan "of Creation" – 2017 (GoK, 2013[8]).

In 2018, the National Council for Sustainable Development adopted a new National Development Strategy 2018-2040 ("*Zhany Doorgo – kyrk kadam*"). One of the government's medium-term priority areas to 2023 is to improve the population's living conditions, including better (regional) infrastructure as well a safe environment conducive to human health. In the transport sector, the strategy foresees a gradual transition to environmentally friendly modes of transport through the use of electric vehicles and electrification of railways (GoK, 2018[9]). The quality of public transport services is also addressed by the Development Programme 2018-2022 "Unity. Trust. Creation" (GoK, 2018[10]). One of the objectives of the Road Transport Development Strategy 2012-2015 was to improve the technical condition of motor vehicles based on the experience of other countries, and to limit the operation of those whose emissions of harmful pollutants exceed the established standards (GoK, 2012[11]).

Recommended actions for the Kyrgyz Republic within the framework of the UN Partnership for Action on Green Economy (PAGE) include introducing at the national level processes for implementing economic modelling to guide the transition to a green economy and sustainable development.[6] However, the economic situation means the country cannot implement the planned measures with regard to climate change (adaptation and mitigation) or transition to green economy (to be reflected in the upcoming Green Economy Concept) entirely through internal resources.

As the global climate regime is evolving, donors and international financial institutions (IFIs) are already starting to invest significant resources to support non-Annex I Parties. International carbon finance mechanisms, such as the Green Climate Fund (GCF), are known to rely to a great extent on country-based systems for programme and project identification and implementation. Those countries that develop the necessary skills to prepare sound public expenditure programmes and identify a pipeline of cost-effective projects will be more competitive and will stand better chances of benefiting from international support.

In order to be successful, the Ministry of Economy, as a major player in climate change policy in the country, will need to develop the necessary practical skills to prepare economically sound public investment programmes that can compete effectively for support and leverage funds from both budgetary and donor sources. These programmes need to be also integrated into national development strategies and medium-term budgetary processes (such as medium-term expenditure frameworks or MTEFs). In addition, government administrations need to be willing to apply good practices in public expenditure management, such as accountability, transparency and efficiency.

Based on information from previous work by the OECD in this field, Kyrgyzstan has introduced sectoral MTEFs in health, education and agriculture; however, donor funds are not integrated in the MTEFs. Although the Kyrgyz Government has accumulated some experience with MTEF design, the practice needs to be extended to other (environmental) sectors, including actual implementation. The Kyrgyz Government will need to ensure that it puts in place climate-related investment programmes which will identify the most cost-effective projects to be supported with public funds.

1.3. What is this report about?

In 2017, the OECD and Kyrgyzstan joined forces to analyse how a public investment programme could spur the development of cleaner public transport, and reduce air pollution and GHG emissions from public transport in large urban centres in the country. It was agreed that the main focus of the programme would be to support the shift to modern buses powered by clean fuels, such as compressed natural gas (CNG) and liquefied petroleum gas (LPG).

The preparation of the programme (henceforth the "project") involved four main activity areas and outputs: 1) an initial scoping and analytical stage; 2) development of a programme costing methodology; 3) design of a programme in line with international good practices; and 4) preparation of an analytical report and training. Activity areas 2 and 3 constituted the backbone of the project, which aimed to demonstrate in practice how to use scarce public funds to encourage the private sector to invest in clean and socially important projects.

The programme implementation will require institutional arrangements that ensure transparent and cost-effective decision-making. The report analyses several institutional options. The institutional set-up proposed in this study includes three levels: 1) a programming entity; 2) an implementation unit; and 3) a technical support unit. Their roles and responsibilities are presented in detail in the report.

This report is the culmination of the investment programme preparation process, and presents the results of the scoping analysis. It is organised as follows:

- Chapter 2 presents the CPT Programme, and provides estimates of its costs and expected environmental and socio-economic benefits. The chapter also lays out the financing strategy and optimal co-financing level.
- Chapter 3 presents market analyses for clean technologies and fuels in the bus transport sector in Kyrgyzstan and, on this basis, assesses the viability of the investment programme. The production and import of buses were examined to assess domestic capacity for meeting the need for bus replacements.
- Chapter 4 discusses the institutional arrangements for managing the CPT Programme.
- Chapter 5 presents an overview of the project cycle management (PCM) procedures developed for each project pipeline identified as part of this programme.
- Chapter 6 briefly describes the main demographic, macro-economic and environmental issues in Kyrgyzstan relevant to the transport sector. It also presents an overview of the urban public transport system, level of GHG emissions and air pollution in the main urban centres and the major health risks associated with the main air pollutants.
- Chapter 7 describes the current policy and regulatory framework in the transport sector.
- Annex A presents an overview of clean technologies and fuels in the transport sector, while Annex B explains the use of the OPTIC (Optimising Public Transport Investment Costs) model. Annexes C-E contain sample project application and appraisal forms.

Notes

1. This brief review draws on a more detailed analysis presented in Chapter 6.

2. Wind power plants are only economically feasible in areas with a sufficient average annual wind speed and a constant wind direction. In Kyrgyzstan's mountainous terrain, such conditions can only be found in remote and sparsely populated areas (GoK, 2016[1]).

3. See World Bank (WB) country data on Kyrgyzstan at: https://data.worldbank.org/country/kyrgyz-republic.

4. Russian: ГОСТ = state.

5. Personal communication with the Center for Renewable Energy and Energy Efficiency Development (www.creeed.net).

6. UN PAGE Kyrgyzstan (www.un-page.org). See also: www.kg.undp.org/content/kyrgyzstan/en/home/projects/partnership-for-action-on-green-economy.html.

Bibliography

Eckstein, D. and et al. (2019), *Global Climate Risk Index 2019: Who Suffers Most From Extreme Weather Events? Weather-related Loss Events in 2017 and 1998 to 2017*, Briefing Paper, Germanwatch, Bonn, https://www.germanwatch.org/sites/germanwatch.org/files/Global%20Climate%20Risk%20Index%202019_2.pdf. [2]

GoK (2018), *Development Programme of the Kyrgyz Republic for the period 2018-2022*, Government of Kyrgyzstan, Bishkek, http://www.un-page.org/files/public/the_development_program_of_the_kyrgyz_republic_for_the_period_2018-2022.pdf. [10]

GoK (2018), *National Development Strategy of the Kyrgyz Republic for 2018-2040*, Government of Kyrgyzstan, Bishkek, http://donors.kg/images/National_Development_Strategy_of_KR_2018-2040_final_ENG.docx. [9]

GoK (2016), *Third National Communication of the Kyrgyz Republic under the UN Framework Convention on Climate Change*, Government of Kyrgyzstan, Bishkek, https://unfccc.int/sites/default/files/resource/NC3_Kyrgyzstan_English_24Jan2017.pdf. [1]

GoK (2015), *Intended Nationally Determined Contribution - Submission fo the Kyrgyz Republic*, Government of Kyrgyzstan, Bishkek, https://www4.unfccc.int/sites/submissions/INDC/Published%20Documents/Kyrgyzstan/1/Kyrgyzstan%20INDC%20_ENG_%20final.pdf. [4]

GoK (2013), *National Sustainable Development Strategy for the Kyrgyz Republic for the period 2013-2017*, Government of Kyrgyzstan, Bishkek, https://www.un-page.org/files/public/kyrgyz_national_sustainable_development_strategy.pdf. [7]

GoK (2013), *Priorities for Adaptation to Climate Change in the Kyrgyz Republic till 2017 (in Russian)*, Government of Kyrgyzstan, Bishkek, http://www.ecology.gov.kg/page/view/id/124. [3]

GoK (2013), *Programme for the transition of the Kyrgyz Republic to sustainable development for 2013-2017, (in Russian)*, Government of Kyrgyzstan, Bishkek, http://cbd.minjust.gov.kg/act/view/ru-ru/53067. [8]

GoK (2012), *Strategy for Development of Road Transport in the Kyrgyz Republic for 2012-2015 (in Russian)*, Government of Kyrgyzstan, Bishkek, http://cbd.minjust.gov.kg/act/view/ru-ru/93738?cl=ru-ru. [11]

Levina, M. (2018), *"Smog over Kyrgyzstan capital city: causes, effects, and solutions"*, The Times of Central Asia, 27 January, http://www.timesca.com/index.php/news/26-opinion-head/19261-smog-over-kyrgyzstan-capital-city-causes-effects-and-solutions (accessed on 30 August 2019). [6]

NSC (2016), *Environment in the Kyrgyz Republic, Statistical Compilation 2011-2015*, National Statistical Committee of the Kyrgyz Republic, Bishkek, http://stat.kg/media/publicationarchive/8c0e9d22-6bb6-4145-b1d6-8311da33521d.pdf. [5]

Laws and regulations

(listed by most recent publishing date, in Russian)

Presidential Decree No. 221 of 31 October 2018 "On National Development Strategy of the Kyrgyz Republic for 2018-2040", http://stat.kg/ru/ukaz-prezidenta-kyrgyzskoj-respubliki-o-nacionalnoj-strategii-razvitiya-kyrgyzskoj-respubliki-na-2018-2040-gody.

Resolution of Jogorku Kenesh of the Kyrgyz Republic No. 2377-VI of 20 April 2018 "On approval of the Development Programme of the Kyrgyz Republic for the period 2018-2022", http://mineconom.gov.kg/storage/documents/109/15393398945bc07676beab4_pdf.pdf

Government Resolution of Kyrgyz Republic No. 549 of 2 October 2013 "On approval of priority areas for adaptation to climate change in the Kyrgyz Republic until 2017", http://cbd.minjust.gov.kg/act/view/ru-ru/94766?cl=ru-ru.

Government Resolution No. 218 of 30 April 2013, "On approval of the draft Programme for the transition of the Kyrgyz Republic to sustainable development for 2013-2017", http://cbd.minjust.gov.kg/act/view/ru-ru/53066.

Presidential Decree No. 11 of 21 January 2013 "On the National Sustainable Development Strategy of the Kyrgyz Republic for the period 2013-2017", http://cbd.minjust.gov.kg/act/view/ru-ru/61526.

Government Resolution No. 677 of 4 October 2012 "On approval of the Strategy for Development of Road Transport in the Kyrgyz Republic for 2012-2015", http://cbd.minjust.gov.kg/act/view/ru-ru/93738?cl=ru-ru.

2. Main elements of the Clean Public Transport Programme

This chapter introduces the proposed Clean Public Transport Programme. The programme is designed to be implemented in two phases: Phase 1, a pilot phase that includes urban transport in two selected cities (Bishkek and Osh); and Phase 2, an extension of the programme to cover suburban areas of the pilot cities and inter-city public transport in Kyrgyzstan. The chapter summarises its expected environmental and socio-economic benefits, the costs involved, as well as a possible financing strategy and optimal co-financing level.

2.1. What are the objectives of the Clean Public Transport Programme?

The overall objective of the proposed Clean Public Transport (CPT) Programme is to reduce emissions that form smog in urban centres (emissions from ground-level sources), which includes reducing emissions of pollutants such as carbon monoxide (CO), sulphur dioxide (SO_2), nitrogen oxides (NO_x) and particulate matter (PM). The programme is also designed to contribute to Kyrgyzstan's climate change mitigation efforts and the transition to a green economic model of development. The programme will help to reach the country's declared goal of reducing emissions of greenhouse gases (GHGs) by 11.5-13.8% by 2030, compared to 1990 emission levels, as specified in the intended nationally determined contribution (INDC) prepared by the Government of Kyrgyzstan for the 2015 Paris Climate Conference (GoK, 2015[1]) – see Box 1.1 in Chapter 1 and Section 7.5.[1]

In 2010, the transport sector in Kyrgyzstan emitted 2.1 million tonnes of carbon dioxide equivalent (CO_2e). Although this represents a cutback of 1 million tonnes of CO_2e on 1990 levels (a decrease of 32%), this still lags behind Kyrgyzstan's total GHG emissions, which decreased by 52% in 1990-2010 – from 30.7 million tonnes of CO_2e to 14.7 million tonnes of CO_2e (GoK, 2016[2]).

As can be seen in Figure 2.1, transport contributed relatively little to the country's overall GHG emissions – at 10% in 1990 and 15% in 2010. Within the transport sector, almost all GHG emissions can be attributed to road transport – 93% in 1990 and 99% in 2010 (see also Section 6.3.1).

Figure 2.1. Transport's share of GHG emissions in Kyrgyzstan, 1990 and 2010

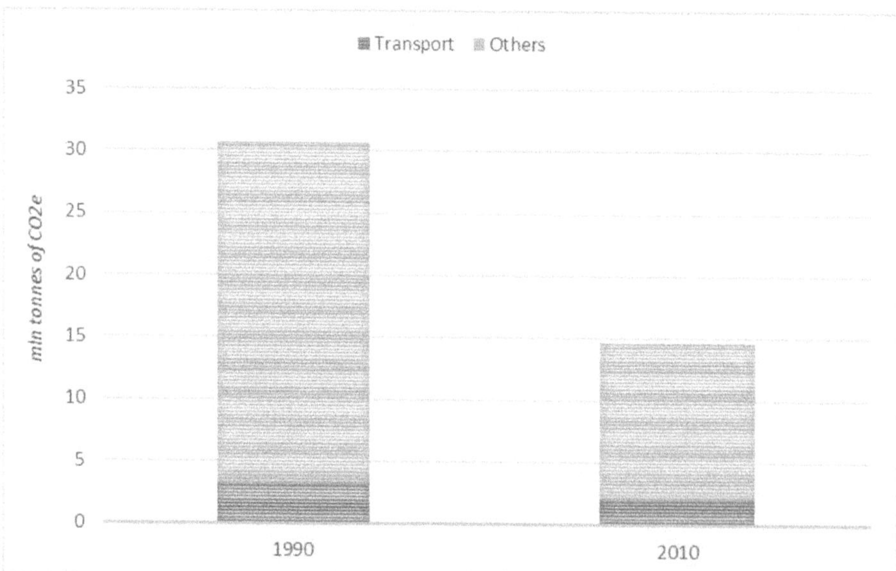

Note: For conversion to CO_2 equivalents, global warming potential values for non-CO_2 gases in the IPCC Fifth Assessment Report, 2014 (AR5) were used (see: www.ipcc.ch/assessment-report/ar5). Non-methane volatile organic compounds are not reflected due to lack of disaggregated data.
Source: (GoK, 2016[2]), *Third National Communication of the Kyrgyz Republic under the UN Framework Convention on Climate Change*, https://unfccc.int/sites/default/files/resource/NC3_Kyrgyzstan_English_24Jan2017.pdf.

A closer look at the data published in the Third National Communication to the UNFCCC reveals that emissions of harmful air pollutants in Kyrgyzstan decreased by 51% between 1990 and 2010 (Figure 2.2). However, when considering solely mobile sources, the decline was only 33%. So whereas in 1990 the contribution of the transport sector to overall air pollution was 49%, in 2010 it had increased to 67%. Within the transport sector, road transport is primarily responsible for all emissions (98% in 1990 and 100% in 2010).

Figure 2.2. Emissions of air pollutants from mobile and stationary sources in Kyrgyzstan, 1990 and 2010

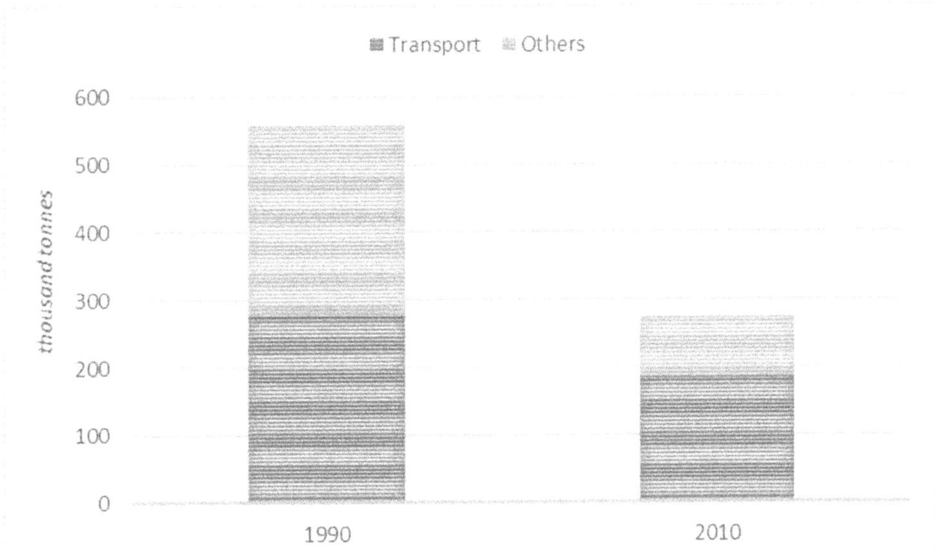

Note: Air pollutants include NO_x, CO and SO_2. The total emissions value is based on a simple summation of individual pollutant emission weights.
Source: (GoK, 2016[2]), *Third National Communication of the Kyrgyz Republic under the UN Framework Convention on Climate Change*, https://unfccc.int/sites/default/files/resource/NC3_Kyrgyzstan_English_24Jan2017.pdf.

2.2. What will the programme involve?

In practice, the overall environmental objectives of the CPT Programme will be accomplished by supporting investments in replacing the bus fleet used in urban, suburban and inter-city public transport with modern vehicles powered by cleaner fuels or electricity.

By modernising the bus fleet, the reliability and efficiency of public transport will be increased and the domestic market will be encouraged to produce, or at least assemble, modern buses and trolleybuses.

The study conducted a market analysis of cleaner fossil fuels and sources of power (see Section 3.1) which identified four groups of investment projects ("pipelines") to replace the old urban, suburban and inter-city bus fleet:

1. Investment in vehicles fuelled by compressed natural gas (CNG)
2. Investment in electricity-powered vehicles (trolleybuses and battery trolleybuses)
3. Investment in vehicles fuelled by liquefied petroleum gas (LPG)[2]

4. Investment in vehicles fuelled by diesel Euro 5 and Euro 6 emissions standards (see Annex A.

Given Kyrgyzstan's ageing bus fleet, the proposed investment "pipelines" are intended to support the purchase of new vehicles, rather than only modernising engines. These proposed investment pipelines should be accompanied by other investments – either from public or private sources – such as in new trolleybus lines, CNG/LPG refuelling and electricity charging stations and other supporting activities to improve the transport system in urban centres (e.g. the creation of bus lanes, improvement of bus stops and smart traffic control).

Two cities, Bishkek and Osh, were identified to participate in the pilot phase of the investment programme. In the second phase, the programme is designed to be extended to the suburban areas of the two pilot cities and some indicative (major) inter-city connections in Kyrgyzstan.

Because the bus fleet in Kyrgyzstan consists of too many minibuses (see Sections 6.2.4 for Bishkek and 6.2.5 for Osh), priority is given to replacing part of the minibus fleet with regular buses. The City Hall of Bishkek, for instance, estimates it would need 600-800 buses of average capacity to serve the city centre (and later, more than 40 surrounding new settlements) and to gradually replace the minibus fleet. The minibus fleet runs almost entirely on diesel, while in the bus fleet there are a few units powered by cleaner fossil fuels (e.g. around 10 CNG vehicles in Bishkek). Electric transport (trolleybuses) make up less than 3% of the public transport fleet in Bishkek and Osh (combined average).

Achieving this will require significant resources, both private and public. Transport fares, however, are very low – starting at USD 0.12 per ride in Bishkek and USD 0.09 per ride in Osh – and access to credit is constrained. These cities, which own the main public transport fleets in their municipalities, have already incurred loans for public transport programmes, mainly through the European Bank for Reconstruction and Development (EBRD), and therefore their creditworthiness is low. Without state support and tariff increases, the modernisation of the public transport fleet will continue to lag.

The CPT Programme is designed to be implemented in two phases, discussed below:

- Phase 1 (pilot phase) covers a limited number of buses in the centres of pilot cities (Bishkek and Osh). The pilot phase would replace old trolleybuses and expand the CNG bus fleet to replace diesel-fuelled minibuses. This would involve purchasing 115 trolleybuses and 288 new CNG buses.
- Phase 2 (scaling-up phase) would involve the further expansion of the CNG fleet in to the remaining parts of the pilot cities (suburbs) as well as inter-city connections linking rural areas in Kyrgyzstan. This would involve purchasing a total of an additional 870 CNG buses and 90 modern diesel buses.

2.2.1. Phase 1 (pilot phase)

Two cities were identified for the pilot phase: Bishkek and Osh. The pilot phase in each of the two cities will take two years, including a one-year preparatory phase (see Section 2.6).

City of Bishkek

Bishkek is the capital of Kyrgyzstan. With a population of 1 027 200 it is the most populated city in the country.[3] It lies in the Chui River valley near the foot of the Kyrgyz range of the Ala-Too Mountains at an elevation of 750-900 metres and is usually regarded as Central Asia's greenest city (in terms of trees per capita).

Bishkek is a separate administrative unit (independent city – *shaar*) and serves also as an administrative centre (apart from 2003-2006) of the surrounding Chui *oblast* (region), which is Kyrgyzstan's northernmost region. The capital is the financial centre of the country (home to the country's national bank, commercial banks and other financial institutions). In the past, it used to be an important junction on several trading routes (also between Europe and Asia). During the Soviet era, a major intrastate connection was constructed in Kyrgyzstan – a 605 km-long highway between Bishkek (then, Frunze) in the north and Osh in the south.

Since 2011, Bishkek has participated in a programme to renew part of the trolleybus fleet which was co-financed by the EBRD (see Section 6.2.4).

The CPT Programme proposes purchasing 216 new public transport vehicles in the pilot phase in Bishkek:

- replacing 78 old trolleybuses with the same number of modern trolleybuses
- purchasing another 20 trolleybuses to strengthen the existing fleet (some of the trolleybuses could be equipped with electric batteries) [4]
- replacing 78 old diesel buses with the same number of CNG buses
- replacing 200 old diesel minibuses with 40 CNG buses.

Since most heavy-duty diesel engines in Kyrgyzstan do not meet the Euro VI standards (see Section 6.2), introducing Euro V and Euro VI diesel engines might seem an effective way to modernise the public transport fleet. However, the fuel consumption of Euro V/VI engines is higher than old diesel engines so beneficiaries would not see their operating costs reduce. Given the currently very low transport fares in Kyrgyzstan (see Section 3.2.3), the amount of public support needed to purchase Euro VI diesel buses would be very high. For this reason, it remains the least preferred option.

The key costs and benefits of the pilot implementation are provided in Table 2.1. The total cost of the CPT Programme for Bishkek is estimated to be KGS 2 209 million (USD 31.81 million), of which KGS 1 263 million (USD 18.18 million) will be co-financed by the programme and KGS 946 million (USD 13.62 million) will be invested by private or public bus operators and/or the city of Bishkek.

Table 2.1. Key costs and benefits of the pilot phase of the CPT Programme in Bishkek

	Unit	Value	
Total number of new trolleybuses	#	98	
Total number of new CNG buses	#	118	
Total costs of buses replaced	KGS mln	2 209	
Co-financed by the programme	KGS mln	1 263	
Co-financed by private/municipal bus operators	KGS mln	946	
		Normative pollution factors*	**Real pollution factors***
Total CO_2 reduction	tCO_2/year	6 370	11 862
Total CO reduction	kg/year	29 115	29 115
Total NO_x reduction	kg/year	116 403	116 403
Total PM reduction	kg/year	2 755	2 755
Total SO_2 reduction	kg/year	2 603	2 603

Note: *For a discussion of normative and real pollution factors, see Section 2.3.3 and Annex B.
Source: OECD calculations, OPTIC Model.

As shown in Table 2.1, the CO_2 emission reductions from this pilot phase would be high – a reduction of 6 370 tCO_2/year. However, NO_x emissions could see the largest decrease, which could fall by 116 403 kg/year.

City of Osh

Osh is the second largest city in Kyrgyzstan in terms of population – 299 500[5] – and the only other city with a trolleybus network and a well-developed public transport system. It is referred to as the "capital of the south", partly given its 3 000-year history as the oldest city in Kyrgyzstan. It is located in the Fergana Valley at an altitude of 963 metres above sea level.

The city used to be an important outdoor bazaar along the Silk Road. Although Osh (as well as other towns in the south of the Kyrgyz Soviet Socialist Republic) began to be industrialised only in the 1960s (as opposed to Bishkek mentioned above), the city's industrial base largely collapsed after the break-up of the Soviet Union and has recently only started to revive.

Osh is also the only city other than Bishkek with the administrative status of independent city (*shaar*). The City of Osh also serves (from 1939) as an administrative centre of the surrounding Osh *oblast* (region), the southernmost region in Kyrgyzstan and regarded as the country's southern hub for industry and trade.

Similar to Bishkek, Osh has participated since 2014 in an EBRD programme to renew part of its bus fleet (see Section 6.2.5).

The CPT Programme proposes purchase 187 new vehicles for public transport in the pilot phase in Osh, including:

- purchasing 17 new trolleybuses, continuing the existing EBRD programme that has replaced 23 trolleybuses to date
- replacing 50 old diesel buses with the same number of CNG buses
- replacing 600 old diesel minibuses with 120 CNG buses.

As Table 2.2 shows, the total cost of this phase in Osh would amount to KGS 1 879 million (USD 27.28 million), of which the CPT Programme could support KGS 774 million (USD 11.24 million), while public and private bus operators, and/or the city of Osh, would contribute KGS 1 104 million (USD 16.03 million).

Table 2.2. Key costs and benefits of the CPT Programme's pilot phase in Osh

	Unit	Value	
Total number of trolleybuses	#	17	
Total number of CNG buses	#	170	
Total costs of vehicles replaced	KGS mln	1 879	
Co-financed by the programme	KGS mln	774	
Co-financed by private/municipal bus operators	KGS mln	1 104	
		Normative pollution factors*	Real pollution factors*
Total CO_2 reduction	tCO_2/year	5 744	12 237
Total CO reduction	kg/year	33 944	33 944
Total NO_x reduction	kg/year	132 611	132 611
Total PM reduction	kg/year	3 247	3 247
Total SO_2 reduction	kg/year	3 078	3 078

Note: *For a discussion of normative and real pollution factors, see Section 2.3.3 and Annex B.
Source: OECD calculations, OPTIC Model.

As shown in Table 2.2, the expected NO_x reduction would 132 611 kg/year. In terms of CO_2 emissions, the reduction is estimated to be 5 744 tCO_2/year.

Summary of pilot phase

Overall, in both cities, the pilot phase would see 115 new trolleybuses and 288 new CNG buses purchased. These numbers assume that Kyrgyzstan has the market capacity to supply this quantity of modern vehicles, that private and municipal bus operators have the capacity to invest in these new assets over a one-year period, and that the government has the capacity to invest in the necessary support infrastructure.

The purchase of 98 new trolleybuses in Bishkek and 17 in Osh will in a broader sense add to and learn from the experience of previous (EBRD-supported) replacements that started in 2011 and 2014 in Bishkek and Osh, respectively. Also, both pilot cities have a large number of minibuses (usually diesel-fuelled) in their public transport fleets that are in urgent need of replacement. Therefore, 200 old diesel minibuses will be replaced in Bishkek and 600 in Osh by 40 and 120 CNG regular buses, respectively.

The investment costs of the pilot phase of the CPT Programme would amount to KGS 4 088 million (USD 59.36 million), of which KGS 2 037 million (USD 29.58 million) would need to come from the public purse (Table 2.3).

Table 2.3. Key costs and benefits of the CPT Programme's pilot phase

	Unit	Value	
Total number of trolleybuses purchased	#	115	
Total number of new CNG buses	#	288	
Total cost of vehicles replaced	KGS mln	4 088	
Co-financed by the programme	KGS mln	2 037	
Co-financed by private/municipal bus operators	KGS mln	2 051	
		Normative pollution factors*	Real pollution factors*
Total CO_2 reduction	tCO_2/year	12 114	24 099
Total CO reduction	kg/year	63 059	63 059
Total NO_x reduction	kg/year	249 013	249 013
Total PM reduction	kg/year	6 002	6 002
Total SO_2 reduction	kg/year	5 681	5 681

Note: *For a discussion of normative and real pollution factors, see Section 2.3.3 and Annex B.
Source: OECD calculations, OPTIC Model.

2.2.2. Phase 2 (scaling-up phase)

The second phase of the programme is designed to replace the remaining old bus/minibus fleet in Bishkek and Osh, i.e. those supplying the suburban routes, as well as some inter-city connections.

Public transport in Kyrgyzstan is dominated by diesel minibuses; currently regular buses only service a small number of urban and inter-city routes. Therefore, the second phase of the CPT Programme proposes replacing half of the minibuses with minibuses powered by clean fuels, and the other half with regular buses (more than 10 metres long) which can carry up to five times more passengers.

The calculation of the number of buses to be purchased in Phase 2 took into consideration the number of old diesel buses (with engines of up to Euro IV standard) and minibuses currently providing public passenger transport services. Due to the lack of reliable data on the existing inter-city bus fleet, these figures have been estimated. This estimation also considers the possibility that the overall number of minibuses will be reduced and a certain share of these minibuses (about 50%) will be replaced with regular buses. Overall it will involve 960 new vehicles: 870 CNG and 90 diesel-powered ones.

The key costs and benefits of both programme phases are shown in Table 2.4 (please note that the second column includes the overall result for both phases). While no sensitivity analysis for the phases was performed, changes in the programme's cost-effectiveness might occur if the prices used for the costing change (e.g. passenger fares; see Box 4.1 in Chapter 4).

Table 2.4. Key input and output parameters of the assessed CPT Programme phases

	Unit	Phase 1 (Bishkek and Osh)	Phase 1 + Phase 2 (suburban routes in Bishkek and Osh; inter-city)
Total number of trolleybuses purchased	#	115	115
Total number of buses purchased	#	288	1 248
Modern diesel	#	0	90
CNG		288	1 158
LPG	#	0	0
Total number of minibuses purchased	#	0	0
Modern diesel	#	0	0
CNG or LPG	#	0	0
Total costs of buses/trolleybuses/minibuses purchased	KGS mln	4 088	13 691
co-financed by the programme	KGS mln	2 037	5 799
co-financed by private/municipal bus operators	KGS mln	2 051	7 892
Total CO_2 reduction	CO_2 t/year*	12 114	68 506
Total CO reduction	kg/year	63 059	306 608
Total NO_x reduction	kg/year	249 013	1 236 180
Total PM reduction	kg/year	6 002	29 022
Total SO_2 reduction	kg/year	5 681	27 291

Note: *Normative pollution factors, see Section 2.3.3 and Annex B.
Source: OECD calculations, OPTIC Model.

2.3. What will the costs and benefits be?

2.3.1. Renewed public transport fleet

In total, the programme will result in 403 new urban public transport vehicles in the pilot phase (115 trolleybuses and 288 CNG buses). The pilot and scaling-up phase will result in a total of 1 363 new urban, suburban and inter-city public transport vehicles (115 trolleybuses, 1 158 CNG buses and 90 diesel buses).

The programme objectives have been translated into straightforward and measurable targets:

- Increase the ratio of new buses (less than five years old) used for urban, suburban and inter-city public transport in Kyrgyzstan from 5.7% of the fleet (2017 baseline) to 38.0% after the pilot phase, and to 83.6% after the scaling-up phase.
- Increase the ratio of new trolleybuses (less than five years old) in the fleets of Bishkek and Osh from 44.1% (2017 baseline) to 91.8% after the pilot phase.
- Decrease the ratio of minibuses in the public transport fleet in Kyrgyzstan from 86.0% (2017 baseline) to 83.1% after the pilot phase and to 66.3% after the scaling-up phase.
- Increase the ratio of CNG-fuelled buses in the public transport fleet in Kyrgyzstan to 4.6% after the pilot phase and to 23.2% after the scaling-up phase.

The investment distribution between the pilot cities of Bishkek and Osh, and other cities/regions of Kyrgyzstan, is shown in Figure 2.9. To some extent, the proposed CPT Programme will build on the existing investment programme in urban public transport financed by a loan from the EBRD (see Sections 6.2.4 and 6.2.5).

2.3.2. Using the OPTIC Model to estimate costs and benefits

The costs and benefits of the CPT Programme were estimated using an Excel-based model called Optimising Public Transport Investment Costs (OPTIC). This analytical tool has been developed by the OECD to help public authorities prepare and estimate, as precisely as possible, the costs and environmental benefits of green public investment programmes (Box 2.1). The model was first designed and tested in Kazakhstan (OECD, 2017[3]). The assumptions surrounding cost calculation and emission reductions factors are described in Annex B in the section "Programme costing for Phase 1 (pilot phase) and Phase 2 (scaling-up phase)".

Box 2.1. The OPTIC model

The Optimising Public Transport Investment Costs (OPTIC) model was developed along with this study and is one of the main outputs of the project.

OPTIC's spreadsheet-based model is a simple, easy-to-use decision support tool prepared exclusively to calculate and optimise total programme costs, as well as the CO2 emission reductions and reductions of other pollutants from urban public transport (CO, NOx, PM, SO2) that could be potentially achieved by implementing the proposed project pipelines. The model helps calculate the optimal level of subsidy that can be offered to potential beneficiaries.

Optimisation of costs and benefits implies achieving given targets at the lowest possible cost for the public financier. If underlying economic conditions in the country change over the programme period (e.g. tariffs are increased, interest rates on commercial loans are lowered) and/or available public financing is reduced or augmented, both targets and subsidy levels can be re-calculated (or optimised) and adjusted accordingly.

The model consists of seven modules: 1) assumptions; 2) emission factors; 3) transport sector overview with information on current bus fleet and age; 4) determining of the subsidy level; 5) cost calculation; 6) emission reductions calculation; and 7) programme costing and environmental effects.

2.3.3. Emission reductions

In order to estimate the environmental outcomes of the CPT Programme, the model uses two different sets of pollution factors: normative and real. As discussed in Annex B, this was necessary as normative pollution factors declared and checked in laboratory conditions differ from actual pollution factors measured in the urban transport cycle. Normative emission factors take into account various modern emission standards for heavy-duty diesel engines, and estimations for CNG and LPG-fuelled engines. The emission factors introduced by the standards, however, are based on maximum emission levels according to specific norms. Real emissions may vary, mainly because normative emissions are tested in laboratory conditions and not in actual traffic. This is a concern mostly for diesel engines, where emission reductions depend on the emission reduction equipment installed. In this case, the real level of emissions was also calculated taking into account the results published by the International Council on Clean Transportation (ICCT),[6] based on real-world exhaust emissions from modern diesel cars (Franco et al., 2014[4]). Emissions from CNG and LPG are less problematic because they use cleaner fuels. A detailed discussion of emissions factors can be found in Annex B to this report.

The most significant reductions from this programme are expected to be in NO_x emissions, which are estimated to decline by 1 854 270 kg/year (Table 2.5). CO_2 emissions are estimated to decline by 102 759 tCO_2/year.

Table 2.5. Estimated key costs and benefits of the entire CPT Programme

Type	New buses (number)						Investment	Public support	Emission reduction per year				
	Bus			Minibus									
	Diesel	CNG	LPG	Diesel	CNG or LPG	Trolleybus	KGS mln	KGS mln	CO_2 (t)*	CO (kg)	NO_x (kg)	PM 2.5 (kg)	SO_2 (kg)
Bishkek	0	848	0	0	0	98	9 509	3 972	39 988	195 082	744 468	18 521	17 519
Osh	0	250	0	0	0	17	2 679	1 071	22 839	82 398	337 450	7 704	7 255
Other cities	90	60	0	0	0	0	1 503	755	5 679	29 128	124 263	2 798	2 517
TOTAL	90	1 158	0	0	0	115	13 691	5 799	68 506	306 608	1 236 180	29 022	27 291

Note: * Normative pollution factors
Source: OECD calculations, OPTIC Model.

Figure 2.3 presents the possible reductions of greenhouse gases and air pollutants from both phases of the CPT Programme in Bishkek and Osh, including their suburban networks and main inter-city connections. As only these two cities have a well-developed urban public transport network (other cities essentially only use inter-city connections[7]), the main environmental impact is expected to be in the pilot cities as well.

Figure 2.3. Aggregate annual emission reductions resulting from the CPT Programme in Kyrgyzstan, 2021-26

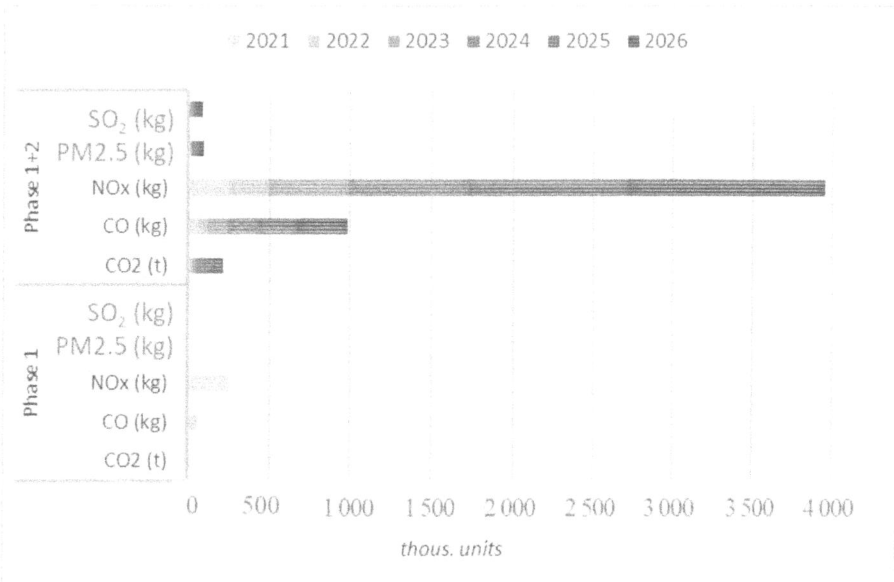

Source: OECD calculations, OPTIC Model

Figure 2.4 projects environmental outcomes for the city of Bishkek, including the second (scaling-up) phase, over the six years of project implementation. These investments can bring significant emission reductions. Whereas CO_2 emissions will be reduced by 43.1% (52 711 tonnes/year) compared to the baseline, the combined reduction of air pollutants will be 86.7% (153 tonnes/year) after the scaling-up phase.

Figure 2.4. Difference between old and new fleet in Bishkek – carbon dioxide and air pollutant emissions, 2020-26

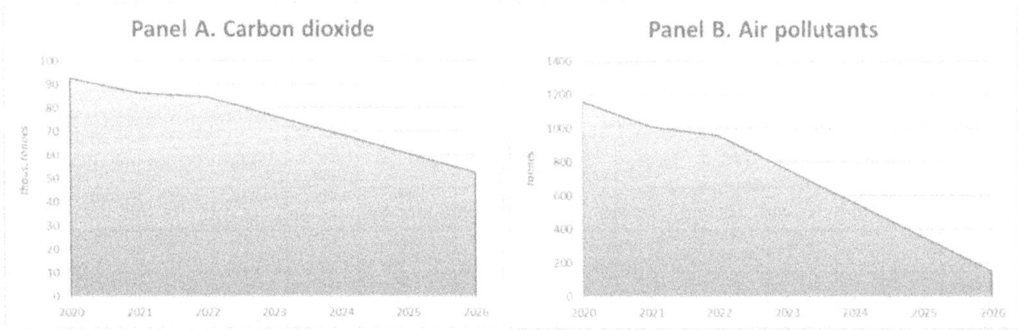

Note: The values reflect only emissions from vehicles to be replaced (baseline value) and the new fleet (target value), not the total emissions from public transport in Bishkek. Air pollutants include CO, NO_x, PM2.5 and SO_2 and the total emissions value is based on the simple summation of individual pollutant emission weights.
Source: OECD calculations, OPTIC Model.

Figure 2.5 projects the environmental outcomes for Osh, including the second (scaling-up) phase, over the three years of project implementation. Whereas CO_2 reduction will be 59.6% (15 494 tonnes/year) compared to the baseline, the combined reduction of air pollutants will amount to 90.6% (45 tonnes/year) after the scaling-up phase.

Figure 2.5. Difference between old and new fleet in Osh – carbon dioxide and air pollutants emissions, 2020-23

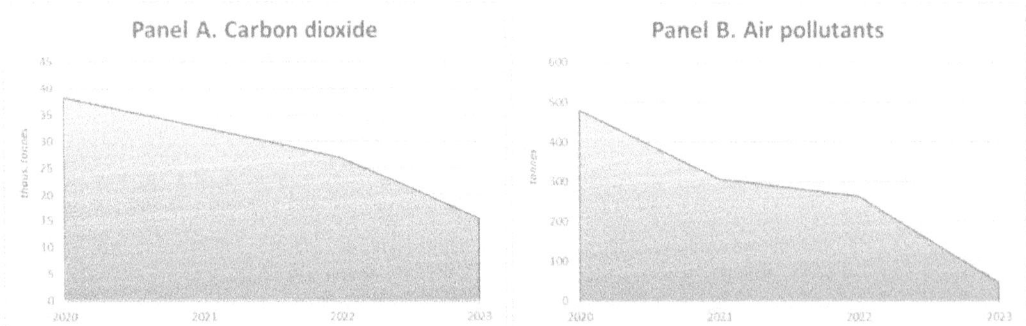

Note: The values reflect only emissions from vehicles to be replaced (baseline value) and the new fleet (target value), not the total emissions from public transport in Osh. Air pollutants include CO, NO_x, PM2.5 and SO_2 and the total emissions value is based on the simple summation of individual pollutant emission weights.
Source: OECD calculations, OPTIC Model.

Figure 2.6, Figure 2.7, and Figure 2.8 contrast possible GHG and air pollution reduction resulting from the CPT Programme's phases and scenarios with current emissions levels from the existing public transport fleet.

CO_2 and NO_x promise the greatest emission reductions. Obviously, significant emission reductions start accumulating with the implementation of Phase 2 of the CPT Programme. By the end of Phase 2, CO_2 emissions are estimated to decrease by about 68 506 tonnes/year (a reduction of 47.3% compared to baseline). These reductions are estimated using the normative pollution factors approach (Figure 2.6).

Figure 2.6. Potential carbon dioxide reductions resulting from the CPT Programme

(tonnes/year)

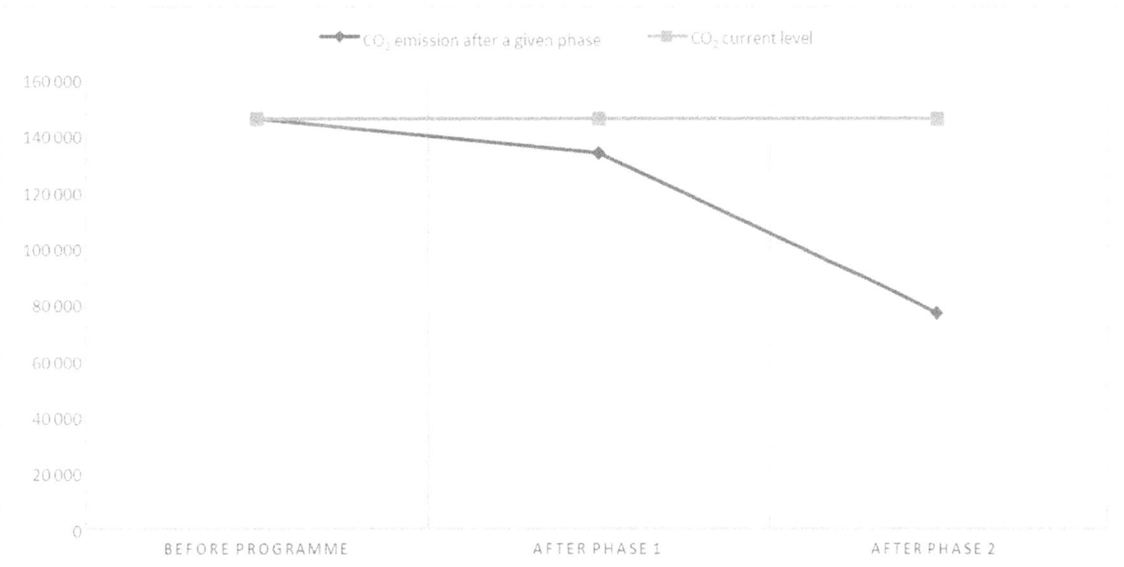

Note: The values reflect only emissions from the vehicles to be replaced (baseline value) and the new fleet (target value), not the total emissions from public transport in Kyrgyzstan.
Source: OECD calculations, OPTIC Model.

In the case of NO_x emissions, this reduction is estimated to amount to about 1 236 tonnes/year (a reduction of 86.4% compared to baseline). CO emissions reductions will amount to 307 tonnes/year (meaning a reduction of 94.0% compared to baseline) (Figure 2.7).

Figure 2.7. Potential carbon monoxide and nitrogen oxides reductions resulting from the CPT Programme

(tonnes/year)

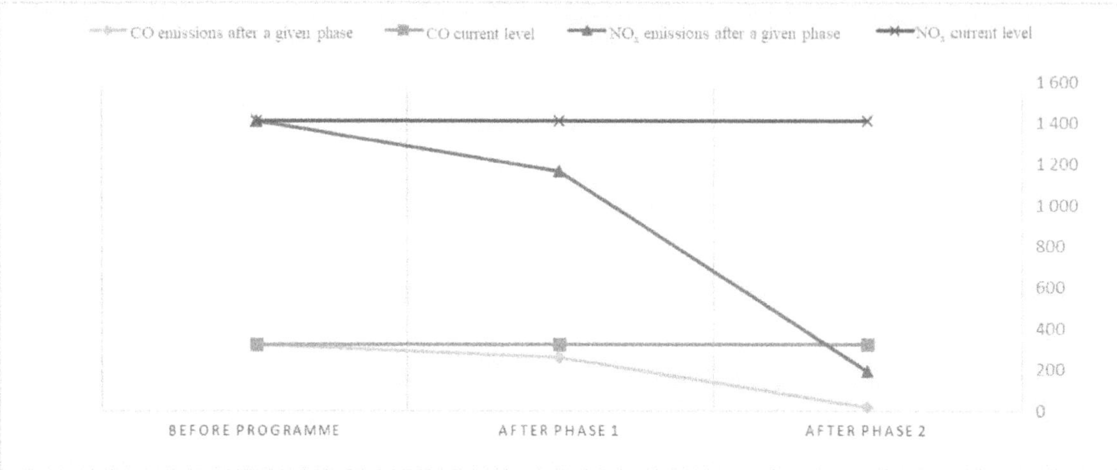

Note: The values only reflect emissions from the vehicles to be replaced (baseline value) and the new fleet (target value), not the total emissions from public transport in Kyrgyzstan.
Source: OECD calculations, OPTIC Model.

In terms of relative improvement, the best result will be achieved for SO_2 emissions, which will be reduced by 99.6% (or 27 tonnes/year) after the scaling-up phase. Particulate matter (PM) emissions will decrease by 29 tonnes/year (a reduction of 98.7% compared to the baseline) (Figure 2.8).

Figure 2.8. Potential particulates and sulphur dioxide reductions resulting from the CPT Programme

(tonnes/year)

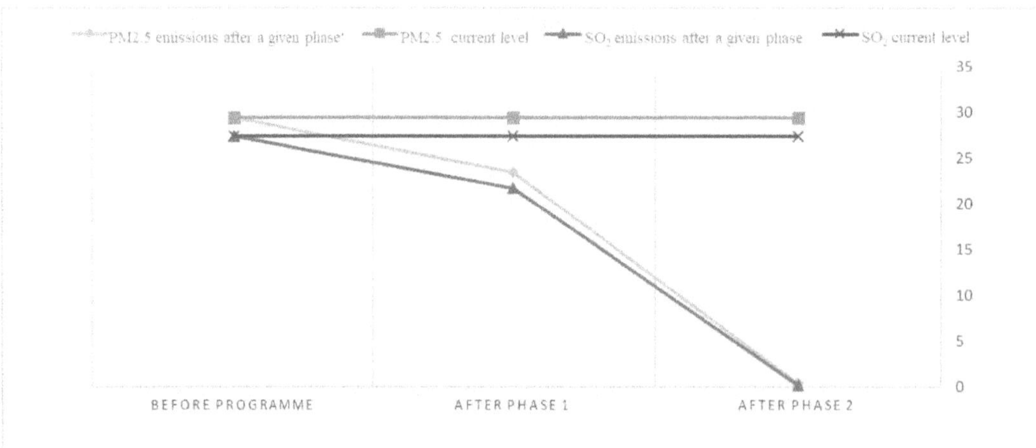

Note: The values only reflect emissions from the vehicles to be replaced (baseline value) and the new fleet (target value), not the total emissions from public transport in Kyrgyzstan.
Source: OECD calculations, OPTIC Model.

2.3.4. Investment costs and financing options

The pilot phase (Phase 1) covers a limited number of buses in the centres of the pilot cities of Bishkek and Osh. It would involve purchasing 115 trolleybuses and 288 new CNG buses at a cost of KGS 4 088 million (USD 59.36 million), of which KGS 2 037 (USD 29.58 million) in public financing will be required.

The scaling-up phase (Phase 2) takes into account the replacement of buses in suburban areas of Bishkek and Osh, as well as a rough estimate of the replacement of some inter-city buses. This would involve the replacement of 870 CNG buses and 90 modern diesel buses, at a cost of KGS 9 603 (USD 139.44 million), of which KGS 3 762 (USD 54.63 million) are required as public co-financing.

The total investment cost of both Phase 1 and Phase 2 of the CPT Programme is estimated at KGS 13 691 million (USD 198.8 million), excluding preparation and implementation costs. Of this total cost, KGS 5 799 million (USD 84.21 million) in public support will be needed.

Figure 2.9 presents the overall CPT Programme costs for investors (i.e. private and municipally-owned public transport companies) and public sector financiers (both national and international) in the pilot phase (Phase 1) and in the scaling-up phase (Phase 2).

Figure 2.9. Total investment costs of the CPT Programme in Bishkek, Osh and other cities

(KGS and USD)

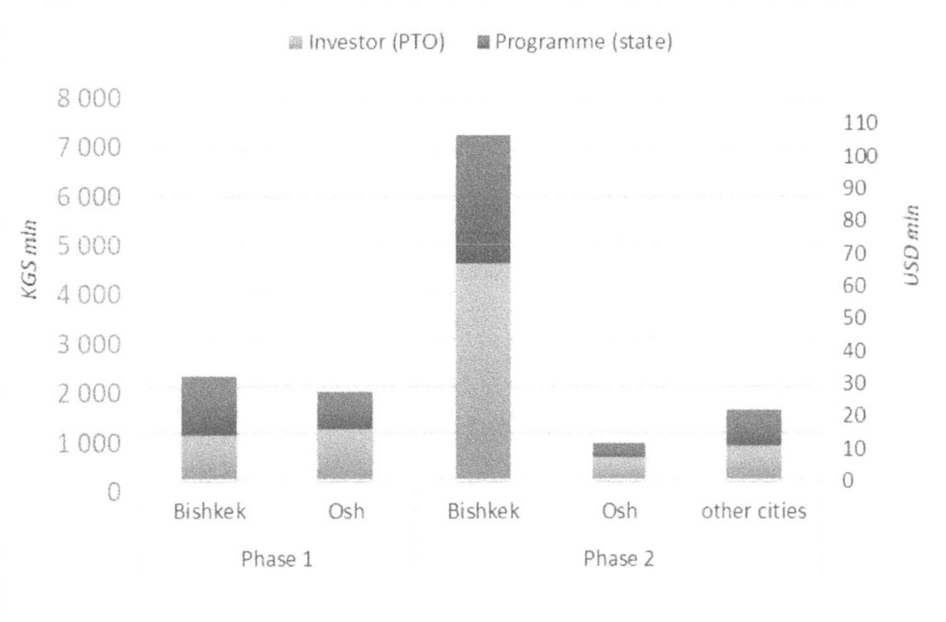

Note: PTO – public transport operator.
Source: OECD calculations, OPTIC Model.

Table 2.6 summarises the size, results and associated costs of the CPT Programme for Phases 1 and 2, assuming that the programme is implemented directly by a government-established implementation unit (IU). The annual amounts were estimated by dividing the public co-financing required in Phase 2 (i.e. excluding the pilot phase) by the five years of programme implementation in the second phase.

Table 2.6. Summary of CPT Programme costs, Phases 1 and 2

(KGS million)

City	Investment costs	Public co-financing							
		Total public co-financing	Year						
			1	2	3	4	5	6	7
Preparation costs (including fundraising)	1.2	1.2	0.6	0.6	0	0	0	0	0
Pilot phase	4 088	2 037	0	2 037	0	0	0	0	0
Implementation unit (operating costs)	14.4	14.4	0	0	2.9	2.9	2.9	2.9	2.9
Second phase	9 603	3 762	0	0	752	752	752	752	752
Total	13 706	5 814	0.6	2 037	755	755	755	755	755

Source: OECD calculations, OPTIC Model.

The CPT Programme preparation costs (including fundraising) assume that two people will be employed on a full-time basis during the first year, at a cost of KGS 288 000 (USD 4 180), based on an average monthly salary for administrative employees of KGS 16 000 (USD 230) and 50% overheads (social security and other administrative costs).

The CPT Programme preparation costs in the second phase (including fundraising) assume that two people will be employed on a full-time basis during the first year of Phase 2 at a cost of KGS 576 000 (USD 8 360), using the same calculations above. In addition, the implementation unit would employ eight people on a full-time basis, whose costs are estimated to amount to KGS 2.3 million (USD 33 500) annually in the second phase of the programme.

Table 2.7 mirrors Table 2.6, but all costs are recalculated in US dollars.

Table 2.7. Summary of CPT Programme costs, Phases 1 and 2

(USD million)

City	Investment costs	Public co-financing							
		Total public co-financing	Year						
			1	2	3	4	5	6	7
Preparation costs (including fundraising)	0.02	0.02	0.01	0.01	0.00	0.00	0.00	0.00	0.00
Pilot phase	59	30	0	29	0	0	0	0	0
Implementation unit (operating costs)	0.21	0.21	0.00	0.00	0.04	0.04	0.04	0.04	0.04
Second phase	139	54	0	0	11	11	11	11	11
Total	199	84	0.01	29	11	11	11	11	11

Source: OECD calculations, OPTIC Model.

It will be costly for the public financier to cover these costs even if part of the individual costs is covered by bus operators (see Table 2.4 above). The most likely financing source for the CPT Programme will be the resources of public transport operators (both public and private) combined with state budget support (a subsidy in the form of a grant) to motivate bus operators to allocate their own financial resources. The most likely financing scheme is depicted in Figure 2.10.

In the future (at a later stage of the CPT Programme or in other public investment programmes), commercial loans combined with public support in the form of loan guarantees and grants from public sources could be given to public transport operators. From initial discussions, a portion of the existing credit line that the Government of

Kyrgyzstan has with the Asian Development Bank (ADB) could be devoted to the CPT Programme. This credit could then be on-lent to operators or municipalities. Commercial loans, while a theoretical possibility, should be used only after the exploration of other loan possibilities, including in particular on-lending of loans incurred by the state from international sources.

Figure 2.10. Financing from own sources and public grant

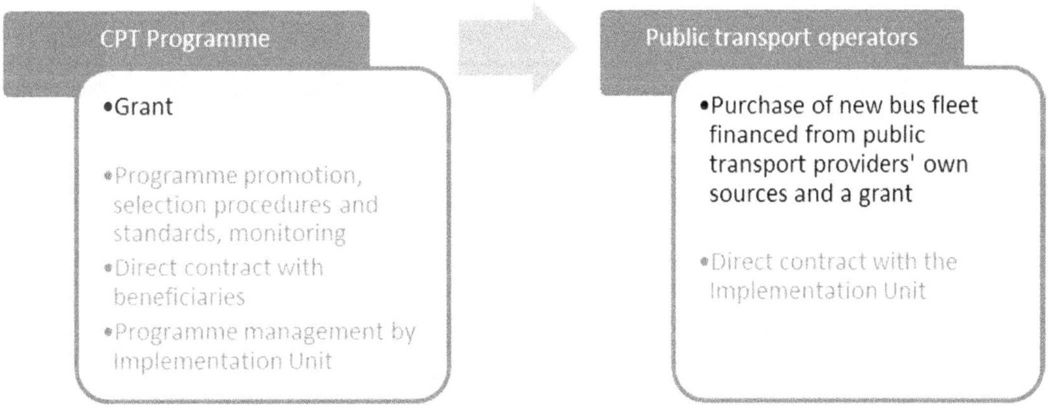

2.4. What is the optimal co-financing level?

Calculating the optimal level of public funds for co-financing the costs of the purchase of the new, cleaner vehicles is an important element of the analysis. Estimates suggest that the level of public funds should not exceed the rates provided in Table 2.8 below. These rates, which represent the optimal subsidy level per type of pipeline, were calculated using the OPTIC Model based on the net present value (NPV) of each type of investment (see Annex B).

The calculation of these rates takes into account current fares and the daily distances covered by operators (which are not optimal).

Table 2.8. Summary of public support for the CPT Programme

Programme pipeline	Estimated public co-financing
Trolleybus	80%
Buses and minibuses with engines fuelled by CNG	37%
Buses and minibuses with engines fuelled by LPG	39%
Buses and minibuses with engines fuelled by modern diesel (Euro 5/V and Euro 6/VI)	65%
CNG stations	Provided by the private sector
LPG stations	Provided by the private sector
Side investments	Provided by cities

Note: Percentage values denote the level of public support from the bus purchase costs.
Source: OECD calculations, OPTIC Model.

There are two issues of note regarding the calculation of these optimal subsidy levels. First, when a public transport operator modernises its fleet, the operator will not need to replace buses in the near future (in particular, considering buses that are more than 15 years old which replacement would be necessary in any case). Thus, only the price difference between modern (low-emission) buses and traditional buses is taken into account when calculating the subsidy level.[8] Second, some fuels will be cheaper than diesel. For example, CNG and LPG are cheaper than diesel even taking into account increased consumption. Therefore, savings in fuel costs for public transport operators are also taken into account when calculating the subsidy level.

Figure 2.11 and Figure 2.12 contrast purchase price and fuel cost for the different types of buses, as an aid for decision making. As seen in Figure 2.11, while the purchase price of (or the initial investment in) cleaner fuel buses is significantly higher than for a traditional diesel bus, the much lower fuel costs over the useful lifetime of the cleaner bus allow for additional savings.

Figure 2.11. Relationship between purchase price and fuel costs for diesel and cleaner buses

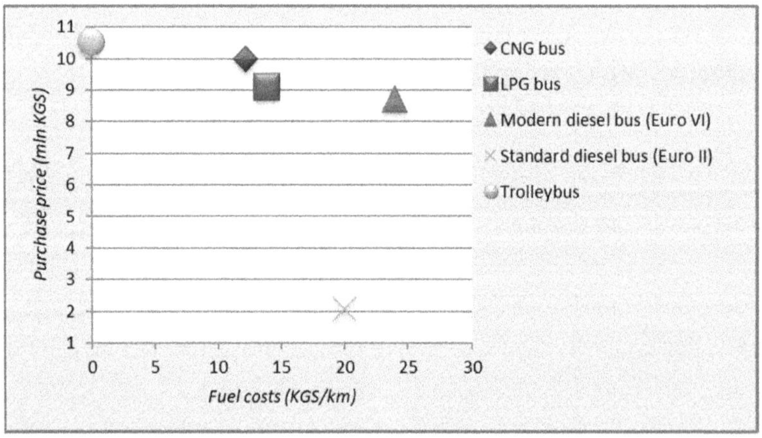

Source: OECD calculations, OPTIC Model.

Similarly, Figure 2.12 shows that CNG fuel is cheaper than diesel, and the fuel consumption of CNG buses per 100 kilometres is lower. Although trolleybus consumption appears to be high, given the low price of electricity, it is the most economical option in terms of running costs. The potential savings from using storage batteries and the low pollution levels from electric transport make trolleybuses a particularly attractive option for investment (for exact fuel consumption values, see Table B.1 of Annex B). However, during the winter months, when there is not enough water in the Toktogul Dam, trolleybuses need to use electricity generated by thermal power stations rather than the usual hydropower, which temporarily worsens its environmental benefits (see Section 6.1.4).

Figure 2.12. Relationship between consumption and fuel price for diesel and cleaner buses

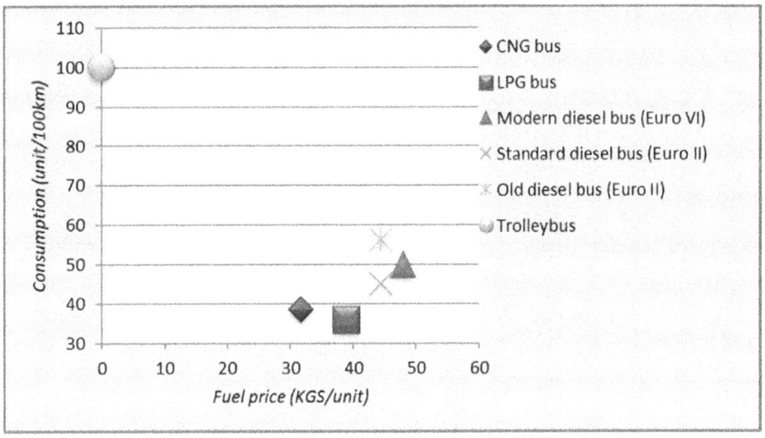

Source: OECD calculations, OPTIC Model.

It is essential to monitor market developments regularly (e.g. changes in bus/trolleybus and fuel/electricity prices, development of the market for new engines, and availability of other financing sources) and how they interact with the CPT Programme design. Such market changes need to be reflected in the programme, and the subsidy level provided by the state adjusted accordingly. The section on "Programme costing for Phase 1 (pilot phase) and Phase 2 (scaling-up phase)" in Annex B provides an indicative calculation of the optimal subsidy level based on bus and fuel prices at the end of 2018. These, however, are offered more as an illustration of how the subsidy level needs to be calculated, rather than as absolute values. The model provides an opportunity to adjust and optimise the programme assumptions and its effects by changing the basic data as appropriate.

2.5. What will the implementation set-up be?

The institutional set-up proposed in this study includes three levels: 1) a programming entity; 2) an implementation unit; and 3) a technical support unit. The analysis suggests that the Ministry of Economy could act as the programming entity. Programme implementation, which should be a separate and distinct function from the programming role, could be performed by local banks that sign a co-operation agreement with the Ministry of Economy following a successful public tender bid to provide this service. Other potential implementation units could be the Investment Promotion and Protection Agency (IPPA), the State Agency for Environmental Protection and Forestry (SAEPF), and the Regional Environmental Centre for Central Asia (CAREC). Regardless of the choice, the implementing entity should have a degree of independence to ensure that decisions are made using rules and criteria in line with the programme objectives, and not subject to undue political influence (see Section 4.2).

Inter-ministerial co-operation is vital for the successful implementation of the programme. Such a programme can help increase the profile of the environment and climate on the transport policy agenda. In transitioning to clean public transport, the Ministry of Economy would benefit from closer co-operation with other ministries, in particular the Ministry of Finance, in order to mobilise existing funds and potential external financing sources in order to achieve low-carbon mobility in the country.

2.6. What will the timeframe look like?

Given that the CPT Programme will be co-financed with public funds, a preparation period (Figure 2.13) will be needed before the first phase to include the programme provisions in the state budget process, and to identify and apply for funding from additional sources (including donors).

The experience of other countries with similar publicly supported investments suggests that such programmes are best implemented over the medium to long-term and linked to government targets. It was agreed with stakeholders that the CPT Programme would begin with a pilot phase. The major constraint is likely to be procurement procedures. The pilot phase could thus take up to a year.

The results of the pilot phase will be evaluated to decide whether it will be necessary to continue with the second phase. If so, it is proposed that the second phase of the CPT Programme be carried out over a period of five years and then reviewed in detail. A decision can then be made as to whether it should be extended or brought to a close, depending on possible new policy objectives and government goals or market developments.

Figure 2.13. Proposed timeline

(years)

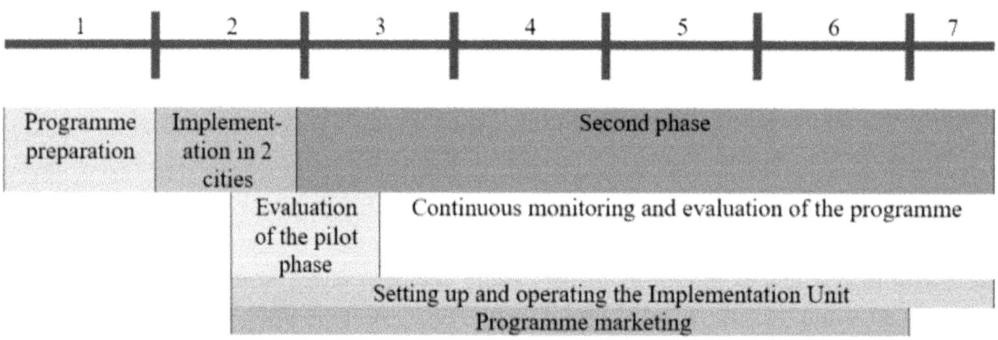

In addition, there should be annual evaluations of the CPT Programme to see whether the projects are helping to meet government objectives and to revise elements if necessary. Since the programme is designed to be co-financed through the state budget, any change should be co-ordinated with the existing multi-year budget and its requirements. On this basis, annual financial plans for financing through the regular annual budget should be prepared.

2.7. Conclusions

As the OPTIC Model calculations have shown, the total cost of implementing the CPT Programme will be substantial. Since new technologies are more expensive before they reach market maturity, public financial support will be necessary to help the public transport operators (both municipal and private) to upgrade to a modern and environment-friendly vehicle fleet.

The investment programme foresees public grants – and prospectively, commercial and preferential loans and public loan guarantees – as the most targeted support options. Finance is available, primarily through national public authorities (grants), or international/development financial institutions (preferential loans and grants). In the future, the involvement of national commercial banks (commercial loans) and national public authorities (loan guarantees) could broaden the scheme and its financing options.

When calculating the optimal level of public support (subsidies in the form of grants), the programme analysis took into account several contributory factors – such as the lower running costs of alternative fuel vehicles (as these fuels/sources of power are less expensive), lower operational and maintenance costs (due to higher reliability of new vehicles) and the overall need to replace the vehicles that have been fully depreciated.

For these economic reasons (i.e. achieved savings in operational costs), it is not necessary for the CPT Programme to be completely grant-financed. The programme is designed to increase investment by public transport operators in the vehicle fleet without making the replacement too profitable based on public resources (or to support purchases that would/could take place without public support).

In any case, applying a robust methodology – to estimate the costs of the investment programme, set the optimal level of subsidy and forecast the expected environmental benefits – can make the CPT Programme more credible for both national and international public financiers.

Notes

1. 21st Conference of the Parties of the United Nations Framework Convention on Climate Change (UNFCCC COP21). For more information on COP, see https://unfccc.int/process/bodies/supreme-bodies/conference-of-the-parties-cop.

2. It is important to note that while buses powered by LPG are given medium priority (see Section 5.1.2), no LPG buses are foreseen in the investment plans of the cities of Bishkek and Osh. Although LPG is used in Kyrgyzstan (mainly by private users, including public transport operators), CO_2 emissions from LPG-powered engines are higher than from CNG-powered ones (see Section 3.1 and Annex A to this report). Therefore, it is suggested that the programme should financially support buses powered by CNG rather than LPG. For this reason, the results of the OPTIC (Optimising Public Transport Investment Costs) Model do not include LPG buses. The model can, however, be used to include LPG buses should policy makers decide to evaluate this option in the future.

3. As of end of 2018. See NSC on resident population at: http://stat.kg/en/opendata/category/39.

4. Even though trolleybuses have only small batteries, they are cheaper to run (in terms of operational and maintenance costs) than electric buses. They can travel on the battery for a limited

number of kilometres (depending on the battery capacity), but most of the route is powered by the city's electrical wire network, which allows the trolleybus batteries to be charged while driving.

5. As of end of 2018. See NSC on resident population at: http://stat.kg/en/opendata/category/39.

6. International Council on Clean Transportation (www.theicct.org).

7. Other cities face affordability constraints in further developing their urban public transport services. For example, Naryn (capital of Naryn *oblast*) has only one trolleybus line.

8. Given that most public transport operators would rather buy used public transport vehicles, the price of a used bus served as the basis for the calculation.

Bibliography

Franco, V. et al. (2014), *Real-World Exhaust Emissions from Modern Diesel Cars. A Meta-Analysis of Pems Emissions Data from EU (Euro 6) and US (Tier 2 Bin 5/Ulev II) Diesel Passenger Cars*, International Council on Clean Transportation, Berlin, http://www.theicct.org/sites/default/files/p. [4]

GoK (2016), *Third National Communication of the Kyrgyz Republic under the UN Framework Convention on Climate Change*, Government of Kyrgyzstan, Bishkek, https://unfccc.int/sites/default/files/resource/NC3_Kyrgyzstan_English_24Jan2017.pdf. [2]

GoK (2015), *Intended Nationally Determined Contribution – Submission of the Kyrgyz Republic*, Government of Kyrgyzstan, Bishkek, https://www4.unfccc.int/sites/submissions/INDC/Published%20Documents/Kyrgyzstan/1/Kyrgyzstan%20INDC%20_ENG_%20final.pdf. [1]

OECD (2017), *Promoting Clean Urban Public Transportation and Green Investment in Kazakhstan*, Green Finance and Investment, OECD Publishing, Paris, https://doi.org/10.1787/9789264279643-en. [3]

3. Economic analysis of the Clean Public Transport Programme

This chapter summarises the economic analysis conducted to assess the viability of the deigned Clean Public Transport Programme. It begins with a general overview of clean technologies and fuels in the transport sector, as well as a specific review of the energy market in Kyrgyzstan. It then describes the economic aspects of purchasing and running buses, and finally assesses potential sources of government financing available for the programme.

A market analysis was undertaken to determine the feasibility of the Clean Public Transport (CPT) Programme and its potential focus and scope.

Globally, the transport sector relies almost entirely on oil with about 94% of transport fuels being petroleum products. According to prognoses, these will dominate in road transport until at least 2050 (although the exact fuel mix might vary), even in the most stringent mitigation scenario (Sims and Schaeffer, 2014[1]).

There is often a time lag between when new technologies first appear in OECD countries and when they reach developing countries, which import mostly second-hand vehicles. It may take five years or longer lag for new technologies to reach second-hand vehicle markets in large quantities.

As part of the CPT Programme proposal, a detailed analysis was done of the key parameters, as well as the advantages and disadvantages of the various fuel options available for the programme, e.g. compressed natural gas (CNG)/liquefied natural gas (LNG), liquefied petroleum gas (LPG), diesel, and electricity to power trolleybuses. This chapter summarises the main findings, while Annex A to this report, especially Table A.3, contains the detailed analysis.

Apart from cleaner technologies and fuels, this chapter also discusses domestic production and import of buses, bus (trolleybus, minibus) fares for urban transport, and the co-financing available for investment projects.

3.1. Overview of clean technologies and fuels in the bus transport sector

This section provides an overview of the three cleaner fossil fuel options available in Kyrgyzstan:

- compressed natural gas (CNG)
- liquefied petroleum gas (LPG)
- diesel fuel (Euro 5) combined with Euro 6/VI engines.

The section also describes electricity as a power carrier, especially if sourced from cleaner fossil fuels (natural gas) or renewable energy (wind, solar, hydro power).

3.1.1. Compressed natural gas (CNG)

CNG can be used in traditional petrol (internal combustion engine) automobiles that have been modified or in vehicles specially manufactured for CNG use. Although vehicles can use natural gas as either liquid (i.e. LNG) or gas (i.e. CNG), most vehicles use the gaseous form. Besides fossil gas (CNG and LNG), methane vehicles can also be fuelled with biomethane or power-to-methane – a concept that converts electrical energy into chemical energy using water and carbon dioxide (also called power-to-gas).

CNG combustion produces fewer undesirable gases than other fuels and is safer in the event of a spill, because natural gas is lighter than air and disperses quickly when released. CNG vehicles have been introduced in a wide variety of commercial applications, from light-duty (<3.5t) to medium-duty (<7.5t) and even heavy-duty (>7.5t) vehicles.

The energy efficiency of driving on CNG is typically similar to gasoline or diesel, but produces up to 25% less tailpipe emissions (CO_2/km) because of differences in fuel carbon intensity. Lifecycle greenhouse gas (GHG) analysis suggests lower net reductions for natural gas fuel systems, however, in the range of 10-15%. This is because methane emissions are largely associated with leakage – i.e. unburnt methane leaking into the atmosphere – from the production of natural gas and the filling of CNG vehicles (in smaller amounts basically throughout the whole supply chain, ranging from 0.2% to 10% with a mean of 2.2% and median 1.6%) (T&E, 2018[2]).

In cars, the GHG savings range from -7% to +6% compared to diesel. In heavy duty vehicles (HDVs), such as buses, the range is -2% to +5% compared to best-in-class diesel trucks and depending on the fuel and engine technology. Therefore, CNG vehicles perform similarly to petrol vehicles and only slightly better than diesel ones (T&E, 2018[2]).

On the other hand, CNG vehicles require larger fuel tanks than conventional petrol-powered vehicles and the cost of fuel storage tanks is a major barrier to rapid and widespread adoption of CNG as a fuel. Denser storage can be achieved by liquefaction of natural gas (LNG), which is successfully being used for long-haul HDVs and ships. The indicative average distance between LNG refuelling points for HDVs is 400 km (T&E, 2018[2]).

3.1.2. Liquefied petroleum gas (LPG)

Also known as propane-butane, LPG is a flammable mixture of hydrocarbon gases used as a fuel in heating appliances, cooking equipment and vehicles. In some countries, LPG has been used since the 1940s as an alternative to petrol for spark ignition engines.

LPG has a lower energy density than either petrol or fuel-oil, so the equivalent fuel consumption is higher by about 10%. Many governments (not including Kyrgyzstan) impose less tax on LPG than on petrol or fuel-oil, which helps offset the greater consumption of LPG.

However, as mentioned in Chapter 2, CO_2 emissions from LPG-powered engines are higher than from CNG-powered ones. Therefore, the results of the OPTIC (Optimising Public Transport Investment Costs) Model do not include LPG buses. However, as LPG is already being used in Kyrgyzstan (mainly by private users, including public transport operators), the OPTIC Model can be used to include LPG buses should policy makers decide to evaluate this option in the future. For this reason, buses powered by LPG are given medium priority (see Section 5.1.2).

LPG burns more cleanly than petrol or fuel-oil – causing less wear on engines – and is especially free of the particulates present in the latter.

3.1.3. Diesel with Euro 6/VI engines

Diesel engines are one of the most common combustion engine choices for buses and other commercial vehicles, globally. For the time being, buses that run on diesel and biodiesel – brought to the market mainly by blending with conventional diesel – constitute by far the largest part of the bus fleet. The vast majority of the minibus fleet in Kyrgyzstan is composed of light and medium-duty commercial vehicles (see Section 6.2).

A standard diesel city bus emits fewer carbon emissions per passenger than cars, and lower emissions can be achieved by encouraging more passengers to shift to public transport (see Annex A). Since the 1990s, the Euro emission standards[1] – which define the acceptable limits of nitrogen oxides (NO_x), total hydrocarbons (THCs), non-methane hydrocarbons (NMHCs), carbon monoxide (CO) and particulate matter (PM) – have considerably reduced pollutant emissions of new vehicles sold in the European Union (EU) and the member states of the European Economic Area (EEA).

The biggest improvement in absolute terms has been achieved in reducing CO emissions (a Euro 6 vehicle emits 6.2 grams per kilometre less than a Euro 1 vehicle), whereas in relative terms the biggest improvement has been in PM emissions (a reduction of 98%) (Figure 3.1; see also Table A.1 and Table A.2 in Annex A to the report).

Figure 3.14. The impact of Euro standards on air pollution from light commercial diesel vehicles

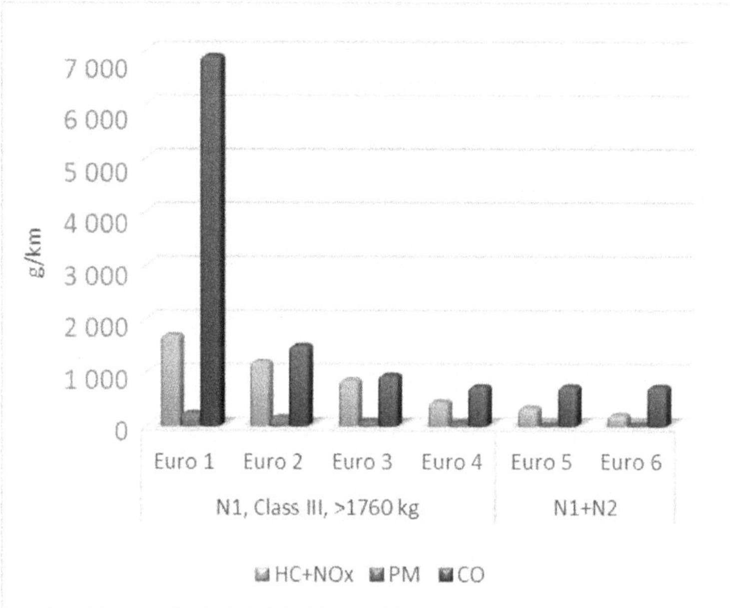

Note: N1: commercial vehicle not exceeding 3.5t (light-duty truck); N2 : commercial vehicle exceeding 3.5t but not 12t (truck).
Source: DieselNet (www.dieselnet.com).

On the other hand, a shift from Euro V to Euro VI for heavy-duty vehicles will require considerable investments by manufacturers and public transport agencies, and a major outlay by bus manufacturers. Similar to light-duty vehicles shown in Figure 3.1, the shift to Euro VI engines will also have a significant environmental cost in the form of emissions of particulates from engine exhaust (in particular, as compared to Euro I-IV categories).

Using biofuels, such as ethanol (for internal-combustion-engines) and biodiesel (for spark-ignition-engines) blends with conventional fuels (i.e. petrol and diesel) creates large a potential for further CO_2e emission reductions due to their lower fuel carbon intensity (CO_2/megajoule). However, the GHG impact assessment is rather complex.

However, as mentioned in Section 4.5.1, the support for diesel-fuelled vehicles requires strengthening regulatory measures to assure lower negative environmental impact of these vehicles.

3.1.4. Electricity

Due to current limits in battery capacity and in driving range (generally 100-200 kilometres for a small to medium-sized car), electric vehicles are at present best suited to urban and suburban driving. An urban bus can have a range of 200 kilometres per charge, but the full battery electrification of heavy-duty vehicles and long-haul bus and coach fleets is not likely to be a realistic option in the near future. On the other hand, trolleybuses are, at this point, a more viable electrically-powered alternative for reducing emissions. In addition, trolleybuses can be rendered "autonomous" over portions of their route by storing electricity.

3.2. Main economic variables of Kyrgyzstan's public transport

3.2.1. Energy market in the Kyrgyz Republic

The main suppliers of petroleum products to the Kyrgyz Republic are Kazakhstan, followed by the Russian Federation. Table 3.1 and Table 3.2 present the consumption, export and losses of petroleum products and natural gas respectively in the Kyrgyz Republic.

As can be seen in Table 3.1, the consumption of petrol increased considerably in 2011-16 (by 57%), while the increase in diesel consumption was only moderate (8.2%). This increased consumption needs to be covered by imports as the country's crude oil production is rather minimal (1-2 000 barrels per day over 1992-2019[2]).

Table 3.1. Consumption, export and losses of petroleum products, 2011-16

(conventional fuel equivalent*)

Items	2011	2012	2013	2014	2015	2016
Motor-car petrol	**950**	**1 423**	**1 307**	**1 020**	**1 104**	**1 445**
Consumed	878	1 298	1 201	577	938	1379
Exported	15	7	23	37	47	10
Losses	1	19	1	1	1	1
Surplus, end of year	56	99	82	405	118	55
Diesel fuel	**715**	**908**	**1041**	**943**	**716**	**744**
Consumed	645	788	993	728	629	698
Exported	24	9	13	3	1	-
Losses	1	2	-	-	-	-
Surplus, end of year	45	109	35	212	86	46
Fuel oil	**243**	**169**	**127**	**322**	**505**	**267**
Consumed	183	110	71	285	387	201
Exported	12	3	3	-	-	1
Losses	-	-	1	-	-	-
Surplus, end of year	48	56	52	37	118	65

Note: *Conventional fuel equivalent: thermal unit of fuel used to compare different types of fuel. Combustion of 1 kg of solid (liquid) conditional fuel (or 1 m^3 gaseous) is equal to 29.3 megajoules (7 000 kcal).
Source: National Statistical Committee of the Kyrgyz Republic (http://stat.kg).

As Table 3.2 shows, in contrast to petrol and diesel, the consumption of natural gas slightly decreased over 2011-16 (by 0.02%). Similarly to crude oil, Kyrgyzstan does not produce significant amounts of natural gas – less than 30 million cubic metres per year since 1996 (whereas in 1992 it was 100 million cubic metres).[3] For fossil fuels production, see Section 6.1.3.

Table 3.2. Consumption, export and losses of natural gas, 2011-16

(conventional fuel equivalent*)

Natural gas	2011	2012	2013	2014	2015	2016
Total	**383**	**490**	**355**	**328**	**318**	**331**
Consumed	331	394	311	293	298	325
Exported	-	-	-	-	-	-
Losses	52	96	44	35	20	6
Remainder, end of year	-	-	-	-	-	-

Note: * Conventional fuel equivalent: thermal unit of fuel used to compare different types of fuel. Combustion of 1 kg of solid (liquid) conditional fuel (or 1 m^3 gaseous) is equal to 29.3 megajoules (7 000 kcal).
Source: National Statistical Committee of the Kyrgyz Republic (http://stat.kg).

As can be seen in Figure 3.2, Bishkek city and the adjacent Chui *oblast* (region) were leaders in retail sales of automotive fuel in 2018. In fact, these two administrative units accounted for 50.3% of all sales in 2018.

Figure 3.15. Retail sales of automotive fuel, 2018* (by region)

(KGS million)

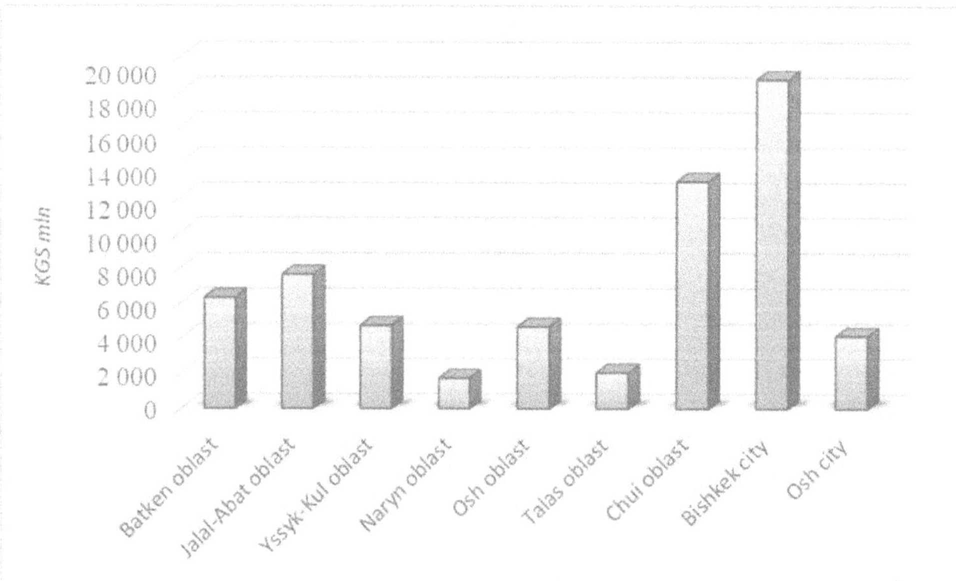

Note: *Preliminary data.
Source: National Statistical Committee of the Kyrgyz Republic (http://stat.kg).

Figure 3.3 shows the growing gap in these sales between the capital and the adjacent Chui region, and between the other pilot city Osh and its region, since 2006 (though sales have been increasing in all four areas).

Figure 3.16. Retail sales of automotive fuel in pilot cities and neighbouring oblasts, 2006-18*

(KGS million)

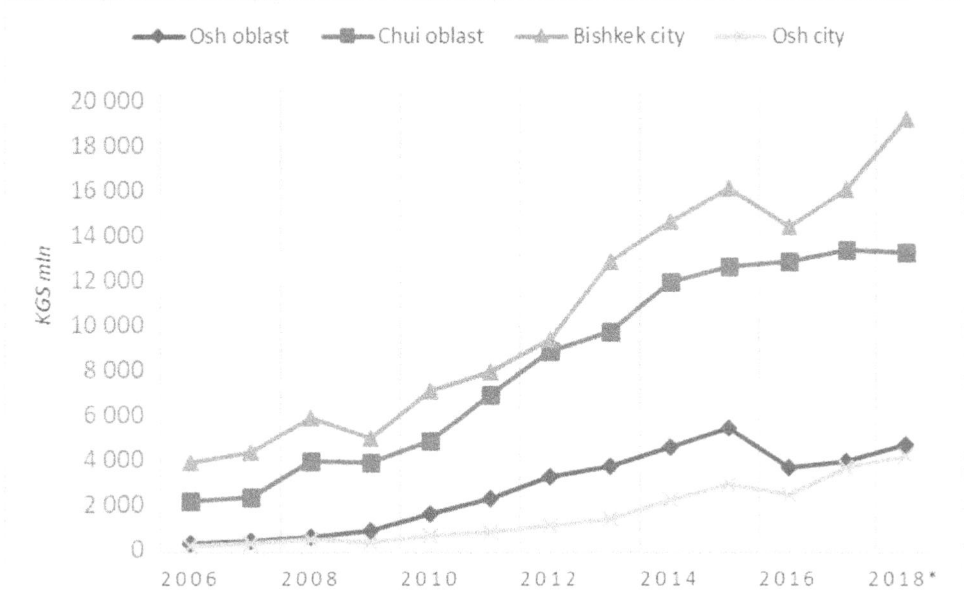

Note: *Preliminary data for 2018.
Source: National Statistical Committee of the Kyrgyz Republic (http://stat.kg).

The national consumption of liquefied petroleum gas is far below 1 000 barrels per day, as seen in Figure 3.4. Consumption fell by 84% between 1992 and 2012.

Figure 3.17. Consumption of LPG in Kyrgyzstan, 1992-2012

(thousand barrels per day)

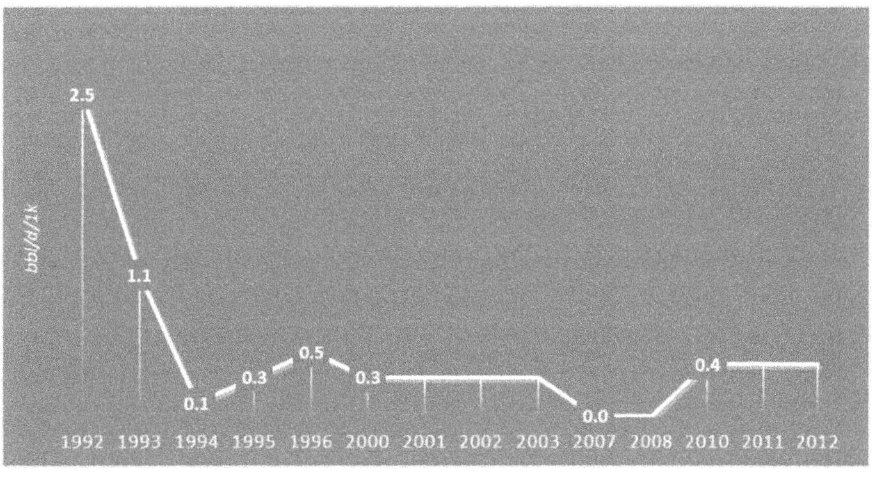

Source: IndexMundi Portal (www.indexmundi.com).

3.2.2. Fuel prices

Table 3.3 presents the retail prices for various fuels in the Kyrgyz Republic.[4] The State Agency for Regulation of the Fuel and Energy Complex (see Section 6.1.4) is responsible for granting energy production licences and setting energy tariffs.

Table 3.3. Retail prices for fuel in the Kyrgyz Republic, 2018*

Item	KGS/litre	USD/litre
Petrol-92	44.12	0.64
Petrol-95	46.53	0.68
Diesel	46.52	0.68
LPG	25.50	0.37

Note: *As of December 2018. There are no data on CNG prices in transport.
Source: National Statistical Committee of the Kyrgyz Republic (http://stat.kg).

In Bishkek, the prices in Gazprom Neft stations were as follows in May 2018:[5]

- Petrol-92: 43.50 KGS/l (USD 0.63)
- Petrol-95: 46.50 KGS/l (USD 0.68)
- Diesel, Euro 5: 45.50 KGS/l (USD 0.70)
- LPG: 25.50 KGS/l (USD 0.37).

From January to December 2018, the price of fuel increased by about 11% and diesel by 24%. It is suggested that for planning purposes higher prices than the actual prices be assumed for LPG and CNG , as eventually prices will have to move towards world levels[6] and excise and other taxes will be imposed in order to generate government revenues. Therefore, the following prices were used in the OPTIC Model (see Section 2.3.1):

- Diesel, Euro 6: 48 KGS/l (USD 0.70)
- Diesel, standard: 44.39 KGS/l (USD 0.65)
- Electricity: 0.03 KGS/KWh (USD 0.0004)
- LPG: 39.02 KGS/l (USD 0.57)[7]
- CNG: 31.71 KGS/kg (USD 0.46).

The share of average per capita expenditure on natural gas – not only in the form of CNG but also for other (main) purposes, such as cooking and heating (apart from electricity generation) – reflects the actual cash expenditures of the population (Table 3.4). Here, we can see that the cities of Bishkek and Osh have the highest per capita expenditures on natural gas by a large margin, driving up the country's average.

Table 3.4. Share of average per capita expenditure on natural gas in the Kyrgyz Republic, 2012-16

(%)

	2012	2013	2014	2015	2016
Kyrgyz Republic	**0.9**	**0.8**	**0.6**	**0.7**	**0.7**
Batken Region	0.3	0.2	0.1	0.1	0.1
Jalal-Abad Region	0.5	0.6	0.4	0.4	0.4
Issyk kul Region	0.0	0.0	0.0	0.0	0.0
Naryn Region	0.0	0.0	0.0	0.0	0.0
Osh Region	0.4	0.2	0.1	0.1	0.2
Talas Region	-	0.0	0.0	0.0	0.0
Chui Region	0.6	0.4	0.5	0.4	0.4
Bishkek	3.1	2.7	2.5	2.7	2.7
Osh (city)	-	1.9	0.4	0.8	1.0

Source: National Statistical Committee of the Kyrgyz Republic (http://stat.kg).

According to the Center for Renewable Energy and Energy Efficiency Development, there is no legislation for biogas plants. Two demonstration plants, however, do exist in the country. They produce 10 million cubic metres of biogas per year from waste. As there is no organised waste collection system, further development of biogas plants is very difficult. At present, biogas is used for electricity production. A by-product of biogas production is a bio fertiliser which is rated as very good.[8]

3.2.3. Domestic bus prices and fares

Kyrgyzstan does not have a very well-developed domestic automobile or bus industry. Since 2011 the production of vehicles has represented only 0.4-0.7% of the total production of industrial goods, measured in KGS. The economic downturn of 2014-15 is visible in this sector as well (Table 3.5).

Table 3.5. Production of industrial goods in the Kyrgyz Republic, 2013-18

(KGS million)

Items	2013	2014	2015	2016	2017	2018
Total	**169 829**	**171 109**	**181 027**	**209 812**	**237 225**	**250 640**
Manufacturing	141 350	140 267	140 604	163 298	181 574	189 802
Production of machinery and equipment not included in other groups	342	408	280	225	373	218
Production of vehicles	1 018	747	608	906	1 190	950
Other production, repair and installation of machinery and equipment	1 306	1 319	1 194	1 302	1 333	2 054

Source: National Statistical Committee of the Kyrgyz Republic (http://stat.kg).

According to the Trend news agency, manufacture of Isuzu buses and Ravon passenger cars in Kyrgyzstan will begin by the end of 2018. There is already a production area in the city of Osh which will begin with the large-scale assembly of Ravon brands. Bus production is planned in Bishkek. SamAvto's products, whose partner is the Japanese company Isuzu, is planned to be launched there (Trend AZ, 2017[3]).

According to AzerNews, nine enterprises from Uzbekistan will open production in Kyrgyzstan. Uzavtosanoat, jointly with AvtoOndoozavod, will open two enterprises for assembling agricultural machinery and trailers. In addition, an Uzbek company together with DT Technik and Avtotsentr Estakada from Kyrgyzstan will open factories for assembling buses and servicing transport, respectively (Aliyeva, 2018[4]).

At present however, as domestic capacity is low, essentially all buses will have to be imported.

The following unit prices of imported vehicles should be assumed in the design of the CPT Programme:

- new trolleybus: KGS 10.5 million (USD 152 000)
- new battery-powered trolleybus (with "autonomous" capability), reference price (imported): KGS 20 million (EUR 255 000; USD 291 000)
- new CNG bus: KGS 10 million (USD 145 000)
- new LPG bus: KGS 9.09 million (USD 132 000)
- new diesel Euro VI bus: KGS 8.7 million (USD 126 000)
- standard diesel bus (reference price): KGS 2.08 million (USD 31 000).

The programme will not include minibuses – either new or used (minibuses are foreseen to be replaced by regular buses).

Fares on urban public transport in Bishkek are determined by the Bishkek Mayor's Office and the City Council. They are fixed as a flat rate and usually paid in cash.

The resolution issued by Bishkek city hall in 26 April 2012 established the following tariffs for passenger transport:

- trolleybus – KGS 8 (USD 0.12)
- bus – KGS 8 (USD 0.12)
- minibus – KGS 10 (USD 0.15)
- minibus after 21:00 – KGS 12 (USD 0.17)
- taxi from 06:00 to 21:00 o'clock – KGS 10 (USD 0.15)
- taxi from 21:00 to 24:00 o'clock – KGS 12 (USD 0.17)
- routes (express): from 12 to 17 KGS (USD 0.17-0.25)
- special prices exist for retirees, e.g. KGS 5 (USD 0.07) with minibus till 17:00.

In Osh, the following tariffs are applied:

- trolleybus – KGS 6 (USD 0.09)
- bus – KGS 8 (USD 0.12)
- minibus – KGS 10 (USD 0.15)

- privileged persons (school students, retirees, disabled people, etc.) – KGS 1 (USD 0.01).

The fare on buses and trolleybuses is paid at the end of the journey as the passenger leaves the vehicle. While passengers do generally follow this procedure, the lack of any fixed system of sale and control of tickets can lead to collection losses. The Bishkek Trolleybus Management employs a very limited number of conductors to collect fares and control tickets.

On minibuses, the fare collected is shared between the driver and his company. The share should guarantee a minimum income for the company. Currently, however, drivers' incomes are very low – less than USD 80 per month. Keeping at least 10% of the cash received from passengers would allow the driver to at least double his income. This issue can only be resolved by introducing regulated ticket sales.

There are no serious technical obstacles to introducing an electronic fare system. While electronic equipment can be installed in vehicles, the sale system needs to take into account the fact that credit and debit cards are not widely used in Kyrgyzstan, especially among the social groups that use public transport.

3.3. Sources and types of financing for investment projects

Financing investment projects must take into account the economic reality of the country. Indeed, the source of revenues for budgets of cities and municipalities in the Kyrgyz Republic are primarily taxes (income and VAT).

According to the Ministry of Finance, when the tax system changed in recent years, these revenues were negatively affected. A new distribution of taxes is now being considered as an option to compensate cities for their revenue loss. In this restricted budget context, government capacities do not appear sufficient to undertake large-scale investment in transportation rolling stock. Such projects can only be financed with the support of international financial institutions, donors, public money and private investment.

In the past international financing institutions and donors have played key roles in the modernisation of the public transport fleet. State budget financing, either directly through the budget or from special funds, has not been used.

Kyrgyzstan has received substantial support from multilateral and bilateral development agencies. According to a private sector assessment conducted by the Asian Development Bank (ADB, 2013[13]), the major development projects promoting business development in the country are supported by the following donors:

- ADB: Asian Development Bank
- EBRD: European Bank for Reconstruction and Development
- GIZ: Deutsche Gesellschaft für Internationale Zusammenarbeit
- IFC: International Finance Corporation
- IMF: International Monetary Fund
- USAID: United States Agency for International Development.

The Central Asia Regional Economic Cooperation (CAREC) Program directs 77% of its investments into the transport sector (as of end of 2017).[9]

In particular, the EBRD has been involved in financing the purchase of new vehicles for urban public transport in Bishkek and Osh. The ADB has also expressed interest in providing loan financing for urban public transport investments, based on an existing credit line established with the government.

Other types of financing that should be considered are:

- **Local banks**: local banks can provide loans as part of the financing mix. Moreover, these banks could manage the project cycle as implementation units (see Section 4.2).
- **Loan guarantees** – the Ministry of Finance can provide loan guarantees to private and municipally-owned public transport enterprises (PTOs) and municipalities can provide loan guarantees to private PTOs.
- **Interest rate subsidies** – public money can be used to cover the difference between the interest rate a commercial bank would need to charge in order to be involved in a given project and the interest rate the borrower has the capacity to pay.

3.4. Conclusions for the CPT Programme

Kyrgyzstan has essentially no domestic production of natural gas, automobiles or buses. Given that the majority of buses – except for new trolleybuses purchased under the EBRD projects – are old and diesel-powered, a support programme aimed at the replacement of ageing public transport fleet is justified.

New models of diesel, CNG or LPG-powered buses offer savings in operating costs (due to lower maintenance costs and cheaper fuel) over old, diesel-powered models. Since Bishkek and Osh already have trolleybuses, these models should continue to be used. Unit prices for CNG, LPG, and electricity are very low compared to world levels; this will have the effect of lowering the calculated public support for the CPT investment programme. Using CNG and LPG to power public transport buses will decrease operating costs, given the lower costs of these fuels compared to diesel. Improved diesel fuels, however, such as Euro V and VI, can also be viable alternatives where CNG and LPG are not available. The Kyrgyz Republic needs to introduce European standards for diesel fuels.

CNG buses are more expensive to buy and may require additional infrastructure in some cities. However, it is also important to point out that diesel buses need special equipment to ensure that emission reductions be met. This equipment increases operating costs, leading some operators to dismantle the equipment. This practice should be discouraged and avoided. For more detailed information, Table A.3 of Annex A to this report compares the key parameters, as well as the advantages and disadvantages of CNG, LPG, and diesel fuel to power buses.

Given that the purchase cost of CNG and LPG-powered buses is higher than new model diesel-powered buses, the programme should provide enough assistance to allow the project to become profitable. This is defined as the point at which the net present value (NPV) of the investment is equal to zero from the point of view of the investing entity (see Annex B). This approach provides an opportunity for direct assistance to the service provider (for example, in the form of a grant) together with a loan, for example from the EBRD or a local bank or banks.

Notes

1. See EU emission standards for passenger cars and light-duty trucks at: www.dieselnet.com/standards/eu/ld.php.

2. For Kyrgyzstan's crude oil production and consumption, see: https://tradingeconomics.com/kyrgyzstan/crude-oil-production; or www.indexmundi.com/energy/?country=kg.

3. For Kyrgyzstan's natural gas production, see: https://knoema.de/atlas/Kirgisistan/topics/Energie/Gas/Erdgasgewinnung.

4. State Agency for Regulation of the Fuel and Energy Complex under the Government of the Kyrgyz Republic (www.regulatortek.kg). For general information about the State Agency in English, see: https://erranet.org/member/kyrgyz-republic.

5. See Gazprom Neft information on LPG at: www.gazprom-neft.kg/article/gaz.

6. For average world price of petrol, diesel and LPG fuels as well as electricity, see: www.globalpetrolprices.com. For natural gas prices for transport (CNG and LNG), see: http://cngeurope.com.

7. See current LPG prices at: www.globalpetrolprices.com/lpg_prices/#hl130. The price at the end of 2018 was about USD 0.37. For planning purposes, however, a significantly higher price was used due to the fact that LPG prices are significantly below world prices at present.

8. Personal communication with the Center for Renewable Energy and Energy Efficiency Development (www.creeed.net).

9. See CAREC Program's project portfolio at: www.carecprogram.org/?page_id=13630.

Bibliography

ADB (2013), *Private Sector Assessment, Update, Kyrgyz Republic*, Asian Development Bank, Manila, http://www.adb.org/sites/default/files/linked-documents/cps-kgz-2013-2017-oth-04.pdf. [5]

Aliyeva, K. (2018), "Uzbekistan to open nine enterprises in Kyrgyzstan", *AzerNews,* 11 January, http://www.azernews.az/region/125337.html (accessed on 30 August 2019). [4]

Sims, R. and R. Schaeffer (2014), "Transport", *Climate Change 2014: Mitigation of Climate Change. Contribution of Working Group III to the Fifth Assessment Report of the Intergovernmental Panel on Climate Change* Cambridge University Press, Cambridge and New York, pp. 599-670, http://www.ipcc.ch/site/assets/uploads/2018/02/ipcc_wg3_ar5_chapter8.pdf. [1]

T&E (2018), *CNG and LNG for vehicles and ships – the facts*, European Federation for Transport and Environment, Brussels, http://www.transportenvironment.org/sites/te/files/publications/2018_10_TE_CNG_and_LNG_for_vehicles_and_ships_the_facts_EN.pdf. [2]

Trend AZ (2017), "Production of UzAvtoprom cars in Kyrgyzstan will begin till the end of 2018", *Trend News Agency,* 25 December, https://en.trend.az/casia/2840029.html. [3]

4. Institutional arrangements and policy framework

This chapter proposes some institutional arrangements for managing the Clean Public Transport Programme as an investment programme. It begins by outlining good practice in setting up institutional frameworks for large environmental investment programmes. It suggests a three-level institutional structure comprising: 1) a programming entity; 2) an implementation unit; and 3) a technical support unit. It also suggests a possible division of responsibilities across these three entities, and describes the minimum operating regulations required to manage the programme. Finally, the chapter reviews the barriers to implementation in the form of regulations and policy distortions and suggests ways of addressing them.

4.1. Institutional arrangements for managing public investment programmes

There are a number of different good-practice institutional forms for managing public environmental expenditure. Simple expenditure programmes (e.g. financing research or education, purchasing simple equipment or standard services) may be managed directly by assigning additional responsibilities to existing government institutions at a variety of levels, using their regular staff and routine budget processes. For larger-scale, targeted programmes – in particular, programmes that involve financing capital investments, such as the Clean Public Transport (CPT) Programme – special institutional arrangements are recommended. These special arrangements may take many institutional forms and involve various types of implementing units (OECD, 2007[1]).

Deciding which form is most appropriate will generally depend on a variety of factors related to the sources of finance, the types of disbursements envisaged, and the legal and political culture of governance in a given country. Regardless of the institutional form, public environmental expenditure management should involve institutional structures and procedures that promote environmental effectiveness, embody fiscal prudence, and use financial and human resources efficiently.

Experience shows that these arrangements can take four basic forms:

1. government implementation units
2. environmental funds or a similar public finance institution
3. directed credit or a line of credit to financial intermediaries (such as commercial banks)
4. outsourcing.

Government implementation units – the most common arrangements – include the following institutional forms:

- government departments with responsibility for procuring goods and services or financing specific projects within the state budget
- project implementation units established in a government department to implement projects within a specific government expenditure programme included in the budget
- autonomous/decentralised government units financed by the budget but created to decouple the delivery of services or administrative tasks from policy formulation.

Regardless of the type of government implementation unit chosen, carrying a programme to completion requires capacity for project selection, implementation and monitoring. This means hiring skilled, trained personnel with a dedicated focus on the programme. Environmental programmes of EUR 50 million (USD 57 million) annually and about 200 contracts per year implemented in Central and Eastern Europe generally need staff of more than 20 people. In the case of the programme discussed in this study, given the relatively small number of contracts and homogenous types of investments required, only 5 people would be needed (see Table 2.6 and Table 2.7 in Chapter 2 for programme implementation costs).

In most instances, the institutional arrangement for large-scale (investment) programmes includes both a management (implementation) unit and a supervisory body. The implementation unit's management and staff are responsible for the day-to-day project cycle activities (identification, selection, appraisal and monitoring of projects), development of the annual expenditure plan and budget, and monitoring and preparation of reports. The supervisory body usually focuses on taking strategic decisions and approving internal operating procedures and rules (including eligibility and appraisal criteria to guide project selection). This division of responsibilities provides a system of checks and balances and improves the accountability of the programme. The supervisory body retains the final decision-making authority to approve financing of the individual projects recommended by the implementation unit's technical staff after the appraisal process (see Section 5.1). In the case of the CPT Programme, supervision will be performed by the programming entity (see below).

Outsourcing or contracting out is a further option if the government department does not have the capacities to fulfil its duties as an implementation unit. This allows an implementation unit to enter into a contract with an outside supplier for the provision of goods and services typically provided internally. If this option is chosen, good practice requires that outsourcing be conducted through competitive tendering.

To take one example, since 1993 the Austrian Federal Ministry for Sustainability and Tourism (BMNT)[1] has delegated the management of the grant schemes for Austria's Environmental and Water Management Fund to a private consulting company, Kommunalkredit Public Consulting (KPC) GmbH. KPC is also responsible for the Austrian Joint Implementation (JI)/Clean Development Mechanism (CDM) programme and serves as one of the four managers of the newly established Climate and Energy Fund. KPC manages more than 3 000 projects annually. Its role is to advise the ministry during the programme development phase and on the development of support programmes, as well as to provide technical, economic and legal assessment of support and consultancy projects. KPC also advises the decision-making bodies of these institutions – such as the BMNT in this case – on drafting contracts, monitoring project implementation and managing disbursements. Significantly, when the management of the Environmental and Water Management Fund was outsourced to KPC in 1993, its administrative costs were immediately reduced by more than half and have fallen since 2000 to only 20% of the 1993 cost.

Figure 4.1 presents the management scheme for the Austrian JI/CDM programme.

Figure 4.1. Management scheme for the Austrian JI/CDM programme

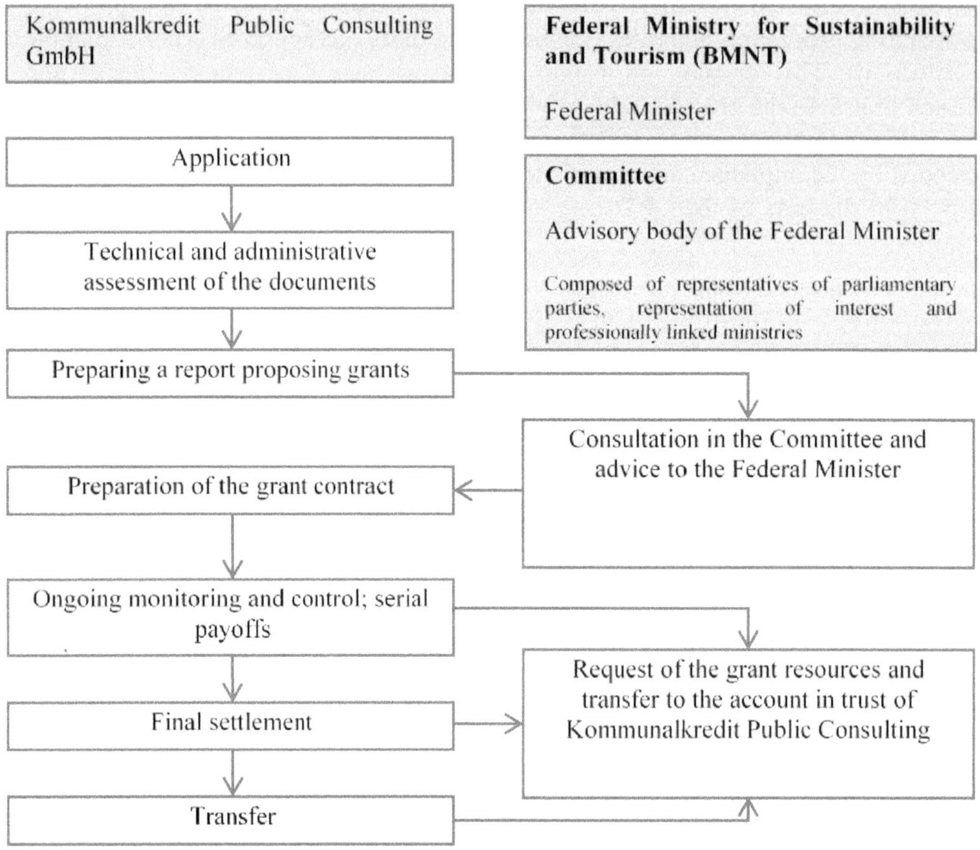

Source: Provided to the OECD by Kommunalkredit Public Consulting

4.2. A proposed institutional set-up for the CPT Programme

In preparing any public investment programme, the public financier needs to ensure that the essential individual elements of the programme are carefully designed and put in place before the programme is launched. This section summarises the main elements of the green public investment programme in Kyrgyzstan designed as part of this study, and explains how and why the project team arrived at the solutions proposed.

Effective programme implementation requires the following elements:

- stable and predictable sources of finance for the programme
- institutional arrangements to manage the programme expenditure, with sufficient resources, qualified staff and instruments to meet its objectives
- well-documented principles, rules and operating procedures for project cycle management (PCM)
- clearly defined and robust criteria for appraisal, selection and financing of investment projects

- clearly defined procurement rules.

To facilitate future implementation of the investment programme, this chapter and the next (Chapter 5) provide detailed information on the following arrangements:

- institutional arrangements comprising three levels: 1) programming entity (PE); 2) implementation unit (IU); and 3) a technical support unit (TSU) – see below
- PCM procedures, including eligibility criteria, project appraisal criteria, project-ranking procedures and financing rules (Chapter 5).

The institutional set-up needs to ensure that sufficient resources are allocated to meet the programme's objectives, and that qualified staff and instruments to implement the programme are made available. In general, programming and project appraisal should be strictly separated. Programming is the responsibility of the programming entity in the government agency appointed to manage the investment programme. Project appraisal is a technical process conducted by competent technical staff recruited on a competitive merit basis and held responsible for their decisions. The implementation unit should be operationally and technically independent and shielded from political pressures by rules and procedures developed by the programme's technical staff. It should also be a separate entity from the TSU.

4.2.1. Defining the programming entity

The programming entity is responsible for designing the programme, including (adapted from (OECD, 2007[1]):

- Defining priority environmental objectives for the investment programme that are specific, measurable, realistic and time-bound.
- Developing an investment programme that responds to the overall environmental and climate-related objectives. This programme should include specific targets, cost estimates, descriptions of eligible project types and beneficiaries, terms of financing, procedures, principles and criteria of project appraisal and selection, procurement rules, programme timeframe and indicators of performance.
- Determining sources of funds and the size of the financial envelope of the investment programme.
- Selecting the best institutional arrangements for managing the investment programme – in particular, deciding whether the programme can be managed directly by existing government institutions at different levels, or whether special institutional arrangements are required.
- Selecting, contracting and monitoring the implementation unit to manage the investment programme.
- Selecting and monitoring the technical support units required to implement the programme.

In Kyrgyzstan the Ministry of Economy should perform the role of the PE. It can use its available staff and resources to undertake its programming duties in consultation with relevant bodies, including other relevant government agencies, professional associations, local municipalities and non-government organisations as appropriate. In addition, representatives of these bodies may be invited to sit on and have an advisory role on the programme supervisory board.

4.2.2. Deciding on an implementation unit

The implementation unit (IU) is charged with drafting the programme's operating regulations, as described in Section 4.3 below. The IU needs to consult with the technical support unit(s) in the drafting and using its operating regulations. Because programming is a political process, it is important that the responsibilities for programming and project cycle management are separated and distinct. The latter role could be fulfilled by a local bank or banks, which would sign a co-operation agreement with the Ministry of Economy based on a successful public tender bid. Other potential IUs include the Investment Promotion and Protection Agency (IPPA), the State Agency for Environmental Protection and Forestry (SAEPF), and the Regional Environmental Centre for Central Asia (CAREC). The IU would provide the Ministry of Economy with information on the forecast number of beneficiaries and their financial needs. It would also manage the project cycle – conducting marketing activities for the programme, identifying beneficiaries and conducting eligibility appraisals of beneficiaries. The IU would communicate to the Ministry of Economy beneficiaries' loan and grant needs so that the ministry can monitor the CPT Programme budget for the given year (or programming cycle) and project types (project "baskets").

4.2.3. Appointing a technical support unit

The technical support unit (TSU) would give specialised assistance, advice and expertise in the areas of energy and fuel efficiency compressed natural gas (CNG), liquefied petroleum gas (LPG), modern diesel buses/trolleybuses, and air pollution and GHG emission reductions. The Investment Promotion and Protection Agency (IPPA), the State Agency for Environmental Protection and Forestry (SAEPF), or the Regional Environmental Centre for Central Asia (CAREC) could play this role – although they cannot act both as IU and TSU. Other TSUs may be identified, as deemed necessary and prudent.

4.3. Fundamental operating regulations

The effective implementation of the programme requires that the implementation unit (IU) define and publicise its operational rules and regulations. At a minimum, the core elements of such rules should include:

- definitions
- general provisions
- definition of eligible projects
- rules for awarding grants
- rules for modifying or terminating a grant contract
- procedures for programme review.

The grant agreement should define in detail the following terms and conditions as a minimum:

- amount of grant award (as an absolute value or as a share of total project investment cost)
- start and end dates of the project to be financed, as well as planned environmental impacts
- date on which the grant, or its instalments, will be transferred to the recipient
- rights of the implementation unit to control the awarded grant as well as the method of recovering the grant if the project fails to meet its stated objectives
- grantee's specific obligations arising under the contract with the programme implementation unit
- conditions under which the contract loses its force
- consequences of contract dissolution.

Typically, a project grant should not exceed 50% of the funds earmarked for the applicable type of project in the approved IU's annual financial plan. This is to enable the leverage of resources from other sources and ensure the commitment of the recipients to implementing the project using their own resources.[2]

Under this particular programme, and given the nature of investments to be financed, it is proposed that the programme can be financed by the state budget within the medium-term expenditure framework (MTEF) process. Financial support should be provided in the form of grants and/or bank guarantees.

There are other procedural rules that need to be considered, for example:

- The grant may be transferred to the applicant all at once or in instalments (tranches).
- A portion of the grant may be transferred in advance (up to 20% of the total value of the project), if project start up is impossible without advance funding.
- The recipient of a grant advance should be required to return to the IU any interest income resulting from holding the grant in its bank account (or the amount could be deducted from future tranches).
- The dates for making grant transfers are determined by the IU, based on funds at its disposal and upon consideration of an applicant's proposal, as presented in the application.
- Financial resources from the grant are transferred exclusively for the purpose of meeting the payments required by the grantee. The recipient should allow the IU full access to original invoices prepared by contractors or suppliers.

The *OECD Handbook for Appraisal of Environmental Projects Financed from Public Funds* includes a detailed discussion of all the rules that need to be considered in defining the procedures for the programme IU. It could be useful in further defining procedural rules for the CPT programme (OECD, 2007[1]).

4.4. Promoting the programme

Promotion is essential for the success of the programme; this is the responsibility of the IU. The promotion package might include the following elements:

- sending programme information to local administrations and potential beneficiaries
- distributing programme rules to local administrations and potential beneficiaries
- maintaining the IU's website with information on rules for awarding grants and application forms
- issuing press releases.

The costs of programme promotion should be included in the programme costs envelope.

4.5. Eliminating policy distortions

Various regulatory barriers may complicate the implementation of even a well-designed investment programme. It is important that before a programme is developed and financed, the Government of Kyrgyzstan reviews the relevant regulatory basis and eliminates any barriers as much as possible. Combining such regulatory improvements with financial support from the state is more likely to lead to the modernisation of the bus fleet in Kyrgyzstan and result in significant reductions in air pollution and GHG emissions.

One of the biggest obstacles for implementing an investment programme in the public transport sector in Kyrgyzstan is the very limited creditworthiness of bus operators. There are several reasons for this, including weak pricing signals for new technologies and fuels (which ultimately favour the old type of buses), a fare system for urban public transport that does not cover the capital cost of new buses, and a tender system that favours short-term contracts and makes it difficult to invest in a new bus fleet.

These distorted policies are the reason why the bus operator market is fragmented, dominated by small companies that lack creditworthiness and that are not attractive to international financial institutions, such as the European Bank for Reconstruction and Development (EBRD). Eliminating these barriers is key for the success of the programme. However, not all of them have to be addressed at the same time and some are interchangeable. For example, a better fare system and long-term contracts will help to increase creditworthiness, but this can also be achieved through loan guarantees or a higher level of public support provided by the CPT Programme.

Some of the key actions needed to remove implementation barriers are presented below.

4.5.1. Strengthen technical regulations in transport

Many of the policy and regulatory barriers identified by this study are similar to challenges experienced in other countries. To ensure the programme's successful implementation, the government will need to:

- **Strengthen (diesel) engine emission norms and bring them closer to European standards.** The Kyrgyz Republic has still not adopted modern emission norms for passenger cars or heavy-duty truck and bus engines. The emission norms are based on old diesel emission standards (Euro IV – introduced in the European Union back in 2005 – and lower). Euro 5 standards are to come into effect in 2019, but only for fuel, not engines. In contrast, Europe instituted the Euro VI standard in 2014 (see Table B.16 and B.17 of Annex B).
- **Strengthen (diesel) fuel standards.** Modern diesel engine emission norms cannot be introduced if the available fuel does not meet certain standards. The engines

include equipment sensitive to low-quality fuel, and sulphur dioxide (SO_2) emissions directly depend on the fuel's sulphur content. It is possible to find Euro 5 fuel in Kyrgyzstan, but by and large the available diesel fuel in the country meets only Euro 3 standards.

- **Strengthen technical inspection standards.** Although buses and minibuses in the country must pass technical inspections (twice a year), these inspections are not strict on emissions. Public transport operators thus have no incentive to improve emissions standards. Standards for technical inspection need to be better enforced.

4.5.2. Introduce adequate financial and pricing signals

The analysis in Chapter 3 shows that the average price of CNG and LPG fuels is much lower than the average price of petrol and diesel, which are also subject to an additional excise tax (see Section 7.1.12).

Although CNG and LPG fuels are cheaper than diesel, CNG and LPG-fuelled buses are more expensive (as they require the installation of additional equipment). Bus operators have not been given clear incentives to shift to cleaner fuels (either from renewable resources or cleaner fossil fuels). Given the significant efficiency gains (and environmental and health benefits) of replacing ageing and inefficient diesel and electricity-powered vehicles,[3] the investment programme (through the government) should provide the necessary financial incentives to attract investment into the sector.

The experience of EU countries shows that the uptake of fossil gases in transport is highest in countries with the lowest tax rates, i.e. where CNG or LPG enjoy tax rates below the EU minimum. In some countries (such as Italy) this can make them half the price of diesel. This support has continued despite the declining EU domestic fossil gas production and increasing dependence – as in Kyrgyzstan – on energy imports from the Russian Federation[4] (T&E, 2018[2]).

The government could therefore consider introducing targeted tax exemptions (including value added tax and import duties) on CNG/LPG vehicles and for owners of refuelling stations. Such fiscal measures could act as a complementary state support mechanism in addition to grants, loans or loan guarantees provided by the government until critical mass is achieved and the system becomes profitable.

4.5.3. Adjust the fare system for urban public transport

Fares should be aligned with good international practices and designed to maximise the social welfare of both passengers and public transport providers (subject to budget and capacity constraints).

The benefit for public transport service providers can be defined as revenues minus costs. The benefit for the user of these services can be expressed as the generalised price citizens are willing to pay before switching to non-public transport alternatives, minus the actual generalised price of the ticket (see Box 4.1). To some extent, the producer benefit and user benefit may be negatively correlated.

Given the economic and financial situation of public transport providers in Kyrgyzstan, the focus should be on the providers' benefits. The user benefit should be minimised as much as possible (ideally close to zero).

In Kyrgyzstan, operators of minibuses are private, whilst trolleybus and bus services tend to be provided by the municipality. Private operators provide business for profit, so passenger fares need to cover their capital and operating costs. As fares on public transport are so low in Kyrgyzstan (see Section 3.2.3), the quality of service provided by private operators is also low, favouring the use of very old buses in order to minimise capital costs (and depreciation).

Box 4.1. Proposing a sensitivity analysis

A sensitivity analysis into how many new buses/trolleybuses could be bought by increasing fares by KGS 2 (USD 0.03), for example, could be very informative.

Generally, the sensitivity analysis should take into account the fact that an increase in the price of tickets may discourage people from using public transport and may make them switch to using private cars, for instance, which can result in higher levels of air pollution. In economic language, public transport fare increases lead to an exposure-response relationship with a high price elasticity of demand; that is, a price increase leads to a decrease in demand for a given service.

Therefore, in order to achieve the desired environmental effects, it is important that private car transport does not substitute for public transport. Further, such an analysis depends, among others, on local circumstances, including the length of routes and the number of passengers. This type of analysis requires significant additional data collection and discussion with the government and municipal authorities, and therefore could not been done during this study – it should be carried out as part of a different study.

An increase in fares is clearly needed and could theoretically be used to co-finance the CPT Programme. The current fare of KGS 6-10 (USD 0.09-0.15) per journey by bus, trolleybus or minibus in Bishkek and Osh – not considering various discounts (as listed in Section 3.5) – is extremely low and would not be sufficient to guarantee the repayment of any eventual loan by bus or trolleybus operators. Thus, if the fares are kept at their current level, the programme and the public budget will be exposed to default by operators and will have to consume the guarantee, implying significant actual costs for the programme.

In addition to higher single fares, subscription fares could also be considered. This option is usually favoured by passengers who do not own a car and are therefore less price sensitive. On the other hand, in developing countries, people who do not own a car usually belong to lower income groups than in the developed world.[5]

Such changes in the fare system, coupled with the introduction of separate bus lanes and smart traffic lights, could improve the overall management of the public road transport sector in the country (see Section 2.2).

Regardless of the fare system, improvements in the payment system should also be implemented. Trolleybus and bus travel times are greatly increased by the "pay upon exit" system. Although electronic payment systems have been tested, they have not yet been successfully implemented (see Section 3.2.3).

4.5.4. Change public tenders for providing public transport in urban centres

Currently, most public transport operators are awarded short-term (one to three years) contracts. This approach encourages a short-term perspective among operators and motivates them to minimise investments so they can make a return in the short contract period. Operators thus tend to choose cheaper – hence, older and more polluting – buses and minibuses.

Shifting to the use of medium to long-term contracts (at least 10 years) would make it possible to award contracts to operators that will invest in a modern bus fleet. This approach, together with an adjusted fare system, regulatory improvements and financial support from the state, is more likely to lead to the modernisation of vehicle fleets.

The review of the urban public transport system in Bishkek and Osh revealed that the majority of operators are private entities: 41 private companies versus 2 public companies in Bishkek, and more than 20 private entities versus 1 public company in Osh (see Section 6.2). In 2016 private companies accounted for 92% of passengers transported in Bishkek (see Table 6.8) and 82% in Osh (see Table 6.11). This indicates that the programme financing needs to be tailored to the private sector, or at least a public-private partnership (PPP).

4.5.5. Encourage (energy) efficiency in public transport

Public transport in Kyrgyzstan is dominated by minibuses; regular buses only service a small number of urban and inter-city routes. While minibuses are needed to close the gap in public transport, they are generally are less efficient than regular buses (in terms of megajoules/passenger-km). Both Bishkek and Osh intend to begin to replace minibuses with modern, higher capacity buses (primarily trolley and CNG buses) that can carry up to five times more passengers.

It doesn't make economic sense to invest in public transport if streets are congested with traffic. Under such conditions, given there are only single-journey fares in Kyrgyzstan, it would not be financially viable for public transport operators to improve the quality of public transport services as foreseen in the recently adopted Development Programme 2018-2022 "Unity. Trust. Creation." (GoK, 2018[3]).

Journey time (and related fuel) savings can be achieved by increasing the operating efficiency of public transport. For example, dedicated bus lanes can reduce the need for inefficient mechanical braking. Kyrgyzstan has a few dedicated bus lanes, though they are often occupied by waiting cars. Eco-driving – i.e. a driving awareness technique that can reduce fuel consumption – can be introduced and taught to trainee bus drivers.

Combining such regulatory improvements with financial support from the state is more likely to lead to the modernisation of the bus fleet in Kyrgyzstan and result in significant reductions in air pollution and GHG emissions.

4.6. Conclusions for the CPT Programme

While there are various institutional set-ups for managing the programme, this chapter has outlined the three most common public support arrangements for providing subsidies (in form of grants) – governmental units, environmental funds and credit lines.

The optimal institutional set-up for managing the resources of the investment programme should be selected only after all elements of the programme are clarified and consensus has been reached on its priorities. Subsequently, the government needs to ensure that resources, qualified staff and instruments are sufficient to implement the programme.

Regardless of the type of institutional set-up chosen, it should involve an institutional structure and procedures that promote environmental effectiveness, embody fiscal prudence, and use financial and human resources efficiently.

It is also advisable for larger (investment) programmes – such as the CPT Programme – to include a supervisory body to adopt strategic documents and take strategic decisions, as well as oversee the implementation capacity of management in terms of project selection, implementation and monitoring (project cycle management). Importantly, both the management and the supervisory body should be protected from political pressures through their operating rules and procedures.

The Government of Kyrgyzstan should also aim to eliminate the policy and regulatory barriers that could hamper the implementation of the CPT Programme. A reflection on other countries' experience could provide an indicative checklist of measures and approaches to tackle these problems.

Notes

1. Known as the Federal Ministry of Agriculture, Forestry, Environment and Water Management (BMLFUW) until January 2018. The new website of the Federal Ministry for Sustainability and Tourism (BMNT) is at: www.bmnt.gv.at.

2. Given the nature of the projects to be financed, the grant should be determined at a level at which the net present value (NPV) for the project is equal to zero (see Section 3.4 and Annex B).

3. Unlike these (cleaner) fossil fuels, electricity-powered vehicles have the advantage of cheap electricity.

4. In 2016, the EU imported 86.7% of its petroleum products and 70.4% of its natural gas, so its energy dependence on natural gas is not significantly lower than on oil, especially given the larger share of imports natural gas from the Russian Federation (39.9%) than oil (31.6%) (EC, 2018[4]).

5. Usually, a single or monthly ticket fare system is considered more operator friendly, and a distance-dependent fare system seems more customer-oriented (and more technically demanding for the operator). A single or monthly ticket fare system is generally more attractive for passengers travelling longer distances, and a distance-dependent fare system more attractive for passengers travelling shorter distances. Finally, with a distance-dependent fare system, the operator can gather information both on the number of trips per route over a defined period and the average length of the route that a passenger travels in a given period. This information may be useful for making better management decisions.

Bibliography

EC (2018), *EU Energy in Figures: Statistical Pocketbook 2018*, European Commission, Brussels, https://publications.europa.eu/en/publication-detail/-/publication/99fc30eb-c06d-11e8-9893-01aa75ed71a1/language-en/format-PDF/source-79929745. [4]

GoK (2018), *Development Programme of the Kyrgyz Republic for the period 2018-2022*, Government of Kyrgyzstan, Bishkek, http://www.un-page.org/files/public/the_development_program_of_the_kyrgyz_republic_for_the_period_2018-2022.pdf. [3]

OECD (2007), *Handbook for Appraisal of Environmental Projects Financed from Public Funds*, OECD Environmental Finance Series, OECD Publishing, Paris, http://www.oecd.org/env/outreach/38786197.pdf. [1]

T&E (2018), *CNG and LNG for vehicles and ships – the facts*, European Federation for Transport and Environment, Brussels, http://www.transportenvironment.org/sites/te/files/publications/2018_10_TE_CNG_and_LNG_for_vehicles_and_ships_the_facts_EN.pdf. [2]

5. Proposed procedures for project cycle management

This chapter presents an overview of the project cycle management procedures developed for each project pipeline identified as part of this green public investment programme. Essentially, the implementation unit should ensure that the programme follows these procedures. A well-designed process – which is the responsibility of the programming entity – should guarantee that only eligible projects compete for public support and that the most cost-effective ones are selected for financing and implementation.

Project cycle management (PCM) comprises several distinct stages: 1) identifying and assessing projects for eligibility; 2) preparing programmes; 3) project development; 4) financing projects; 5) controlling and monitoring project impacts; and 6) maintaining a database of project impacts. Each of these stages is detailed in the sections below.

5.1. Identifying and assessing projects

The first step in the PCM process is to identify eligible projects that respond to the strategic and specific objectives of the national environmental/climate and energy policy, as well as the objectives defined in the CPT Programme. Eligible projects include investments in replacing the public transport fleet in order to reduce air pollution and greenhouse gas (GHG) emissions and improve service quality.

Eligible projects would involve the following activities:

- Replacing old public transport vehicles (buses, trolleybuses and minibuses) with environmentally acceptable models equipped with diesel, CNG or LPG or electricity-powered engines, used for public transport in urban (Phase 1) and suburban routes and inter-city (Phase 2).
- Investing in support activities (studies, construction of CNG filling stations, establishment of a maintenance workshop for new buses, and additional investments that improve public transport services) relevant to the bus replacements in the three pipelines (CNG/LPG, diesel, electric).

Only investment projects (i.e. those involving capital outlays) are eligible for financing under this programme. The list of eligible projects will be reviewed on an annual basis by the implementation unit to ensure that it reflects national environmental/climate and energy policy objectives.

5.1.1. Project eligibility criteria

Clearly specifying the eligibility criteria (in terms of project types, beneficiaries and project costs that will be supported by the programme) and setting robust project appraisal criteria will make programme implementation more transparent and efficient. It will also make the programme credible for financiers – be they public or private, local or foreign.

This section describes the minimum eligibility criteria. These are "knock-out criteria", i.e. failure to meet even one of these criteria at this stage results in rejection of the project (though the option of re-designing the project proposal could be considered). Projects that pass the eligibility assessment but lack sufficient information can be returned to the applicant with a request for clarification. Annex D contains a template of an eligibility evaluation form that can be adapted for project screening.

Eligibility criteria allow the programme to conduct an initial and simple assessment of those projects that appear to address all crucial objectives related to the CPT Programme and that can potentially qualify for financing. The criteria include the types of eligible **projects**, eligible **costs** and eligible **beneficiaries** (project owners) for screening individual projects that apply for public support. The purpose of eligibility criteria is to conduct an initial and simple assessment of those projects that appear to address all the objectives related to the CPT Programme and that can potentially qualify for financing. Eligibility criteria should be simple, straightforward and clearly specified.

The following groups of eligibility criteria could be used to screen projects (detailed lists should be prepared by the Ministry of Economy before the programme launch):

1. Location of the project: limited to urban centres and suburban areas (Phase 1).
2. Types of eligible projects:
    a. the project type should be identified in the list of eligible projects
    b. all proposed costs of the project should be possible to identify in the list of eligible costs
    c. replacement of buses that are more than 10 years old and equipped with below Euro 5/V engines.
3. Types of eligible beneficiaries (project owners):
    a. private public transport operators that currently provide services in eligible urban centres (Phase 1) and suburban areas of the pilot cities or inter-city connections (Phase 2 – for a description of phases, see Section 2.3 and 2.4 above)
    b. municipal public transport operators that already provide services in eligible urban centres and suburban areas of the pilot cities (Phase 2)
    c. pilot cities' administrative governments (for preparing the necessary studies and support investments).
4. Other eligibility criteria: existing city plans for additional (support) investments to improve the city's urban public transport system.

Also, at this stage, a list of eligible vehicle models available on the market could be prepared in order to simplify the procedure and eligibility testing. The list could be updated in the future when new models come on the market. If the type of vehicle proposed for purchase is on the approved list, the IU can proceed without contacting the Ministry of Economy. If not, the project documents, especially technical specifications (which should be delivered by beneficiaries, bus producers or importers on request) should be sent to the Ministry of Economy for evaluation. The Ministry of Economy evaluates whether the vehicle model fulfils the programme objectives – if it does it is added to the list. If it does not fulfil the objectives of the programme, the Ministry of Economy informs the IU, the beneficiary is informed. The project can be re-evaluated if the beneficiary proposes a different vehicle type.

If a project does not comply with the eligibility criteria (i.e. if it receives a "no" response to any of the questions in the eligibility assessment), it is rejected and a written explanation is sent to the applicant. The project may be re-evaluated upon modification and re-submission.

The IU should select employees to help review and evaluate projects. The employees should participate in training by the Ministry of Economy to give them the skills to evaluate whether the project meets the CPT Programme objectives and complies with the eligibility criteria.

5.1.2. Project appraisal criteria

A project that meets the eligibility criteria then needs to be appraised to assess if it is worth funding. The appraisal is also done on the basis of clearly specified and rigorous criteria.

These allow programme managers to compare, rank and select the most cost-effective projects for financing. When these criteria are applied uniformly across all (similar) projects, they can also help reduce management bias in selecting individual projects for financing.

Experience shows that a well-designed appraisal system is fundamental for selecting the most cost-effective investment projects for financing with public resources (see Figure 2.10 above). All projects that pass through the eligibility screening (pre-appraisal) are then appraised and ranked according to a set of appraisal and ranking criteria listed briefly below and scored using an evaluation table (see Annex E). Projects with the highest scores would make the biggest contribution to the CPT Programme objectives and therefore should be the first to be selected for co-financing.

The following appraisal criteria are proposed to evaluate projects in this pipeline:

1. Project preparation:
    a. prepared business plan or strategic plan for implementation of the clean public transport in the city.
2. Project location:
    a. buses to be replaced are operating in polluted districts of the cities (list of polluted districts)
    b. buses to be replaced are used only in the centre of the eligible city
    c. buses to be replaced are used in the city centre and on the outskirts/suburbs of the eligible city
    d. buses to be replaced are used in the city and connecting rural areas outside the eligible city.
3. Project type:
    a. buses have higher priority than minibuses
    b. compressed natural gas (CNG) buses have higher priority than liquefied petroleum gas (LPG) buses
    c. modern diesel buses are assigned the lowest priority.
4. Project size:
    a. replacement of more than 20 buses
    b. replacement of between 10 and 20 buses
    c. replacement of fewer than 10 buses[1].
5. Proposed system of improvements of the urban public transport system in the city:
    a. length of new bus lanes
    b. number of traffic lights with priority for public transport
    c. number of bus stops newly equipped with online information for passengers
    d. number of new bus stops.
6. Environmental efficiency: Cost per reduction of a unit of particulate matter – PM2.5.

The applicants submitting applications and supporting documentation for those projects that pass the cut-off level for financing are then contacted by the IU in writing to inform them that their project has been selected for financing.

5.2. Preparing programmes

Two cities, Bishkek and Osh, were selected for the pilot phase. To implement the pilot phase, it is recommended that a project selection procedure be followed based on negotiations between the city administrations and beneficiaries (operators of the public transport system). The Ministry of Economy, in co-operation with the State Agency for Environmental Protection and Forestry (SAEPF), who are responsible for the overall oversight of the programme, should give clear directions to local administrations, in particular on:

- the amount of funds allocated for the pilot phase for each city
- the maximum share of co-financing from public funds
- the criteria that pilot projects should meet in order to be deemed eligible for financing (see Annex D).

The project cycle management – especially for the second (scaling-up) phase of the programme – will be complex, but in order to keep down administrative and transaction costs (see Table 2.6 and Table 2.7) for beneficiaries, most of the work will be done by the implementation unit (IU).

Programme preparations will consist of negotiations with the IU, signing agreements and designing procedures and forms to be used by the IU.

The IU's main responsibilities should include:

- marketing the programme to potential beneficiaries
- identifying, assessing and selecting eligible projects and beneficiaries; preparing and signing loans; and conducting verification of the projects
- ensuring operations comply with the programme, especially by applying the procedures and criteria established by the Ministry of Economy on selecting beneficiaries and their projects
- reporting regularly on financial and physical implementation to the Ministry of Economy and the Ministry of Finance (every three months)
- preparing forecasts of financial involvement for the next reporting period.

The IU will actively promote the CPT Programme by distributing information about it. This will involve publishing leaflets to be distributed to potential beneficiaries, which define eligible projects, eligible beneficiaries, eligibility criteria, and the type of financing available.

5.3. Financing projects

Once the priority projects have been selected for financing, the proposed financing scheme for each project needs to be designed. This involves determining the amount of the grant required for the project to be viable.

When the proposed financing schedule has been defined, the IU invites the applicant to negotiations and to sign the loan contract. The contract should detail the rights and responsibilities of each party to the agreement, measures to be taken if the beneficiary fails to comply with the terms and conditions of the contract, as well as a disbursement schedule for the financial support.

During project implementation, settling payments with contractors is an important practical issue. The IU will settle payments with contractors.

There are two schemes for organising contracting and paying beneficiaries and contractors:

- Scheme 1: Public support is transferred to the beneficiary (i.e. public transport operator), who organises a tender to select a contractor/supplier (of public transport vehicles). The bank transfers the funds to the beneficiary, who pays the contractor/supplier (of public transport vehicles) upon invoicing (Figure 5.1).
- Scheme 2: Public support is transferred to the beneficiary, who organises a tender to select a contractor, but the contractor is paid directly by the IU. The bank agrees the amount of financing with the beneficiary, but pays the contractor/supplier directly upon delivery of the service and submission of invoice (Figure 5.2).

In both options, if the bus supplier has not already been selected, the beneficiary initiates a tender procedure (in accordance with public procurement law, if the purchases of this beneficiary fall under this law).

Under Scheme 1, at the end of an agreed time period (for example monthly), the Ministry of Economy receives from the IU the list of supported beneficiaries, number and types of purchased vehicles, cost of the purchase and information on the loan provided to the beneficiary. Based on this information, the Ministry of Economy releases the grant amount (calculated as a fixed percentage of the purchase cost). In general, Scheme 1 is more widely used than Scheme 2 (which has benefits under special circumstances, such as lack of trust).

Figure 5.1. Payment scheme 1: beneficiary receives public funds

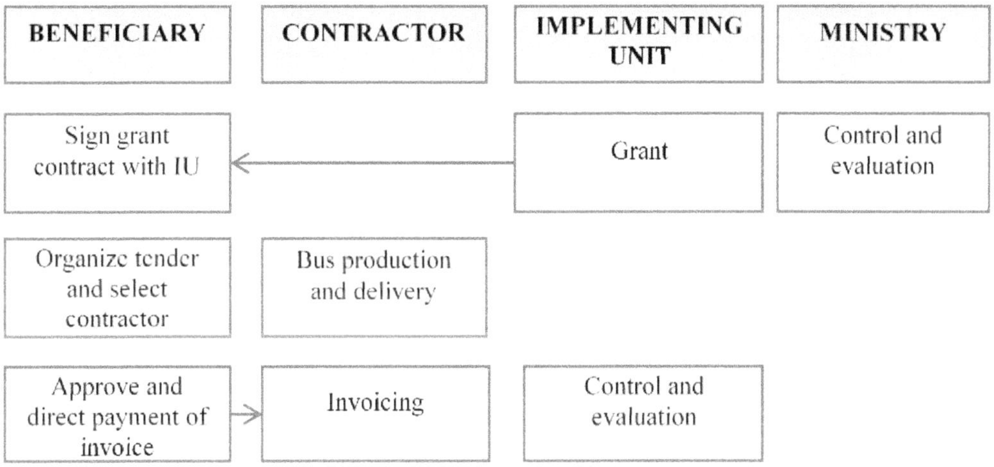

Source: OECD, own graphics.

Figure 5.2. Payment scheme 2: contractor is paid directly

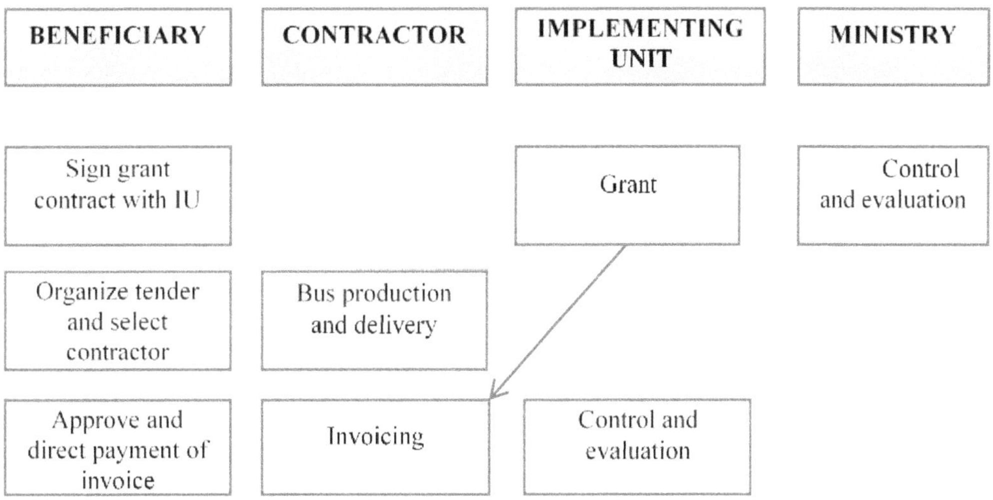

Source: OECD, own graphics.

It is important to highlight again (see Section 2.4) that the rate of financial assistance (subsidy rate) should be set to ensure that it does not replace, but instead leverages, the beneficiary's spending. Thus, public resources should be seen as a last resort for covering the financing gap of green priority projects (following the principle of additionality). For this reason, the level of the subsidy should be kept at the absolute minimum. This optimal minimum can be defined as the rate of assistance that makes environmentally and economically important projects financially viable.

5.4. Controlling and monitoring project impacts

Once implementation has commenced, the IU, as per the contract with the beneficiary, maintains the right to monitor and inspect the implementation of the project in order to:

- compare actual with planned results in physical terms (e.g., number of buses; type of buses)
- determine whether buses are being used to provide public transport in urban/sub-urban centres
- monitor implementation of accompanying investments (e.g., dedicated bus lanes, improved bus stations).

5.4.1. Performance indicators

The following performance indicators could be used by the institution managing the expenditure programme:

- number of buses replaced, 15 years or older, including minibuses
- number of buses replaced, 10 years or older, including minibuses
- number of LPG-fuelled buses replacing outdated buses
- number of CNG-fuelled buses replacing outdated buses
- number of new trolleybuses
- number of model diesel-fuelled (Euro V or better) buses replacing outdated buses
- kilometres of dedicated bus lanes
- tonnes of carbon dioxide (CO_2) reduced per year
- tonnes of particulate matter – PM10 – reduced per year
- tonnes of particulate matter – PM2.5 – reduced per year.

5.4.2. Impact assessment

In contrast to the control and monitoring procedures during project implementation described above, post-implementation control and monitoring (*ex-post* evaluation) involves determining whether the project has met its stated objectives. This is the primary responsibility of the IU, which reports the results to the Ministry of Economy (as manager of the CPT Programme).

Since direct and immediate measurement of project outcomes in terms of air pollution reduction and fuel consumption is very difficult, only the physical outcomes of the project should be monitored, namely:

- the number of buses by engine type and whether buses are used to provide public transport services in urban centres
- verification that emission reduction equipment remains installed in diesel engines
- implementation of accompanying investments.

If the objectives have not been met, the beneficiary may have to return a part or all of the financial support provided under the programme. The contract must clearly rule on such an eventuality.

5.4.3. Maintaining a database of project and programme impacts

A final element of PCM is creating and maintaining a database of project and programme impacts. The Ministry of Economy should determine the best format for the database, such as an Excel-based system or a database software. The following parameters need to be included and maintained in the database:

Programme:

- expenditures by year for each type of project
- actual expenditures compared to those budgeted
- calculated emission reductions by year.

Projects:

- number of projects by type, by year
- physical outcomes by year: number of buses by engine type
- calculated emission reductions by year (estimated based on buses replaced)
- project cost-effectiveness: cost per unit of emission reduction.

The database should be used to inform future beneficiaries, to adjust eligibility and appraisal criteria as needed and to ensure relevance.

5.5. Conclusions for the CPT Programme

The major purpose of the public support under this programme is to provide incentives to local communities and enterprises to undertake green investments and spend more of their own resources on environment-friendly products and technologies.

Some of the main conclusions emerging from the discussion of programming and project cycle management include:

- **Programming is a political process**, focused on defining priorities and goals and setting out rules for the project cycle (e.g. Ministry of Economy). **Appraisal – but simplified – is conducted by professional technical staff** (e.g., the IU), who are held accountable for their decisions. Responsibilities for programming and the project cycle management should be separated.
- **Transparency is key**. Information (on project cycle procedures, eligibility criteria, and achieved results and benefits) should be disseminated widely. All potential applicants should be treated equally; decisions should be explained on time; stakeholders should be invited to participate.
- While a two-step appraisal process is preferable, due to involvement of many small enterprises and banks **the appraisal procedure should be simplified**, as follows: the Ministry of Economy approves the list of buses that are eligible for financing, which makes it simple for banks to approve projects for a financing. If a type of

bus is not on the approved list, it will not be financed and no further assessment is necessary.

- **The process does not stop once a decision to finance a project has been made**: contracting, monitoring project implementation and assessing project outcomes are also essential, as programme managers will learn from this experience.
- **Attracting and retaining qualified staff is key**: the capacity to challenge project owners and to manage the complex process of project appraisal requires experience in the field.

Note

1. The appraisal system should award fewer points to projects involving CNG buses when there are no CNG filling stations in the city or they are not commercially profitable (there are fewer than 100 CNG buses).

6. Macro-economic and environmental overview

This chapter briefly describes the main demographic, macro-economic and environmental issues in Kyrgyzstan of relevance to the transport sector. It presents an overview of the urban public transport system in the country, as well as the level of greenhouse gas emissions and air pollution in the main urban centres. It also analyses the major health risks associated with the main air pollutants. This review forms part of the justification for the need for public support for investments in the transport sector.

6.1. Demographic and macro-economic situation

6.1.1. Geography, territorial division and demographic development

The Kyrgyz Republic is a landlocked country in the north-east of Central Asia, on a territory of 199 951 km^2. It shares a border with Kazakhstan to the north, Uzbekistan to the south-west, Tajikistan to the south, and China to the east and south-east.

Although Kyrgyzstan's altitude ranges between 394 m and 7 439 m above sea level (at Victory (Pobeda) Peak), almost 90% of the country lies above 1 500 m (the average elevation is 2 750 m). According to estimates, less than 20% of the country is suitable for comfortable living (GoK, 2016$_{[1]}$). The territory is characterised by high seismicity (NSC, 2016$_{[2]}$). Kyrgyzstan's high-mountainous landscape is exposed to dangerous processes, with over 20 of the 70 global hazardous natural processes and phenomena that can cause significant damage to the population, economic activities and infrastructure occur in the country (GoK, 2016$_{[1]}$).

Land used by farms makes up about 5% of the country's area, of which 61% is irrigated ploughed fields (3.2% of the total area).[1] Pastures – mostly high-altitude steppes – have a marginal share among the farmlands (0.07%). The rest of the rural area is covered by mountains, forests and glaciers. Negative climatic impacts affecting agriculture include drought and lack of water resources, which could further decrease the already limited arable area.

The nomadic empire called "the Kyrgyz Kaganate" first became part of the Russian Empire in 1876, and in 1936 joined the USSR as the Kirghiz Soviet Socialist Republic (also referred to as Kirghizia). In 1991, Kyrgyzstan proclaimed itself an independent and sovereign state. In 1993, the country officially became the Kyrgyz Republic. All fundamental state institutions and a currency were also established in 1993. A constitution defines the political system of the republic. The President, elected for a six-year term, is head of state and the Prime Minister is head of government.

The national language is Kyrgyz (which belongs to the north-western group of Turkic languages), and Russian is the other official language (since 1997). Both languages are used for administrative purposes and both are relatively widely spoken among the population (depending on the region).[2] According to law, however, the Kyrgyz version of a document is considered to be its original version.

The administrative and territorial division of the Kyrgyz Republic comprises seven *oblasts*[3] (regions) administered by appointed governors; and two cities (Bishkek and Osh), which are administratively independent, with a status equal to a region. The capital of Kyrgyzstan is Bishkek (1 027 200 inhabitants) – also the most populated city in Kyrgyzstan. The second most populated city is Osh (299 500 inhabitants).[4] With the exception of Jalal-Abad city, all other towns have fewer than 100 000 inhabitants.

The Kyrgyz Republic is also organised into 40 administrative *rayons* (districts), 31 towns (including cities of Bishkek and Osh), 9 urban settlements, 3 villages and 453 *aiyl aimak* (village communities). Table 6.1 shows in detail the population density of each region. In 2018, the average population density was 31.3 inhabitants/km^2.

Table 6.1. Population density by region, 2013-17

(people per km²)

	2013	2014	2015	2016	2017
Kyrgyz Republic	**28**	**29**	**29**	**30**	**31**
Batken Region	27	28	28	29	30
Jal-Abad Region	32	33	33	34	35
Issyk-kul Region	11	11	11	11	11
Naryn Region	6	6	6	6	6
Osh Region	40	41	42	43	44
Talas Region	21	21	22	22	22
Chui Region	42	42	43	44	45

Source: National Statistical Committee of the Kyrgyz Republic (http://stat.kg).

The population is unevenly distributed across the country due to its extremely mountainous terrain. Most economic activities take place within settlements, as well as in a relatively small buffer zone of 5 km around settlements. Settlements are usually situated in the lowlands or intermountain basins and mountain valleys, accounting for about one-seventh of the total area (GoK, 2016[1]).

In 2017 the urban/rural population distribution was 34% to 66% (NSC, 2018[3]). In 2018, 34% of the population was below working age, whereas 59% are of working age and 7.5% are above the working age.[5] Over half the population (54%) is under the age of 25. The ethnic composition of the population includes Kyrgyz (73.3%), Uzbeks (14.7%), Russians (5.6%), Dungans (1.1%), Uyghurs and Tajiks (both 0.9%) and other nationalities (3.4%).[6]

The natural population increase in Kyrgyzstan is compared to other Eastern Europe, Caucasus and Central Asia (EECCA) countries in Figure 6.1.

Figure 6.1. Natural increase of population in selected EECCA countries, 2000-13

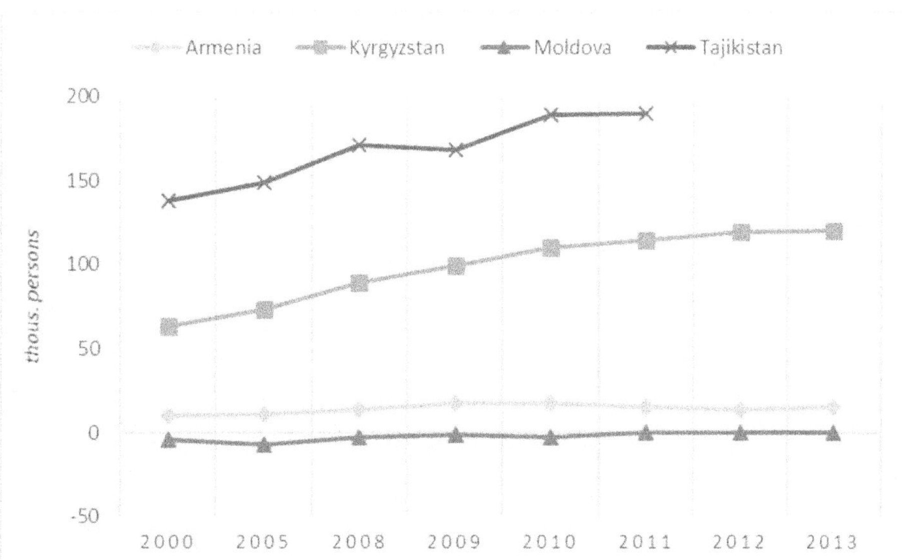

Note: 2012 and 2013 data for Tajikistan not available.
Source: (CIS, 2014[4]), *Commonwealth of Independent States in 2013 – Statistical Yearbook.*

6.1.2. Political and macro-economic situation

The first two decades of independence were marked by struggle. Unmet expectations resulting from prevailing corruption and nepotism culminated in two revolutions. The first revolution took place in March 2005, but it did not live up to expectations and another revolution was carried out in 2010 leading to a change of government in April 2010. After this event, a national referendum was organised and a new Constitution defined the parliamentary form of the government. In this way, Kyrgyzstan became the first parliamentary republic and the only country in Central Asia where the president is limited to a single (six-year) term (World Bank, 2019[5]).[7]

While a certain stability in the political environment was achieved, external shocks as well as a heavy reliance on gold exports have contributed to growth volatility. The estimated gross domestic product (GDP) in 2018 was KGS 557 113 million (USD 8 081.9 million), and has growing at an average annual rate of 4.2% since 2014 (see Figure 6.2).[8] The GDP per capita (purchasing power parity) reached USD 1 331 in 2014, fell to USD 1 163 in 2015, and climbed again to USD 1 272 in 2017 (NSC, 2018[3]). This was caused primarily by the devaluation of the som in 2015 (see Section 6.1.5) – when measured in national currency, GDP per capita has been constantly rising (see Table 6.2).

The decline in economic growth in 2015 is attributable to a significant reduction in industrial production at the Kumtor Gold mine.[9] The healthier 2017 and 2018 figures are mainly based on higher import tax collection; tax revenues as a share of GDP are projected to rise following the implementation of measures to expand the tax base (World Bank, 2019[5]).

Table 6.2. Gross domestic product per capita, 2007-17

Items	2007	2008	2009	2010	2011	2012	2013	2014	2015	2016	2017
thous. KGS	28.1	37.0	39.2	42.4	54.4	58.0	65.0	71.8	75.5	81.8	89.3
thous. USD	0.8	1.0	0.9	0.9	1.2	1.2	1.3	1.3	1.2	1.2	1.3
% of previous year		132%	106%	108%	128%	107%	112%	110%	105%	108%	109%

Source: National Statistical Committee of the Kyrgyz Republic (http://stat.kg); and the World Bank (https://data.worldbank.org) for the year-respective exchange rate.

Figure 6.2 shows the trends in GDP growth and inflation over 2007-17. Over that period, average annual GDP growth was 4.8% and the rate of inflation was 8.5% (since 2012, the pattern has become more stable). Inflation is expected to stay within the National Bank's medium-term monetary targets (5-7%), with the rate for 2019 forecast at 3.0% and for 2020 at 3.5%. GDP growth is expected to be 4.0% and 4.4%, respectively.[10]

Figure 6.2. GDP and inflation growth rates, 2007-17

Source: World Bank (https://data.worldbank.org).

The size of the economy is rather small (as noted above, around USD 8.1 billion in 2018) and its reliance on two volatile sources – i.e. gold mining[11] (10% of GDP) and remittances (27% of GDP in 2018) – makes it vulnerable to external shocks. Exchange rate depreciation (see Section 6.1.5) and economic and financial exposure to the Russian Federation are further severe downsize risks (World Bank, 2019[5]); (Moody's, 2019[6]).

Agriculture is a key economic basis of Kyrgyzstan's economy, both by size of added value generated and by number of people employed. This sector (including fishing and forestry) produces 12-17% (ca. one-sixth to one-eighth) of the country's GDP and provides the processing enterprises with raw materials and the population with food. Unfavourable weather conditions (late spring and early autumn frosts, high temperature, etc.), pollution and uncomplimentary land reclamation conditions (in some areas) limit the comprehensive use of agro-climatic and land resources (GoK, 2016[1]).

Generally, most services (e.g. education, health) and industries (e.g. electricity, water, and gas) are state-owned. On the other hand, the private sector is dominated by small enterprises, and remains the main driver of economic growth. According to data from the National Statistical Committee (NSC), GDP in 2018 was mainly generated by trade (18.2%), followed by manufacturing (15.2%) and agriculture, fishing and forestry (11.7%).[12]

The City of Bishkek and the region of Issyk-Kul report the highest gross regional products per capita (KSG 196 800 and KGS 138 000, respectively). The gross regional product of Osh region (KGS 31 100) is only one-sixth of that of the capital Bishkek (Figure 6.3).

Figure 6.3. Gross regional product per capita, 2017

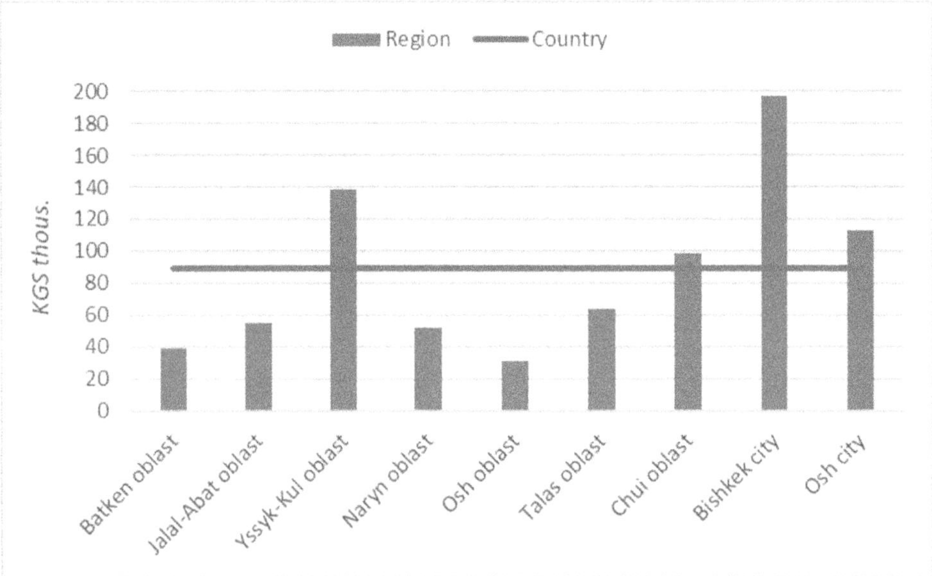

Source: National Statistical Committee of the Kyrgyz Republic (http://stat.kg).

Kyrgyzstan ranked 122nd out of 189 countries on the 2017 Human Development Index (HDI), down from 2010 when it ranked 109th (though, out of 169). Still, the country's HDI value increased by 8.8% between 1990 and 2017 (from 0.618 to 0.672).[13] In 2014, the World Bank re-classified Kyrgyzstan from a low-income to a lower-middle-income country based on its gross national income (GNI) per capita.[14] In 2017, the country reached a GNI per capita of 3 620 (in current international dollars), and is thus approaching the 4 125 GNI per-capita threshold for classification as an upper-middle-income country.[15]

Chronic poverty and related food insecurity and malnutrition, climatic and environmental risks, gender inequalities, disparities in regional economic development and reliance on remittances remain major challenges. Influenced by economic growth over the last decade, poverty has been significantly reduced – in 2017 only 1.5% of the population (91 000 people) were below the international poverty line (USD 1.90 or KGS 43.3 per day per capita), compared to 42.1% (2.1 million people) in 2000.[16]

In 2016, employment was mainly in agriculture, forestry and fishing (26.8%); trade (15.6%); construction (12%); industry (10.1%); and education (8.7%). In 2015, the annual unemployment rate was 7.6% – and fell to 7.2% in 2016. Women account for over half of the unemployed – around 53%. The evolution of the national employment rate is shown in Figure 6.4 (NSC, 2016[7]); (NSC, 2018[3]).

Figure 6.4. Unemployment rate in pilot cities and surrounding regions, 2006-17

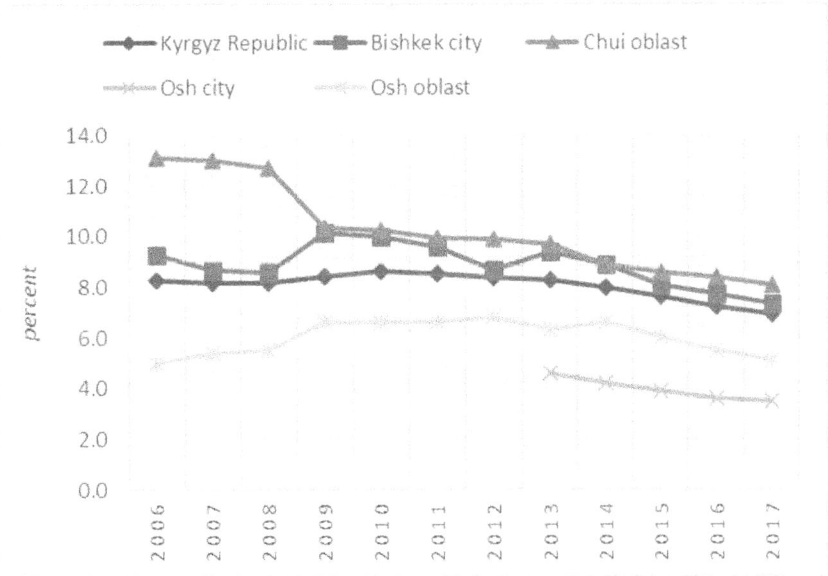

Source: National Statistical Committee of the Kyrgyz Republic (http://stat.kg).

The region of Talas and Osh City report the lowest unemployment rates (2.5 and 5.1%, respectively). On the other hand, women experienced (on a country level) a higher unemployment rate overall of 9%: 8.9% in urban areas and 9.1% in rural areas. Men, in contrast, experienced unemployment rates of 6.5% overall: 7.5% in urban areas and 6.1% in rural areas (NSC, 2018[3]).

The large young cohort entering the working age group (see Section 6.1.1) enhances the country's growth prospects (Moody's, 2019[6]). This will contribute to further GDP growth over the medium-term and help alleviate rural poverty. Remittances will continue to play a decisive role as growth in the agriculture and construction sectors is expected to remain modest (World Bank, 2019[5]).

In 2017, the average nominal per capita monthly income of the population stood at KGS 4 725 (USD 68.6), whereas monthly average nominal wages and salaries per employee, excluding small enterprises, were KGS 15 391 (USD 223.5).

6.1.3. Fossil fuel production and distribution

The country has minimal oil and gas production and depends on imports for these products, especially oil from Kazakhstan (or the Russian Federation) and gas from Uzbekistan (or Kazakhstan). In 2018, domestic production of natural gas stood at 27.3 million cubic metres, crude oil at 200 000 tonnes and coal/lignite at 2 306 000 tonnes. The production of coal/lignite and crude oil has risen seven and three-fold, respectively, since 2006. With about 70 deposits, total coal reserves are estimated to be about 27 billion tonnes, with a proven reserve of 1.3 billion tonnes.

Up to the present day, Kyrgyzstan's economy has been experiencing a permanent shortage of coal due to the underdeveloped railway network (coal's main transportation channel) and increased transportation costs, which have significantly limited market sales (Kyrgyzstan consumes its own nationally produced coal as well as imports from Kazakhstan and the Russian Federation).

Annual natural gas production remains mostly in the range of 20-30 million cubic metres since 2010 (see Figure 6.5). The substantial production increase seen in Figure 6.5 aimed to decrease dependence (and payment disputes) on gas imports from Uzbekistan. Until 2010, domestic gas production was able to cover only about 5% of consumption.[17] Proven natural gas reserves are 5.6 billion cubic metres, but these reserves are difficult to exploit.[18]

The country has about 40 million barrels of proven reserves of crude oil. Currently, it operates seven oil and two gas/oil fields. However, the country only produces 1 000 barrels per day, whereas consumption is 16 000 barrels per day (2017 figures).[19]

Figure 6.5. Fossil fuels in Kyrgyzstan – volumes of production, 2006-18

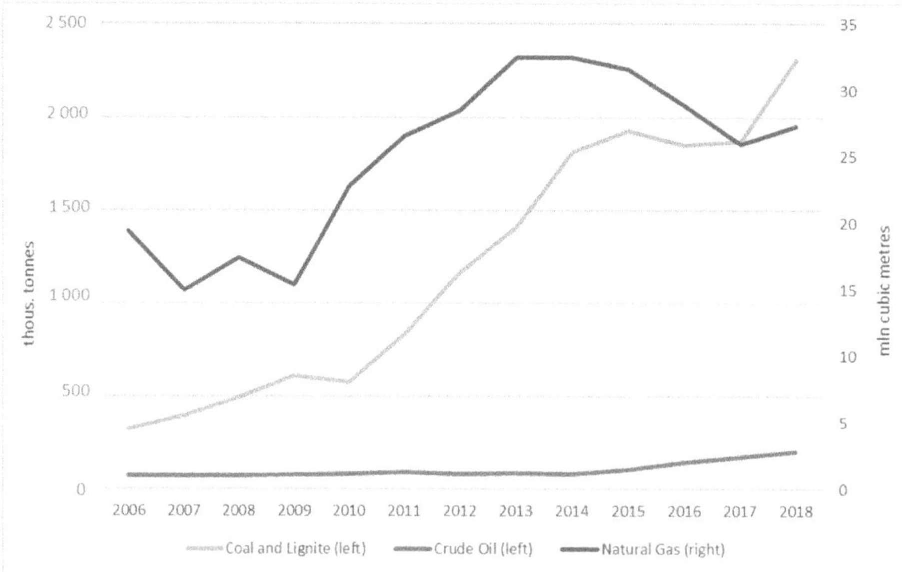

Source: (NSC, 2016[2]), *Environment in the Kyrgyz Republic, Statistical Compilation 2011-2015*, http://stat.kg/media/publicationarchive/8c0e9d22-6bb6-4145-b1d6-8311da33521d.pdf; and the National Statistical Committee of the Kyrgyz Republic (http://stat.kg).

Neftegaz supplies the south of the country with gas, while Gazprom distributes gas over the entire territory using gas from Uzbekistan.[20]

In 2006, Gazprom Neft set up Gazprom Neft Asia, a Kyrgyzstan-based subsidiary company and the largest operator in the Kyrgyz fuel market. The company's assets include 108 filling stations, 8 oil tank farms, and 2 LNG tank farms.[21]

In 2013, a new co-operation agreement in the field of natural gas transmission, distribution and sales in the Kyrgyz Republic was signed between the Kyrgyz and Russian governments. Under this agreement, Gazprom acquired a 100% share in Kyrgyzgaz, the local gas company.

In 2014, Gazprom and Kyrgyzgaz signed a sales and purchase agreement for a 100% share in KyrgyzgazProm (renamed Gazprom Kyrgyzstan), a wholly-owned subsidiary of Kyrgyzgaz. Gazprom Kyrgyzstan has exclusive rights to import natural gas to the Kyrgyz Republic and own the national gas transmission and distribution systems.

In this context, cross-country gas pipelines have been modernised and in early 2018, the Bishkek City Administration had plans to purchase 320-350 natural-gas fuelled buses for USD 50 million from Gazprom. These plans have since been modified (see Section 6.2.4).

As can be seen in Table 6.3, the largest share of energy use comes from electric power, followed by coal and petrol for automobiles.

Table 6.2. Distribution of fuel and energy sources, 2011-16

(tonnes of conventional fuel equivalent*)

Items	2011	2012	2013	2014	2015	2016
Motor-car petrol	950	1 423	1 307	1 020	1 104	1 445
Diesel fuel	715	908	1 041	943	716	744
Fuel oil	243	169	127	322	505	267
Electric power	5 295	5 287	4 827	5 122	4 740	4 633
Coal	1 620	2 041	2 086	2 368	2 750	2 458
Natural gas	383	490	355	328	318	331

Note: * Conventional fuel equivalent: thermal unit of fuel used to compare different types of fuel. Combustion of 1 kg of solid (liquid) conditional fuel (or 1 m^3 gaseous) is equal to 29.3 MJ (7 000 kcal)
Source: National Statistical Committee of the Kyrgyz Republic (http://stat.kg).

Kyrgyzstan ranks among the 15 most energy-intensive countries in the world. Its energy intensity increased over 2010-14 from 181 kilogrammes of oil equivalent (koe) per USD 1 000 of GDP to 204 koe per USD 1 000 of GDP (World Bank, 2017[8]).

As domestic demand for energy is growing and in order to improve the country's productivity and competitiveness, further investments in rehabilitation and new generation capacity will be needed. Clearly, energy efficiency investments are needed on both the supply and demand sides.

Energy security, energy efficiency and sustainable development are declared to be the main priorities of the Kyrgyz Government's energy policy. They have been reflected in and implemented through many national programmes, such as Kyrgyzstan's National Energy Programme 2008-2010, the Strategy for the Development of the Fuel and Energy Complex up to 2025 (GoK, 2008[9]), and the Programme on Energy Saving and Energy Efficiency Policy Planning 2015-2017 (Government Resolution No. 601 of 25 August 2015[22]).

The latter programme focused on securing GDP growth that was less energy intensive. The programme aimed to bring about energy savings of up to 8 million tonnes of oil equivalent by 2025, which would also reduce carbon dioxide (CO_2) emissions by up to 20%. At the same time, the annual GDP growth rate would be maintained at 3% and the annual increase in electricity consumption would grow by 4% (GoK, 2013[10]).

Although GHG emissions from the energy sector dramatically decreased between 1990 and 1995 (especially in comparison to other sectors), the energy sector is still a major consumer of fossil fuels in the country.

6.1.4. The electricity sector

The power sector is the most developed energy subsector in Kyrgyzstan. In 1990-2017, the country produced on average 90.3% of its annual electricity output from hydro power, and the remaining 9.7% from thermal power stations (Table 6.4).[23] These numbers indicate the country's high dependence on hydro resources, which has both positive (such as low electricity generation costs) and negative aspects (such as output sensitivity to seasonal and annual weather variations).[24] In terms of access, almost 100% of Kyrgyzstan's population is connected to the grid,[25] which is remarkable given the country's mountainous landscape.

In 2017, the total installed hydropower capacity was 3 091 MW – ranking Kyrgyzstan seventh amongst the South and Central Asian countries.[26] Hydropower generation was 13 456 GWh. The country has a great number of large and medium-sized rivers offering significant hydropower potential, such as the Naryn River[27] serving Toktogul hydroelectric power plant (HPP), with a generation capacity of 1 200 MW. However, whereas the total potential of hydropower is estimated at 140-170 TWh, only 10% of this has been exploited (IHA, 2018[11]). New generation capacities were added in 2010 (the USD 200 million 360 MW Kambar-Ata 2 hydroelectric power plant on the Naryn River).

While the share of small hydroelectric power stations currently remains insignificant, such stations are important for power supply in mountainous and rural areas where construction of large power lines is economically unprofitable. The total hydro energy potential of 172 rivers and water currents surveyed in the country exceeds 80 billion kWh per year. Technical improvements would enable production of an additional 5-8 billion kWh per year.[28]

The remaining 10% of electricity produced in the country comes from thermal power. The largest thermal power stations are in Bishkek and Osh. The total generation capacity of these two (mainly coal-fired[29]) combined heat and power (CHP) plants equals 716 MW.[30] However, the generation capacity of these CHP plants is larger (18.8%) than their actual production share (9.7%), mainly due to their poor technical conditions. However, the CHPs are important suppliers of heat and electricity in the winter, when consumption is on average 2.9 times higher than in summer (UNISON, 2013[12]).

Table 6.3. Production of electric power in Kyrgyzstan, 2011-16

(million kilowatt-hours)

	2011	2012	2013	2014	2015	2016
Electric power produced – total	**15 158**	**15 168**	**14 011**	**14 572**	**13 017**	**13 118**
Hydroelectric power stations	14 309	14 179	13 097	13 298	11 093	11 498
Thermoelectric power stations	849	989	915	1 274	1 924	1 621

Source: National Statistical Committee of the Kyrgyz Republic (http://stat.kg).

For many years, Kyrgyzstan has been a net exporter of electricity, primarily to Kazakhstan and Uzbekistan (Tajikistan and China), and mainly during the summer months. From 1990 to 2000, annual exports ranged between 6.6 and 9.4 million MWh; however, since 2000, exports have fallen by 87% (to 1.2 million MWh in 2017). These exports have been an important revenue source for the state budget as electricity to neighbouring countries is sold at a higher price than on the domestic market (which is subsidised by the government).

On the demand side, the structure of energy consumption has changed substantially since 1990. Industrial consumption has declined sharply, to 12.4% of fuel and energy resources and 19.1% of total electricity consumed, whereas the housing and utilities sector has risen to 43.5% and 76.6%, respectively. Transport accounted for 39.5% of fuel and energy resources and 0.4% of electricity consumption (GoK, 2013[10]). The electricity sector has some influence on the current state of and prospects for economic development. The sector accounts for about 16% of industrial production and 10% of state budget revenue

(UNCTAD, 2013[13]).[31] Between 2011 and 2018, electricity, gas and steam production accounted on average for 2.2% of country's annual GDP.[32]

These relatively high contributions have been partly caused by the increasing domestic consumption of electricity – which grew between 1990 and 2017 by 51.7% – boosted by the low tariffs stemming from hydropower's low production costs. However, higher domestic consumption (see Table 6.5) has meant lower exports and general shortages on the local market as well. This, combined with three drought years (2014-2016), led to an average annual shortage of 321.5 million kWh in this period. This saw, similar to the 2008-09 energy crisis, a reduction in the power supply to the general population (which uses electricity for heating, for instance) and to enterprises. Electricity needed to be imported from Kazakhstan and Tajikistan during 2014-2016, after which the country improved its efficiency and increased electricity production. As a result, Kyrgyzstan can now cover its own electricity needs and export to neighbouring countries (World Bank, 2017[8]).[33]

Interestingly, not only did electricity exports fall – imports also fell, from 6.4 million MWh to virtually zero in 2004. However, except for the 2014-2016 period, Kyrgyzstan's electricity exports have always exceeded imports.[34]

Table 6.4. Distribution of electric power in Kyrgyzstan

(tonnes of conventional fuel equivalent*)

Electric power	2011	2012	2013	2014	2015	2016
Total	**5 295**	**5 287**	**4 827**	**5 122**	**4 740**	**4 633**
Consumed	3 146	3 495	3 599	3 906	3 758	3 650
Export	981	634	152	25	63	68
Losses	1 168	1 158	1 076	1 191	919	915

Note: *Conventional fuel equivalent: thermal unit of fuel used to compare different types of fuel. Combustion of 1 kg of solid (liquid) conditional fuel (or 1 m^3 gaseous) is equal to 29.3 MJ (7 000 kcal).
Source: National Statistical Committee of the Kyrgyz Republic (http://stat.kg).

The first reform of the electricity sector took place over 1999-2001, starting with the adoption of the Deregulation and Privatisation Programme of the open joint stock company (OJSC) Kyrgyzenergo (Resolution of the Kyrgyz Government No. 239 of 23 April 1997). The programme resulted in transforming the state monopoly into six natural monopolies unbundled by function (one generation, one transmission and four regional distribution companies).[35]

From 2010 onwards, the Government of Kyrgyzstan has undertaken several policy steps to reform the power sector, as demand was exceeding generation capacities. The Mid-Term Power Sector Development Strategy 2012-2017 (GoK, 2012[14]) was approved in 2012 (Resolution of the Kyrgyz Government No. 330 of 28 May 2012), and a detailed action plan for the reform of the energy sector followed in 2013 (GoK, 2013[15]).[36] A medium-term tariff policy (MTTP) for electricity and heating was put in place (Government Resolution No. 660 of 20 November 2014) and amendments were made to the sector laws (Government Resolution No. 295 of 15 May 2012).

Since 2007, the Ministry of Industry, Energy and Fuel Resource has been the main policy-making authority in the electricity sector (in 2009 it changed its name to the Ministry of Energy and Industry).[37] In 2015, the ministry was dissolved and its responsibilities (such as tariff-setting and licensing) were transferred to a new State Committee on Industry,

Energy and Subsoil Use in the following year. An independent (government) regulator – the State Agency for Regulation of the Fuel and Energy Complex – was created in 2014.[38] For a more just allocation of state funds to the power companies, the Kyrgyz Electricity Settlement Centre was established in 2015 to collect and provide data to the regulator. The National Energy Holding Company OJSC was set up in 2016 to facilitate the development of the energy sector (it was transferred state-owned shares in nine energy companies[39]) (Gassner et al., 2017[16]); (IHA, 2018[11]).

The National Energy Programme 2008-2010 and the Strategy for the Development of the Fuel and Energy Complex up to 2025 (GoK, 2008[9]) pointed out that unjustified tariffs combined with low payment collection were leading to financial losses for the generating and transmitting power utilities. Its goals of improving pricing and tariff policies in the energy complex were to be based on introducing the principles of energy sector self-sufficiency and phased elimination of cross-subsidies in the field of tariff formation. Tariffs were to cover all costs of production, transfer, distribution and marketing of electrical and thermal energy and to reflect the entire cost of electricity to each category of consumer. Social support (subsidies) was to be directed to low-end consumers on low incomes through the social protection system (GoK, 2008[9]).

Tariffs were increased in 2006 and 2008, but not in 2010 due to political unrest and the change of government. A tariff increase then took place in 2014 as part of the new (2014-2017) Medium-Term Tariff Policy (MTTP). According to the law on the power industry (Law No. 8 of 28 January 1997) electricity prices should be socially acceptable and non-discriminatory. This has resulted in the lowest tariff levels in the EECCA region. This situation is partly a result of affordable (i.e. subsidised[40]) electricity prices – households' total expenditure ranges between 2.3-2.6% across population groups, which is very low even from the regional perspective. But it is also due to the high system loss from the net supply. This loss is estimated at 30-40%, comprising around one-third in technical losses[41] and two-thirds in commercial losses (metering, billing or payment collection failures, and theft). The overall result is one of the highest losses worldwide (UNCTAD, 2013[13]); (Gassner et al., 2017[16]).

Although a two-tiered residential tariff was adopted in 2015, tariffs were only increased in the upper tier (above 700 kWh), hitting large residential consumers and the industrial sector disproportionally (which accounted only for 19% of residential consumption and 48% of total end-user consumption in 2016 (problem of cross-subsidisation). Despite higher cost-recovery levels, electricity sector revenues in 2016 were still 21% lower than generation costs (compared to 32% in 2014). Although the annual sector deficits declined (to KGS 4.9 billion in 2016, with 49% attributable to electricity and the rest to heating sector), the overall energy sector's debt increased from KGS 200 million in 2010 to KGS 90.7 billion in 2016 (about 20% of GDP and 32% of the country's overall stock of public and publicly guaranteed debt). The upcoming MTTP (2018-2021) aims to increase the lower-tier tariff and to introduce more targeted social safety net schemes, as foreseen in the National Social Protection Programme 2015-2017 (GoK, 2015[17]).

Reducing the consumption threshold for the lowest tariff from 700 kWh to 350 kWh – which is one option to decrease wasteful or uneconomical spending resulting from the lowest tariffs in the region – would result in nearly a 20% reduction in the cost-recovery gap and would relieve the government of its need to provide heavy support (soft loans) to the sector to meet spending requirements (Gassner et al., 2017[16]).

6.1.5. The financial sector

At the end of 2018, Kyrgyzstan's banking sector consisted of 26 financial institutions – the National Bank of the Kyrgyz Republic (NBKR) and 25 commercial banks (including the Bishkek branch of National Bank of Pakistan) together operating 321 branches. The weight of foreign contributions in the capital of the banking system amounted to 47.3% of paid up assessed capital, or KGS 11.1 billion.[42] Of the commercial banks, 15 had a majority share of foreign capital and a further 3 had a minority share. There were also 686 non-bank financial institutions active in the country, including credit companies (such as microfinance organisations and credit unions), insurance companies, investment and pension funds, and stock exchanges (NBKR, 2018[18]).

The NBKR – transformed from the State Bank of the Republic of Kyrgyzstan[43] – licenses, supervises and regulates the activity of financial institutions in the country. It is also in charge of developing a strategy for financial-credit organisations in the Kyrgyz Republic (NBKR, 2018a). In terms of monetary policy, it is responsible for the stability of the som, introduced as the national currency of the Kyrgyz Republic in 1993. The NBKR has pursued a floating exchange rate policy.

In the first half of the 1990s, the banking system was dominated by the three major commercial banks – the Agricultural and Industrial Bank (Agroprombank), the Industrial and Construction Bank (Promstroybank), and the Commercial Bank of Kyrgyzstan – that succeeded the sectoral banks of the Soviet era. These banks not only remained under state control, they also kept a limited number of activities targeted at their focus sector and traditional clientele. In addition, 16 smaller financial institutions were created (either as banks or joint stock companies), which were originally mainly owned by the ministries and state-owned enterprises (i.e. created from their accounts). Their main areas of activity were foreign currency exchange and deposit accounts service.

Since the majority of these new commercial institutions only had a central office and no branches, commercial lending and other banking services to non-state customers – especially beyond the Chui *oblast* – were just as limited after 1991 as before (most banks required 120-200% collateral on loans and charged interest rates of 50-100% which reduced credit access by mainly low-income groups[44]). In 2013, 80% of agricultural companies seeking credit were asked to provide collateral equivalent to 120% or more of the total loan amount, usually in the form of real estate (OECD, 2016[19]).

In 1992, Kyrgyzstan joined the World Bank (WB) and the International Monetary Fund (IMF). In 1995, the country accepted the IMF's obligations under Article VIII of the Articles of Agreement[45] to refrain from imposing exchange restrictions on payments and transfers for current international transactions or from engaging in discriminatory currency arrangements or multiple currency practices without IMF approval.[46] In 1998 – the same year that Kyrgyzstan became a member of the World Trade Organization[47] – the domestic banking sector was negatively hit by the Russian financial crisis, resulting in high inflation (37% in 1999) and currency devaluation (87%),[48] combined with unproportionally large loan portfolios in foreign currency.[49] Influenced by the economic slowdown in 2014-15 and further depreciation of the som against the US dollar (Moody's, 2019[6]), Kyrgyzstan joined Kazakhstan, the Russian Federation, Belarus and Armenia as a member of the Eurasian Economic Union (EAEU) in 2015 (EEC, 2015[20]).

One of the main impediments to creating a competitive and market-oriented banking system in Kyrgyzstan comes from the demand side. Kyrgyzstan has traditionally been a cash-based society and trust in financial institutions is low. Following the Russian financial crisis, three major state-owned banks and other small commercial banks in Kyrgyzstan were forced into bankruptcy and placed under control of the NBKR, causing severe losses to depositors.

In general, access to banking services – especially to automated teller machines (ATMs) and payment terminals – is significantly higher in the capital than in the regions. In places where these services are available, cash withdrawal constitutes 90% of operations with bank cards (over 96% of the volume) (Hasanova, 2018[21]). Citizens' financial literacy (as well as the tax collection rate) was to be enhanced in the second stage of the "State programme to increase the share of non-cash payments and settlements in the Kyrgyz Republic (2012-2017)". For the 2018-2021 period of the programme, the National Bank aims to increase the cash and non-cash turnover ratio to 50/50.[50]

The banking sector is relatively small: at the end of 2018, the assets of commercial banks equalled KGS 219 983 million (of which liabilities made up KGS 182 300 million and equity KGS 37 683 million).[51] Although there is a substantial number of non-bank financial institutions, banks dominate the financial sector, with a share of total assets equalling 92.8% (other local players are mostly underdeveloped and not integrated in the world financial system).[52] The total assets of KGS 237 949 million constituted financial intermediation (assets/GDP) of 42.7%.[53] More than half of these (55%) and nearly a half of the credit portfolio (49%) is held by five major banks (Hasanova, 2018[21]).

Money outside of banks totalled KGS 84 827 million at the end of 2018.[54] This also has an impact on banks that are, in turn, in high demand for attracting additional credit resources. As of March 2019, the average interest rate on newly accepted deposits was much lower than the average interest rate of all deposits (1.33% and 0.17% against 6.33% and 1.41 – national and foreign currency, respectively), whereas the credit portfolio does not show a similar pattern. A high deposit interest rate would encourage savings and deposits. On the other hand, it would also consume banks' revenues that would otherwise be available for loans. Therefore, it might be used as a financial tool to improve liquidity alongside the government securities or refinancing by the NBKR that Kyrgyz banks have taken advantage of in the past.

The total volume of newly issued credits by commercial banks in 2018 equalled KGS 76 612 million (in national currency) and an equivalent of KGS 37 104 million (in foreign currency). In 2008, the amount was KGS 9 083 million (in national currency) and an equivalent of KGS 15 281 million (in foreign currency).[55]

Throughout 2016, the NBKR decreased the base interest rate stepwise from 10.0% to 5.0% (NBKR, 2018[22]). The average weighted annual interest rate of newly issued credits decreased from 25.9% per annum (p.a.) in 2008 to 19.5% p.a. in 2018 (in national currency) and from 20.3% p.a. in 2008 to 9.7% p.a. in 2018 (in foreign currency). Therefore, if it was economically sound to take credit in foreign currency in 2008, it was even more so in 2018 (i.e. the interest rate in foreign currency had been cut by half since 2008 and was only a half than of the one in national currency in 2018). However, of the total amounts of newly issued credits in 2008 and 2018, those in national currency increased 8.4-fold between the years, whereas foreign currency only saw a 2.4-fold increase.[56]

As Figure 6.6 shows, since the early 2000s, interest rates on short-term credit (up to 12-months maturity) have decreased from the peak of 50-60% to be more comparable with medium (1-3 years) and long-term (over 3 years) loans. However, these rates have declined only moderately. At the beginning of 2019, the average weighted interest rates of newly issued three-year loans was 15.8% in national currency (Panel A in Figure 6.6) and 9.2% in foreign currency (Panel B).

Figure 6.6. Average weighted interest rates for newly issued credits, 1996-2018 (by maturity)

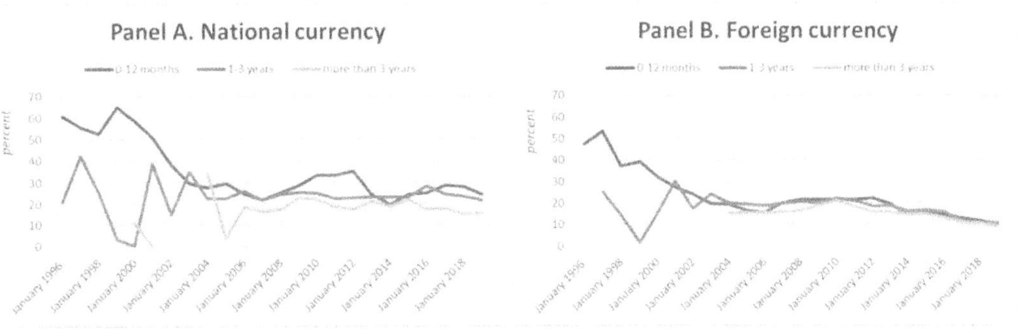

Source: National Bank of the Kyrgyz Republic (www.nbkr.kg).

The general level of dollarisation of the total loan portfolio has decreased significantly, from 63.2% in 2008 to 37.9% in 2018 (on average for the respective year), helping to reduce currency risks.[57] The official average USD/KGS exchange rate in 2010 was 45.99 and 68.84 in 2018, meaning a depreciation of 49.7% (with the sharpest decline in 2015).[58] The National Bank has continued to adhere to the floating exchange rate regime existing in the country. The bank's exchange rate interventions – such as purchasing gold on the domestic market[59] – have helped to smooth the sharp exchange rate fluctuations (NBKR, 2018$_{[22]}$).

As of March 2019, the total deposits of individual persons in commercial banks equalled KGS 73 710 million (64.9% in national currency), those by legal entities equalled KGS 50 127 million (52.9% in national currency), while those by non-residents were KGS 9 932 million (19.8% in national currency).[60] An important milestone was the adoption of the law and respective agency on protecting the deposits of individuals (Law No. 78 of 7 May 2008 "On protection of bank deposits"[61]).

Based on a recent NBKR survey of commercial banks' clients, domestic banks forward 61.9% of the loan portfolio to the production sector (GDP) and 15.0% to finance imports (NBKR, 2018$_{[18]}$).[62]

Only 2% of the total volume of all credits of KGS 130 629 million was in the transport sector, namely KGS 2 570 million (compared to at least 27.5% in the trade sector, for instance). Compared to other sectors – such as trade or agriculture[63] – there is no substantial difference between the ratio of credits taken in national currency (1.9% of all credits) and foreign currency (2.1% of all credits), respectively.

As can be seen in Figure 6.7, the sectoral structure of the loan portfolio also shows high concentration since trade (through banks) and agriculture (through non-bank financial institutions) account for 46.3% of all loans. Whereas in national currency, the largest volume goes to agriculture (KGS 23.4 billion), the largest volume in foreign currency, as well as total volume, is in the trade sector (KGS 19.2 and 36 billion, respectively).

Figure 6.7. Total volume of credits, 2019* (by sector)

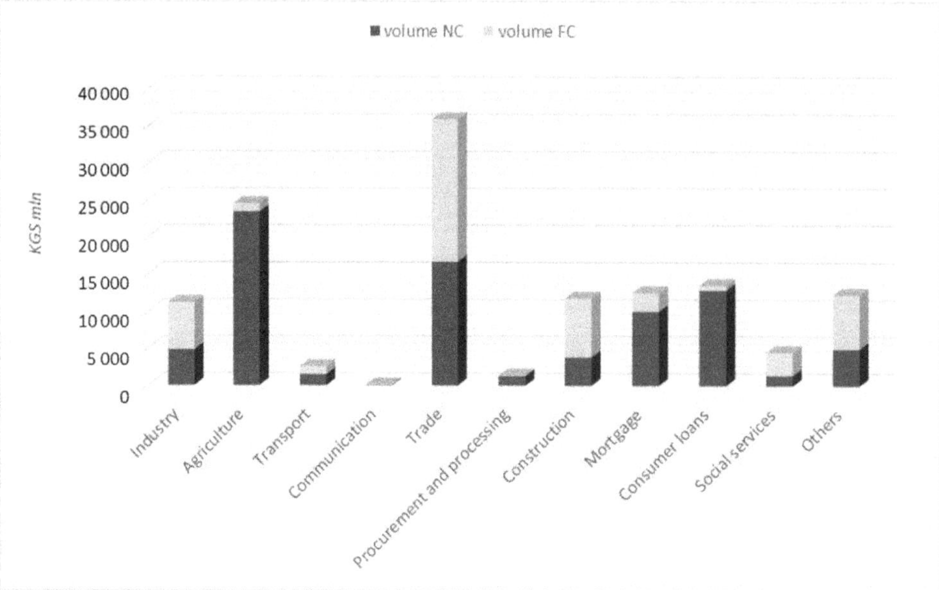

Note: * As of March 2019.
Source: National Bank of the Kyrgyz Republic (www.nbkr.kg).

The transport sector also faced the second highest average weighted interest rate of all sectors,[64] at 16.5% p.a. in March 2019 (compared to only 7.2% p.a in procurement). There is a sufficient share of credits granted with longer tenors (40.5% of all credits); however, this category includes payback periods of three to four years, so the differentiation between mid-term and long-term tenors is not possible from the available NBKR statistics (where one to three years are considered mid-term). Credits with longer tenors made up 30.4% of all credits in national currency and 57.1% in foreign currency.[65] As the available statistics are not broken down into types of customer, it is not possible to say how many SMEs were among the business customers. However, in general 27.9% of firms in Kyrgyzstan identified access to finance as a major constraint (OECD, 2013[23]).

In 2015-2016, the number of borrowers from banks increased by 24.9% (to 361 000 people), while borrowers from non-bank financial institutions and credit unions decreased by 31.8% and 5.3% (to 228 000 and 9 000) respectively (NBKR, 2018[22]).[66] The regional distribution of total loan volumes was uneven, with Bishkek accounting for 56.3% in 2018 (based on average end-of-quarter values), followed by Osh (12.1%) and Jalal-Abad (9.5%).[67]

The loan-to-deposit ratio remained stable and relatively high in both 2008 and 2018, at 93% (average values for these two years).[68] Still, there was sufficient liquidity on the Kyrgyz money market – one of the key segments in the country's financial market – mainly due to an increase in the bank portfolio of liquid and reliable government securities, the notes of the National Bank and availability of refinancing operations conducted by the National Bank (NBKR, 2018[18]). At the end of 2018, the share of non-performing loans in the loan portfolio of the banking system was 7.5% (KGS 9.6 billion).[69]

The comprehensive Banking Law adopted in December 2016 (No. 206 of 16 December "On the National Bank of the Kyrgyz Republic, Banks and Banking Activity"[70]) was supposed to strengthen stability in the banking sector and become an important milestone in the development of banking legislation of the country. However, changes made to the original version approved by parliament have perpetuated the previous vulnerabilities in the legal structure, particularly in governance arrangements (e.g. the audit committee's advisory role vis-à-vis the NBKR Board) (NBKR, 2018[22]); (IMF, 2018[24]).

Another persistent vulnerability is a potential exchange rate depreciation, especially given the relatively large (for a small, low-income economy) government debt burden which is almost all in foreign currency. However, the debt has remained broadly stable since 2015 (55.4% of GDP at the end of 2018) and the debt structure is characterised by highly concessional terms (low interest rates) and very long maturities (hence, interest payments stood at 3.4% of revenue) (Moody's, 2019[6]).

6.2. Transport infrastructure in the Kyrgyz Republic

Due to its mountainous relief, there is no developed railway system in Kyrgyzstan running north to south. International connections are available to Uzbekistan and Kazakhstan. Lack of waterways (including sea access) and high costs of air transport mean that road transport constitutes the main means for the domestic transportation of passengers and freight (in particular to the remote regions of the country). As 95% of freight and 97% of passenger traffic are carried by road, road transport remains one of the most important factors in the country's sustainable socio-economic development and one of the main tools in solving development problems (GoK, 2012[25]).

Moreover, the region is the most important transit country in Central Asia – towards the north-east (from Kazakhstan or the Russian Federation towards Tajikistan and Afghanistan) and towards the south-east (connecting Central Asia with China). In this context, the Central Asia Regional Economic Cooperation (CAREC) corridors link the region's key economic hubs to each other and connect the region to other Eurasian markets (IRU, 2013[26]).[71]

According to the Ministry of Transport and Roads, the total length of public roads in the Kyrgyz Republic is about 34 000 km, including around 18 900 km which are maintained by the road units of the ministry itself (around 4 100 km of international roads, 5 600 km of national roads and 8 900 km of provincial roads). Local government agencies are responsible for developing and maintaining secondary, rural and urban road networks.

Around 67% of the international and national roads are in a sustainable condition, requiring only routine or periodic maintenance. The rest are in poor condition and require rehabilitation or reconstruction. Roads are particularly affected by climate-induced extreme events resulting in landslides and mudslides (ADB, 2012[27]).

6.2.1. Passenger transport

After a decline in passenger and cargo transportation in the first half of the 1990s (due to the economic downturn), the sector has shown an increasing trend since then (GoK, 2016[1]).

In terms of number of passengers transported, Kyrgyzstan ranks high amongst comparable EECCA countries, such as Armenia, Moldova and Tajikistan (Figure 6.8).

Figure 6.8. Passenger transportation by transport enterprises in selected EECCA countries, 2000-13

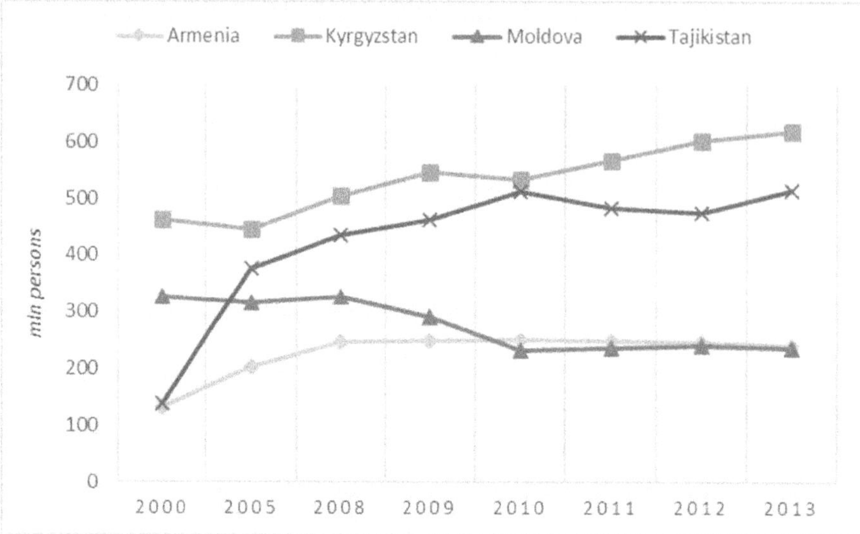

Source: (CIS, 2014[4]), *Commonwealth of Independent States in 2013 – Statistical Yearbook.*

As Figure 6.8 shows, passenger volumes have been increasing since 2005 – not only because of the increase in population, but also due to the growing frequency of work-related trips and lifestyle changes. The growth in the service sector, including the expansion of trade and consumption, has led to the rapid growth of the economy in urban areas and, consequently, in traffic.

The route network in Kyrgyzstan comprises 949 bus routes, including 51 international, 58 interregional, 552 intraregional; and 288 city routes (132 in Bishkek and 56 in Osh). The total length of bus routes in the Kyrgyz Republic is 82 400 km.[72] Generally, however, availability and quality of transport services do not meet the needs of the population. A considerable share of rural settlements lack roads with hard surfaces and a regular bus service.

The total vehicle fleet in the country stands at about 735 000 vehicles, made up of more than 600 000 cars, 93 000 trucks, 10 000 special-purpose vehicles, and more than 32 000 buses and minibuses.[73]

Table 6.6 shows in detail the number of passengers carried by type of transport in Kyrgyzstan. Except for rail transport – where the number of transported passengers shows an overall decrease – all other public transport means have seen an increase in passenger-kilometres, resulting in an average increase in road public transport (bus, trolleybus, car/taxi) of 15% between 2012 and 2018.

Table 6.5. Passengers carried by type of transport in Kyrgyzstan, 2012-18

(million passenger-kilometres)

Transport type	2012	2013	2014	2015	2016	2017	2018*	% change 2012/18
Total	**9 621**	**10 378**	**10 777**	**11 013**	**11 334**	**12 279**	**12 617**	**31%**
Overland transport	**8 019**	**8 279**	**8 597**	**9 046**	**9 532**	**9 664**	**10 221**	**27%**
Railroad	76	56	43	41	41	43	35	-54%
Bus	7 466	7 718	8 000	8 410	8 839	8 932	9 398	26%
Trolleybus	80	78	83	96	106	120	137	71%
Car (taxi)	397	428	471	500	546	569	651	64%
Air transport	**1 602**	**2 099**	**2 180**	**1 966**	**1 801**	**2 615**	**2 396**	**50%**

Note: * Preliminary data
Source: National Statistical Committee of the Kyrgyz Republic (http://stat.kg).

In terms of passenger-kilometres – the measurement unit that best reflects the environmental footprint – the City of Bishkek experienced a similar increase as Kyrgyzstan as a whole over 2010-17 (49% and 51%, respectively). However, as can be seen in Figure 6.9, transport went up by 121% in the Chui *oblast* over the same period.

Figure 6.9. Passenger turnover in pilot cities and surrounding *oblasts* (all transport)

(million passenger-kilometres)

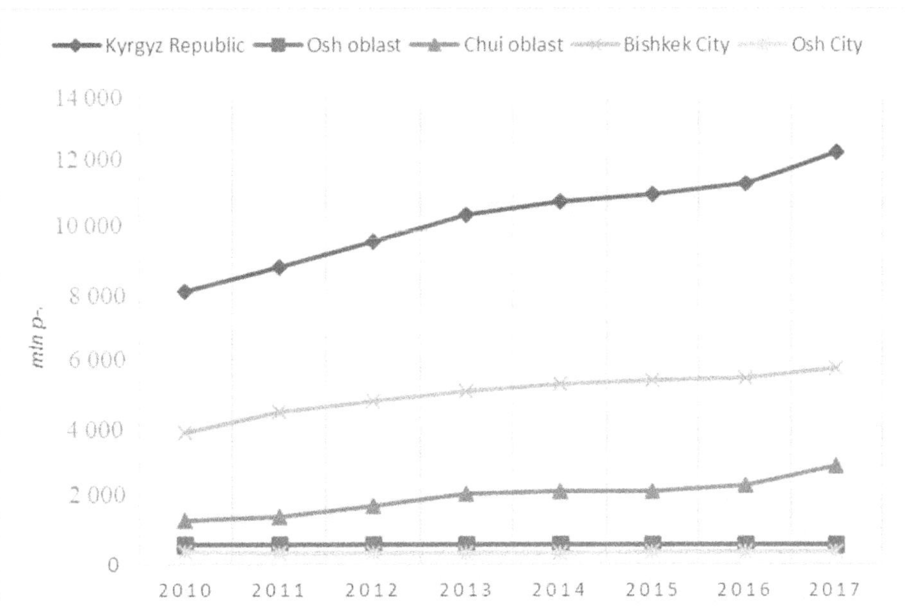

Source: National Statistical Committee of the Kyrgyz Republic (http://stat.kg).

In 2017, in terms of passenger-kilometres, bus transport accounted for the major share (73%) nationally (Figure 6.10). As trolleybus networks are only available in the cities of Bishkek and Osh, trolleybus transport cannot at the moment compete with buses and minibuses (which also may suggest unused potential).

Figure 6.10. Share of transport means in Kyrgyzstan, 2017

(share of passenger-kilometres)

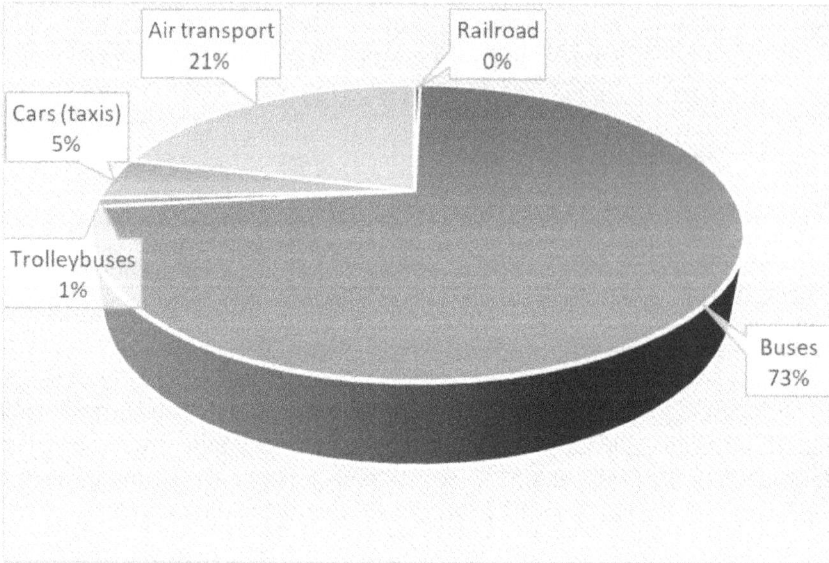

Source: National Statistical Committee of the Kyrgyz Republic (http://stat.kg).

Clearly, automobile transport is the main means of overland transport and its share is constantly increasing. By comparison, the number of passengers transported by railroad is negligible and decreasing steadily.

6.2.2. Freight transport

The domestic freight market faces increasing competition from foreign freight carriers. Due to the inadequate control of vehicles entering the territory of the Kyrgyz Republic, many foreign freight carriers do not observe freight regulations and drive with vehicles that exceed the admissible weight and dimensions. This accelerates the deterioration of highways, as well as affecting both the transportation fleet and traffic safety. For this reason, freight transport has not experienced such an increase as passenger transport (Figure 6.7).

Table 6.6. Freight by type of transport, 2012-18

(million tonne-kilometres)

Type of transport	2012	2013	2014	2015	2016	2017	2018*	% change 2012/18
Total	**2 604**	**2 662**	**2 497**	**2 525**	**2 466**	**2 641**	**2 778**	**7%**
Overland transport								
Rail	923	1 002	1 010	918	807	937	951	3%
Motor vehicle**	1 372	1 392	1 265	1 402	1 501	1 527	1 624	18%
Pipeline transport	209	157	136	146	141	164	193	-8%
Water transport	**2**	**2**	**3**	**2**	**1**	**-**	**-**	**-77%**
Air transport	**99**	**110**	**83**	**57**	**17**	**13**	**10**	**-90%**

Note: * Preliminary data; ** excluding departmental transport since 2014.
Source: National Statistical Committee of the Kyrgyz Republic (http://stat.kg).

The amount of transported goods rose steadily from 27.4 million tonnes in 2006 to 41 million tonnes in 2013. After an abrupt drop in 2014 to 28.9 million tonnes, the amount is slowly increasing once again.[74]

According to the NSC, 133 legal entities employing about 5 000 individuals are involved in transporting goods.[75]

6.2.3. Greenhouse gas emissions

Kyrgyzstan's greenhouse gases (GHG) emissions are relatively low. According to the information presented by the country in its communication on its intended national determined contribution (INDC; see Section 7.5), in 2010 the country's contribution to total global GHG emissions from fossil fuel combustion was 0.023%, while its population was 0.079% of the world's total population. In other words, per capita GHG emissions in Kyrgyzstan are less than one-third of the world average (GoK, 2016[1]). In 2013, its global contribution to GHG emissions increased to 0.034% of world emissions, at 15.5 million tCO_2e (USAID, 2017[32]).

In 2010 the country's overall GHG emissions, excluding the land use, land-use change and forestry (LULUCF) sector, amounted to 12.8 million tCO_2e, or 12.56 million tCO_2e including the LULUCF sector (total net emissions) (Table 6.13). In the base year, 1990, total GHG emissions excluding LULUCF amounted to 28.39 million tCO_2e or 28.43 million tCO_2e including the LULUCF sector (total net emissions).

Table 6.7. Overview of national GHG emissions, 1990/2000/2010

(gigagrams of CO_2e)

	1990	2000	2010
CO_2 emissions, excluding LULUCF/LUCF	20 532	4 957	6 363
CO_2 net emissions/removals by LULUCF/LUCF	837	576.9	558.3
CO_2 net emissions, including LULUCF/LUCF	21 369	5 534	6 922
GHG emissions, excluding LULUCF/LUCF	28 392	9 287	12 802
GHG net emissions/removals by LULUCF/LUCF	40.5	-229.2	-243.7
GHG net emissions, including LULUCF/LUCF	28 433	9 058	12 558

Source: (GoK, 2016[1]), *Third National Communication of the Kyrgyz Republic under the UN Framework Convention on Climate Change*, https://unfccc.int/sites/default/files/resource/NC3_Kyrgyzstan_English_24Jan2017.pdf.

After a major increase around 1998-90 and a subsequent drop in the first half of the 1990s, Kyrgyzstan's GHG emissions reached a low point in 2001, since when the trend has been again slightly upward. In the period 1990-2012, the country's GHG per capita emissions decreased by 68% (Figure 6.11). This is the second most significant decline among the 11 former Soviet Union countries (after Moldova). In 2012, 7 EECCA countries were below the world's average of per capita CO_2 emissions. Kyrgyzstan's value of 2.46 tCO_2e per capita is only about one-third of the global average of 7.55 tCO_2e per capita (2012 values).

Figure 6.11. GHG emissions per capita in EECCA countries, 1990 and 2012

(tonnes of CO_2e)

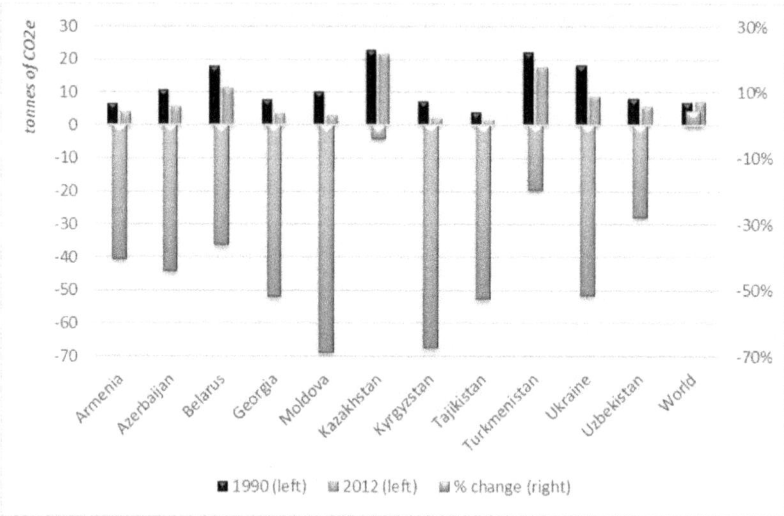

Source: World Bank (https://data.worldbank.org).

In 1990-2012, Kyrgyzstan's GHG emissions were the third lowest in total terms (Table 6.14). Kyrgyzstan managed the second most significant reduction of total CO_2 emissions over this period (after Moldova).

Table 6.8. Total GHG emissions in EECCA countries, 1990 and 2012

(kilotonnes of CO_2e)

	1990	2012	% change
Armenia	24 730	12 319	-50.2%
Azerbaijan	78 097	56 537	-27.6%
Belarus	185 412	109 647	-40.9%
Georgia	38 221	14 628	-61.7%
Moldova	38 030	11 351	-70.2%
Kazakhstan	372 291	366 502	-1.6%
Kyrgyzstan	**33 283**	**13 795**	**-58.6%**
Tajikistan	21 668	15 365	-29.1%
Turkmenistan	81 332	92 178	13.3%
Ukraine	953 112	404 900	-57.5%
Uzbekistan	169 358	177 224	4.6%
World	38 232 170	53 526 303	40.0%

Source: World Bank (https://data.worldbank.org).

Kyrgyzstan's low emissions – in total values as well as per capita – are largely because 90% of total electricity generation is supplied by the hydroelectric power plants. However, the impacts of climate change are expected to decrease water flow after the 2030s, consequently reducing the hydropower resources potential. As a result, with a predicted annual GDP growth of 4%, electricity demand will likely outstrip the hydropower capacities.

According to the World Resources Institute's Climate Analysis Indicators Tool (WRI CAIT),[76] Kyrgyzstan's GHG emissions in 2013, excluding the land-use change and forestry (LUCF) sector, were mainly from the energy sector (61.1%), followed by agriculture (28.4%), industrial processes (5.7%), and waste (4.8%). Emissions from the transport sector are included in the energy sector and account with other fuel combustion for approximately 71% of emissions within the energy sector (USAID, 2017[32]).

Again according to WRI CAIT, the country's energy emissions decreased by 5 million CO_2e between 1992 and 2013, mainly due to decreases in manufacturing and construction and other fuel combustion.[77] In transportation, a significant decrease in fuel consumption occurred between 1993 and 1997 due to changes in the country's vehicle fleet; the number of trucks and buses decreased significantly while cars increased. In 2014, around a quarter of the CO_2 emissions of the Kyrgyz Republic came from transport.

Table 6.9. Kyrgyzstan's major GHG emission trends, 2000-14

(kilotonnes of CO_2e)

	2000	2010	2011	2012	2013	2014
CO_2	4 635	6 384	7 656	10 131	9 842	9 608
CH_4	3 486	3 968	4 130	4 291	3 540	3 591
N_2O	1 452	1 465	1 516	1 567	n.d	n.d.

Source: World Bank (https://data.worldbank.org).

While total GHG emissions in Kyrgyzstan decreased by 52% over 1990-2010, the decrease in the transport sector was only 32%. Within the transport sector, almost all GHG emissions can be attributed to road transport – 93% in 1990 and 99% in 2010 (Figure 6.12).

Figure 6.12. GHG emissions from transport in Kyrgyzstan, 1990 and 2010

(kilotonnes of CO_2e)

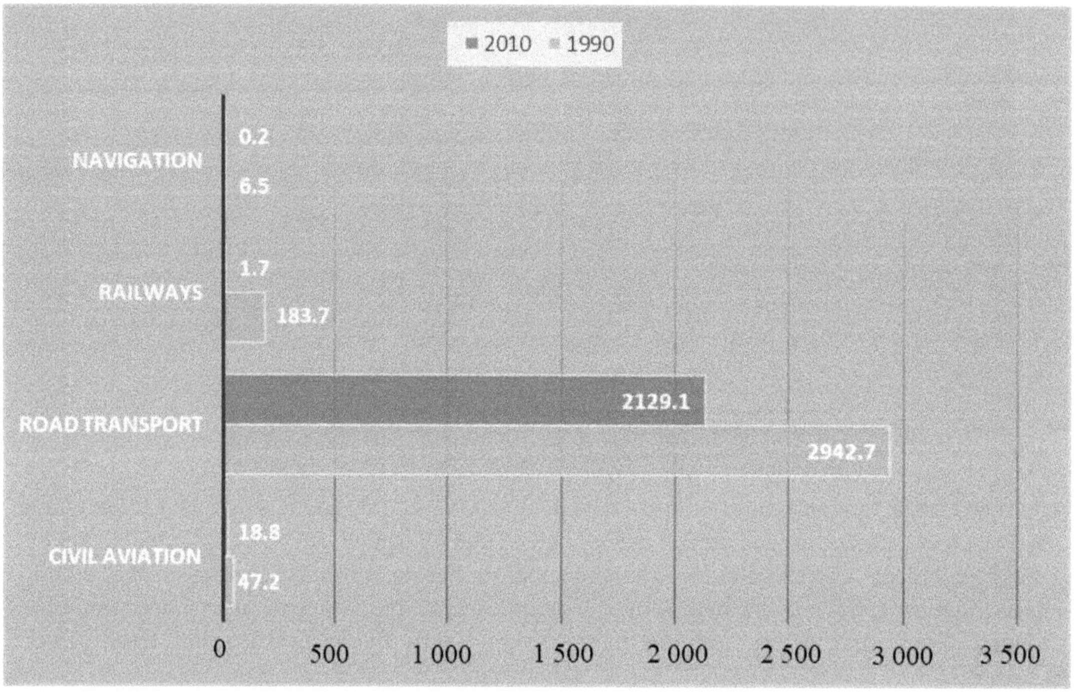

Note: For conversion to CO_2 equivalent, global warming potential values for non-CO_2 gases in the IPCC Fifth Assessment Report, 2014 (AR5) were used.[78] Non-methane volatile organic compounds (NMVOCs) not included (due to conversion difficulties and insignificant values).
Source (GoK, 2016[1]), *Third National Communication of the Kyrgyz Republic under the UN Framework Convention on Climate Change*, https://unfccc.int/sites/default/files/resource/NC3_Kyrgyzstan_English_24Jan2017.pdf.

The CO_2 emissions from transport include emissions from the combustion of fuel for all transport activity, regardless of the sector, except for international marine bunkers and international aviation.

Over 1990-2018, CO_2 emissions from transport increased overall, though with a significant drop in 2014 (Figure 6.13). The transport sector was the biggest contributor to Kyrgyzstan's CO_2 emissions (as a percentage of total fuel combustion) from 2009 to 2015, when it was overtaken by the electricity and heat production sector until 2018.

Figure 6.13. CO_2 emissions by sector in Kyrgyzstan, 1990-2018

(% of total fuel combustion)

Source: World Bank (https://data.worldbank.org).

The transport sector's average contribution to CO_2 emissions over 1990-2018 was 25.8%, compared to 31.9% for the electricity and heat production sector (Table 6.16). However, in 2018, transport was well above its long-term average value (34.8%), while electricity and heat production was around its average (32.7%).

Electricity and heat production experienced the most significant increase in terms of CO_2 emissions as a total of fuel combustion over 1990-2018, followed by the transport sector – by 15.5 and 8.4 percentage points, respectively. These two sectors (in the same order) also contributed most to the country's CO_2 emissions (see mean values in the table). However, the most significant change took place in manufacturing industries and construction, namely a decline by 30.5 percentage points over 1990-2018.

Table 6.10. Sectoral shares in CO_2 emissions in Kyrgyzstan, 1990 and 2018

(% of total fuel combustion)

	1990	2018	Change 1990/2018	Mean value 1990-2018
	%	%	Percentage points	%
Transport	26.44	34.82	8.38	25.78
Electricity and heat production	17.22	32.67	15.45	31.87
Manufacturing industries and construction	37.11	6.60	-30.52	19.99
Residential buildings and commercial and public services	0.00	3.37	3.37	2.47
Other sectors (excluding residential buildings and commercial and public services)	19.19	22.55	3.35	19.89

Source: World Bank (https://data.worldbank.org).

CO_2 emission trends for liquid and gaseous fuel consumption are shown in Figure 6.14. These followed a similar pattern up until 2006, but diverge from then onwards. As the majority of liquid fuel is consumed by transport, the increasing trajectory of the liquid fuel consumption in Figure 6.14 is a proxy for the percentage share of CO_2 emissions from the transport sector.

Figure 6.14. CO_2 emissions from liquid and gaseous fuel consumption in Kyrgyzstan, 1992-2014

(kilotonnes)

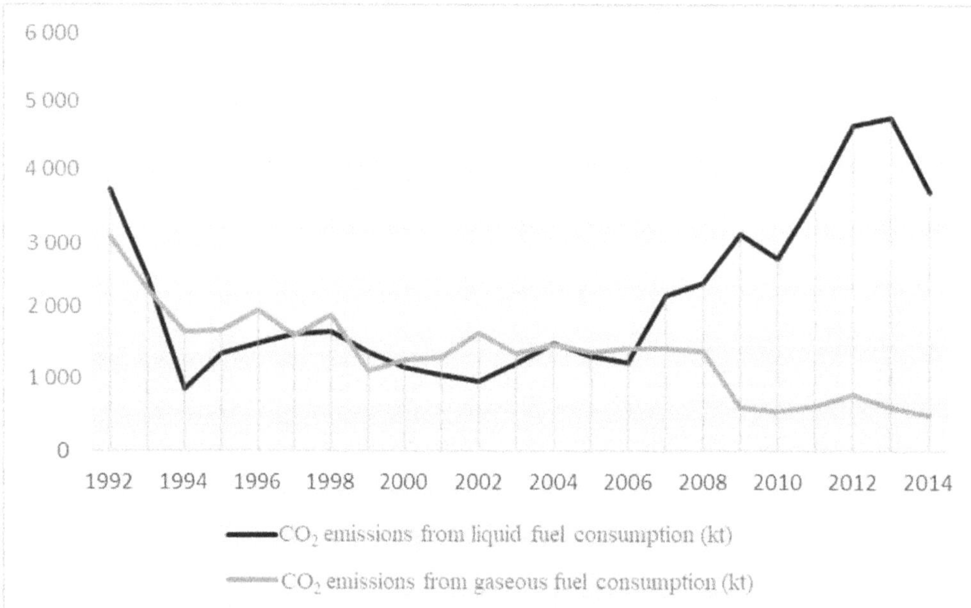

Source: World Bank (https://data.worldbank.org).

6.2.4. Vehicle fleet

In Soviet times, the urban public transport systems in Bishkek and Osh were served by monopolist public transport companies. Following independence in 1991, a new open market was established for all branches, including passenger transport services.

Passenger transport is now provided by more than 252 legal entities, including 35 operating as taxis, and involving more than 12 000 natural persons. In addition, 69 enterprises (agencies) of the structural divisions of the Ministry of Transport and Roads are involved in the transport branch.

As the population looking for work and/or working increased in the capital, so did the minibus share in the urban transport market. In the early 1990s, the first private minibuses appeared (so-called "*marshrutki*"). These vehicles tended to be second-hand foreign minibuses, and most were not even originally designed as passenger carriers (Kadyraliev, 2011[29]). Nowadays, the insufficient number of high-capacity buses in large cities such as Bishkek and Osh has led to the growth of minibuses, which have taken over 95% of the bus routes. Most minibuses are old and poorly maintained, and crowded (IRU, 2013[26]).

In the cities of Bishkek and Osh, traffic volumes on the roads have increased dramatically in recent years (JICA, 2013[29]). The current capacity of the road network cannot accommodate this increasing traffic volume. According to the general plan, the city roads are designed for 40 000 – 45 000 cars, but today about 500 000 cars use them (Mokrenko, 2017[31]). In the last 10 years, only 14 new roads have been constructed.[79] Furthermore, public transport vehicles are not separated from private vehicles on the roads (i.e., there are no dedicated transport lanes). Trolleybuses, buses and minibuses also use the same bus stop. Long queues at the bus stops, particularly in rush hours, remain an important problem. Both cities are therefore subjected to traffic congestion and an increased risk of accidents.

In addition, the rolling stock is generally ageing dramatically (e.g. see Table 6.9 for Bishkek), reaching the end of its operational life and contributing substantially to air pollution.

While the tariffs for passenger transport are regulated by the state, and the prices of fuel, electric power, materials and technical equipment are constantly increasing, the lack of revenue growth for carriers makes it difficult to update their rolling stock on time and improve their services (e.g. training of drivers, safety).

In the case of minibuses, fares are a source of direct income for the drivers, who therefore tend to carry as many passengers as possible. Even though traffic laws do not permit a minibus to carry standing passengers, many minibuses operate with standing passengers and take more than the nominal (legal) passenger numbers. Since other buses cannot fully cover minibus capacity, without intervention by the government, minibuses are unlikely to disappear.

A trolleybus network is much complex than a bus or minibus network. The basic technical conditions for the operation of the vehicles include a traction power supply system with substations, cable lines, overhead lines as well as various fittings and masts. Here too, the network has seen underinvestment over many years, and the current system would not have the capacity to extend the operation of the trolleybus network. Moreover, the latest generation of trolleybuses may not be able to operate on the current network because they require a stable voltage level.

The expansion of the trolleybus network would therefore need significantly higher capital for the purchase of vehicles and modernisation of the related infrastructure. This has also to be included in the investment costs.

Trolleybuses, on the other hand, use local electricity, 90% of which is locally produced by hydroelectric power plants. This reduces the price and risk compared to imported conventional fuels or gas.

6.2.5. Public transport in Bishkek

The Urban Transportation Department in the Bishkek City Mayor's Office was established in 2008 and is responsible for organising public transport networks in the city. It grants licences to the operators of both the public and private public transport sectors (JICA, 2013[29]).[80]

Passenger transport in the city is carried out by:

- municipal enterprise "Bishkek Trolleybus Management"
- municipal enterprise "Bishkek passenger motor transportation enterprise"
- private carriers (minibus routes).

In 2016, passenger transport was distributed as in Table 6.8.

Table 6.11. Passengers on non-electric public transport in Bishkek, 2016

	Thousand passengers	Share of total
Total	**360 609**	
Buses (state)	28 863	8%
Minibuses (private)	331 745	92%

Source: National Statistical Committee of the Kyrgyz Republic (http://stat.kg).

According to the NSC, Bishkek's urban public transport fleet comprises approximately 17 900 units (Table 6.9).

Table 6.12. Ownership and age of Bishkek's urban public transport fleet, 2016

(No. of vehicles)

	Total	Ownership		Year of manufacture, <5 years			Year of manufacture, 5-10 years			Year of manufacture, 10-15 years			Year of manufacture, 15+ years		
		Business	Individual	Total	Business	Individual	Total	Business	Individual	Total	Business	Individual	Total	Business	Individual
Buses	**2 037**	1 222	815	**49**	39	10	**563**	550	13	**32**	24	8	**1 393**	609	784
Minibuses	**15 730**	1403	14 327	**166**	149	17	**547**	195	352	**3077**	218	2859	**11 940**	841	11 099
Trolleybuses*	100	public		52			18			25			5		

Note: *For trolleybuses, the totals reflect estimates after implementation of the EBRD project involving the purchase of 52 trolleybuses (see below).
Source: National Statistical Committee of the Kyrgyz Republic (http://stat.kg), City of Bishkek, and authors' estimates.

The management of city transport at the Bishkek City Hall gives slightly different figures for the ages of the urban public transport fleet (Table 6.10). Even when taking into account the data discrepancies, we can see from Table 6.9 and Table 6.10 that 70-75% of all minibuses in the capital are over 15 years old. If we assume the useful life of a minibus is normally seven years, well over 90% exceed this. The situation for the bus fleet is only slightly better than for minibuses – around 70% of vehicles are beyond their useful life (usually 12 years). However, this is according to data from NSC, as the City Hall of Bishkek reports no vehicles older than 15 years in the stock.

As can be seen in Table 6.9, trolleybuses fare somewhat better – only 5% fall into the oldest category (15+ years) and over 50% are less than 5 years old. Trolleybuses also have a longer useful life (between 15 and 20 years), so at least 95% of trolleybuses are still within their useful life limits.

Table 6.13. Age of urban public transport fleet in Bishkek

(No. and share of units)

Fleet by age	<5 years	5-10 years	10-15 years	>15 years	Total
Buses	10 (2%)	205 (44%)	253 (54%)	0	468
Minibuses	0	400 (10%)	800 (20%)	2 800 (70%)	4 000

Note: Rounded, estimated figures. The most likely reason that these figures differ from national data for the city of Bishkek may be that the national data do not deregister old vehicles.
Source: Bishkek City Hall

During the Soviet period, minibuses were also present, and three local bus companies and an inter-city bus company were operating. Natural gas was also used as a fuel, but subsequently the government switched to diesel buses.

After the year 2000, the bus fleet already consisted of ageing second-hand vehicles, but as these were not replaced the fleet has shrunk. In 2009, as the market developed rapidly with a huge number of operators and overlapping routes, the city administration launched improvements such as purchasing new vehicles from China and re-arranging existing routes giving priority to municipal vehicles in the city centre (Kadyraliev, 2011[29]).

According to the city transport management at Bishkek City Hall, the city currently has 120 buses in working order. A further 50 buses are in maintenance or technical repair. Additionally, there are 96 buses that need capital repair and 192 buses that are damaged and on the write-off inventory (i.e. no longer in service). Of the bus fleet, 10 operate on methane and the rest on diesel. Ten of these buses are 11 metres in length; the remainder are 8.4 metres long.[81]

The public transport situation is made more difficult by the fact that 42 new settlements have appeared around the city in the past 20 years or so. In addition, the city subsidises the public transport system to the tune of about KGS 300 million (USD 4.36 million) a year.

At present, the Bishkek bus network comprises 16 routes, with lengths varying from 26 to 56 km.[82] The main share of passenger traffic in Bishkek is provided by minibuses, operated by 41 private operators. There are 122 minibus routes adding up to around 2 280 km, serving practically the entire city with a daily average of 2 700 minibuses (for the list of minibus routes in Bishkek, see Annex F). The city estimates that it still needs 600-800 additional buses of average capacity (not trolleybuses) to serve the city centre and gradually replace the minibus fleet.

In 2018, the Bishkek City Administration signed an agreement with Gazprom to purchase 320-350 CNG buses. The investment was planned to be financed from a municipal bond issue underwritten by Gazprombank (approx. USD 50 million). Over the course of the negotiations, however, the city withdrew from this agreement, citing expensive conditions (12% interest rate, due already in 2019). Instead, the city has decided to purchase buses in a phased procurement approach over 2019-2020. It will cover the purchase of 42 buses from its own funds, at a cost of KGS 382 million (USD 5.55 million) and plans to request KGS 800 million (USD 11.62 million) from the Republican budget. The city is in the first phase of tendering and is planning to purchase 120 large CNG buses

The trolleybus is the only mode of electric transport in Kyrgyzstan and is operated by municipally-owned companies. There are seven trolleybus routes with a total length of 210 km in Bishkek. Currently, 86 trolleybuses are in operation in the city, with a reserve of 10 trolleybuses that are in maintenance or technical repair.[83]

In November 2017, the Bishkek Trolleybus Management ordered a total of 52 trolleybuses from two suppliers;[84] 14 have already been delivered with the rest expected in June/July 2018. The Russian manufacturer Trolza is to supply 37 vehicles and the Belarusian company Belkommunmash is to supply 15. All vehicles are 12 m long. Trolza also previously supplied 44 trolleybuses to Bishkek in 2013 and 23 to Osh in 2017 (MRI, 2017[31]). Bishkek City Hall estimates that another 100 trolleybuses are needed. To support this effort, the city obtained a EUR 5.4 million (USD 6.1 million) loan and EUR 2.5 million (USD 2.8 million) grant under a European Bank for Reconstruction and Development (EBRD) programme.[85]

An electronic payment pilot was conducted in March/April 2018 on trolleybus lines No. 11 and 14 in order to attract new passengers. Using the Balance.kg application on smartphones, the fare was fixed at KSG 1 (USD 0.01). This campaign was initiated by the Beeline company, a mobile telecom services company, and the Bishkek City Hall. In practice, however, the payment mechanism had several flaws and requires further development.

The city is also holding bilateral discussions with the Asian Development Bank (ADB) concerning a USD 50 million loan for urban public transport. It is ready to take out a loan if the city council supports a tariff increase. It was agreed that ADB needs to define the loan terms.

The city is also interested in the following measures:

- a pilot project (5-10 km) of "autonomous" (i.e. battery-equipped) trolleybuses
- a strategy for public transport development that includes planning for a new route network and an investment plan
- new route planning (and re-planning existing routes) together with optimisation of the minibus and bus network (the city expects to add five new bus routes and two new trolleybus routes)
- replacement of 600 minibuses, with the remaining minibuses to serve areas without trolleybus access.

The city is making a second attempt to start a study into the expansion and optimisation of the urban public transport system (EBRD-financed).[86] This would be a master plan for city development up until 2025. A tender has been announced and the city hopes the 18-month project will start in February 2019. The study will cover tariff policy issues, legal issues, and procedures to reduce the number of minibuses. The aim is to solve traffic jams, air pollution, service levels and routes by 2025.

The Bishkek City Development Agency also reports that the ADB will finance the preparation of a feasibility study for a public-private partnership (PPP) arrangement to attract investors and maintain routes. They also report that a feasibility study on E-ticketing has been prepared and they plan to conduct a tender to select a private partner to implement this measure.

6.2.6. Public transport in Osh

The public transport network in Osh comprises two trolleybus routes and three bus routes operated by the municipal transport enterprise. Additionally, private operators run 48 minibus routes.[87]

The network involves a hub and spoke system with all routes running through the city centre. The routes are licensed centrally by the Public Transport Agency. However, many routes still have duplicate services. The total network length of the routes is 1 726 km, of which 120 km are covered by buses, 54 km by trolleybuses and 1 542 km by minibuses.[88]

Table 6.14 shows passenger transport in the city of Osh.

Table 6.14. Non-electric passenger transport in Osh, 2016

	Thousand passengers	Share
Osh city	**20 634**	
Buses (state)	3 834	18.6%
Minibuses (private)	16 800	81.4%

Source: National Statistical Committee of the Kyrgyz Republic (http://stat.kg).

Minibuses account for the highest market share. According to the NSC, in 2016 the city of Osh had a total of 530 buses and 2 332 minibuses, mostly Mercedes-Benz Sprinters over 15 years old.[89] The city of Osh, on the other hand, reports that there are 86 and 40 operational conventional diesel buses and trolleybuses, respectively. At the same time, about 1 166 minibuses operate in the city. Recently, the city replaced 23 trolleybuses and 30 high-capacity buses (diesel-powered) under an EBRD-financed programme. The project involved a sovereign loan of EUR 5.7 million to be on-lent to the City of Osh and proposed co-financing of EUR 3.1 million grant provided by international donors.[90]

Table 6.15. Ownership and age of urban public transport fleet, Osh, 2016

(No. of vehicles)

	Total	Ownership		Year of manufacture, <5 years			Year of manufacture, 5-10 years			Year of manufacture, 10-15 years			Year of manufacture, 15+ years		
		Business	Individual	**Total**	Business	Individual	**Total**	Business	Individual	**Total**	Business	Individual	**Total**	Business	Individual
Buses	**530**	362	168	**32**	32	0	**98**	98	0	**4**	1	3	**396**	231	165
Minibuses	**2332**	156	2 176	**20**	18	2	**58**	15	43	**318**	41	277	**1936**	82	1 854
Trolleybuses*	**40**	public		**23**			7			**8**			**2**		

Note: * For trolleybuses, the totals reflect estimates after implementation of the EBRD project involving purchase of 23 trolleybuses (see below).
Source: National Statistical Committee of the Kyrgyz Republic (http://stat.kg), City of Osh, and authors' estimates.

The EBRD-financed programmes mean that the situation with the trolleybuses fleet is similar to Bishkek – the majority (around 60%) of the fleet is younger than five years old, while the fully depreciated vehicles (aged 15 years and more) make up only a very small segment (5%). The age of the bus and minibus fleet is a little higher than in Bishkek – about 75% of buses have reached their useful life limits (12 years) and at least 97% of minibuses are over 7 years old (the usual useful life for minibuses, depending on mileage and service). Only 17% of minibuses are less than 15 years old.

The city has limited facilities for maintenance and repairs, which aggravates an already ageing fleet. The city states that it plans to replace a further 17 trolleybuses and purchase 250 new buses.[91]

6.3. Greenhouse gas emissions and air pollution in the Kyrgyz Republic

6.3.1. Air pollution

The Agency of Hydrometeorology at the Ministry of Emergency Situations of the Kyrgyz Republic (Kyrgyzhydromet) is responsible for monitoring air quality. This monitoring is carried out at 14 stationary points in five cities, covering about 64% of the country's urban population.

The following pollutants should ideally be measured – sulphur dioxide (SO_2), oxides of nitrogen NO_x), formaldehyde (CH_2O), and ammonia (NH_3) – however, air pollution data in the Kyrgyz Republic cities are not readily available or reported. Indeed, Kyrgyzhydromet's stationary posts have outdated laboratories and lack emissions analysers that can specify pollution data in detail. The agency uses its own method to calculate pollution and report on air quality (Mokrenko, 2017[31]). Reports on air pollution, including poor air quality events, are posted on the Kyrgyzhydromet website after the event; real-time data are not available.

The main sources of atmospheric air pollution are power plants, mining and processing industries, construction materials industries, as well as the municipal and private sector. Large cities in Kyrgyzstan suffer especially from air pollution caused by human activities, including vehicle emissions, as well as heating homes and facilities using coal. In Bishkek, the coal-fired thermal power plant is a huge emitter.

As can be seen in Figure 6.15 (Panel A), since 2015 there have been more stationary sources of air pollution in the city of Bishkek than in the surrounding Chui *oblast* (36 vs. 34). The volume of emissions in Bishkek was also almost three times higher than for Chui *oblast* (31 700 tonnes vs. 11 900 tonnes in 2015), yet its geographical area is over 100 times smaller (170 km^2 vs. 19 900 km^2).

Figure 6.15. Emission of air pollutants from stationary sources in Bishkek, Osh and surrounding regions, 2011-15

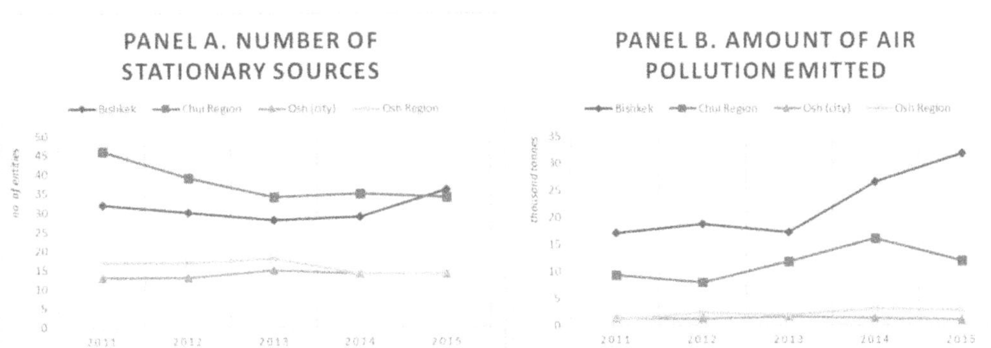

Source: (NSC, 2016[2]), *Environment in the Kyrgyz Republic, Statistical Compilation 2011-2015*, National Statistical Committee of the Kyrgyz Republic, Bishkek, http://stat.kg/media/publicationarchive/8c0e9d22-6bb6-4145-b1d6-8311da33521d.pdf.

In addition, Bishkek's location, situated between mountains, contributes to inversions that trap pollutants in the ambient air. Additionally, trees are being cut down in squares and parks, and also along roads to expand them.

According to the Kyrgyzhydromet report, in May 2018 the city of Bishkek registered high concentrations of nitrogen dioxide (NO_2), nitric oxide (NO) and formaldehyde (CH_2O), exceeding the maximum allowable concentrations. A local NGO – MoveGreen – monitors air quality (PM2.5); in the winter concentrations often exceed 100 microgrammes per cubic metre, which exceeds the maximum permissible 24-hour average concentration defined by the World Health Organization (WHO) by at least four times.

Table 6.17 lists other air pollutants (probably from 2015 or shortly before), showing that the city of Bishkek significantly outweighs the city of Osh and both the surrounding regions.

Table 6.16. Emissions of air pollutants in Bishkek, Osh and surrounding regions

(kg per capita)

	NO_x	CO	NMVOC	SO_2	Total
Osh oblast	0.98	7.61	1.60	1.71	11.90
Chui oblast	4.95	18.08	4.21	3.83	31.06
Bishkek City	22.12	176.91	31.81	21.99	252.83
Osh City	3.98	28.42	5.56	1.82	39.78

Source: (GoK, 2016[1]), *Third National Communication of the Kyrgyz Republic under the UN Framework Convention on Climate Change*, https://unfccc.int/sites/default/files/resource/NC3_Kyrgyzstan_English_24Jan2017.pdf.

Due to power outages in previous years (see Section 6.1.4) and natural gas price increases, most people living in private houses have switched to coal. As they burn coal at low temperatures, a significant part of the fuel turns into harmful toxic gases, mainly carbon monoxide – one of the components of smog. Moreover, local residents often use car tyres and other waste as fuel to heat their homes, which, when burned, form dark smoke and emit particulates.

The impact of motor transport on the environment in Kyrgyzstan is defined by the intensity of transportation and the technical condition of the vehicle fleet. As motor vehicles age, and in the absence of an efficient system of technical inspection and maintenance, the vehicles emit harmful substances that exceed defined norms. According to the State Agency for Environmental Protection and Forestry (SAEPF), the annual total pollutant emissions into the atmosphere in Bishkek amount to 240 000 tonnes, of which 180 000 tonnes are from motor vehicles (Levina, 2018[33]).

The replacement of outdated buses with modern diesel-powered buses or the expansion of trolleybuses networks in the place of diesel-powered vehicles would help reduce pollution by particulate matter, as well as NO_x and SO_2. The introduction of an effective technical inspection system for cars would also reduce harmful substances in the atmosphere.

6.3.2. Influence of air pollution from diesel engines on human health

Diesel engines emit carbon dioxide (CO_2), carbon monoxide (CO), nitrogen oxides (NO_x), sulphur dioxide (SO_2) and particulate matter (PM). The air pollution from diesel engines, especially older ones, poses major environmental and health risks to the population (**Error!**

Reference source not found.). Increased air pollutants carry a risk of mortality, in particular among people over 65 (Pope et al., 1995[34]). Above all, diesel exhaust is a Group 1 carcinogen,[92] causing lung cancer and being linked to bladder cancer.

Particulates from road transport are mainly of three types:

- primary particles emitted from the exhaust pipe liner of vehicles: the primary ultrafine particles emitted by diesel vehicles are mainly formed of soot carbon
- ultrafine secondary particles that are formed in the outside air: these particles are formed from the exhaust pipe liner of the vehicles and therefore cannot be filtered out by the vehicle
- primary particles coming from tyre, clutch, brake or road wear.

Box 6.1. The impact of diesel exhaust emissions

Carbon dioxide (CO_2): non-toxic, but as a greenhouse gas it causes climate change.

Carbon monoxide (CO): a temporary atmospheric pollutant in some urban areas, chiefly from the exhausts of internal combustion engines. Carbon monoxide is absorbed through breathing and enters the bloodstream through gas exchange in the lungs. It is toxic when encountered in concentrations above about 35 ppm.

Nitrogen oxides (NO_x): NOx refer to a mixture of nitric oxide (NO) and nitrogen dioxide (NO_2). They are produced during combustion, especially at high temperatures. Due to reactions and photolysis by sunlight, they are the main source of tropospheric ozone. NO_x may react with water to make nitric acid, which may end up in the soil where it makes nitrate, which is of use to growing plants. NO_x in combination with other pollutants creates urban smog. High concentrations of nitrogen dioxide are harmful to humans because they cause inflammation of the airways.

Sulphur dioxide (SO_2): SO_2 pollution levels from diesel mainly depend on the quality of the fuel. If the fuel contains more sulphur, the diesel exhaust will contain more SO_2. Sulphur dioxide emissions are a precursor to acid rain and atmospheric particulates. Inhaling sulphur dioxide is associated with increased respiratory symptoms and diseases, and difficulty in breathing.

Particulate matter (PM): the major pollutants with negative health effects are PM (2.5 and 10). The particles are so small they can penetrate into the deep regions of the lungs. It is estimated that approximately 3% of cardiopulmonary and 5% of lung cancer deaths are attributable to PM globally. Exposure to PM2.5 reduces life expectancy by about 8.6 months on average.

Since 2000, PM pollution has been estimated to cause 22 000 to 52 000 deaths every year in the United States. It also contributed to about 370 000 premature deaths in Europe in 2005, and 3.22 million deaths globally in 2010, according to a study of the global burden of disease (Lim et al., 2012[35]).

There is no evidence of a safe level of exposure to PM, or a threshold below which no adverse health effects occur. The World Health Organization Air Quality Guidelines values for PM in 2005 were as follows (WHO, 2013[36]):

- for PM2.5: 10 micrograms per cubic metre (μg/m³) for the annual average and 25 μg/m³ for the 24-hour mean (not to be exceeded on more than 3 days/year)
- for PM10: 20 μg/m³ for the annual average and 50 μg/m³ for the 24-hour mean.

Figure 6.16 and Figure 6.17 compare the increased emissions of health-damaging substances by old diesel-powered engines (especially those aged at least 15 years) with modern diesel engines and alternative fuels, compressed natural gas (CNG) and liquefied petroleum gas (LPG).

Figure 6.16. Assumed amount of health-damaging substances emitted per distance travelled (normative)*

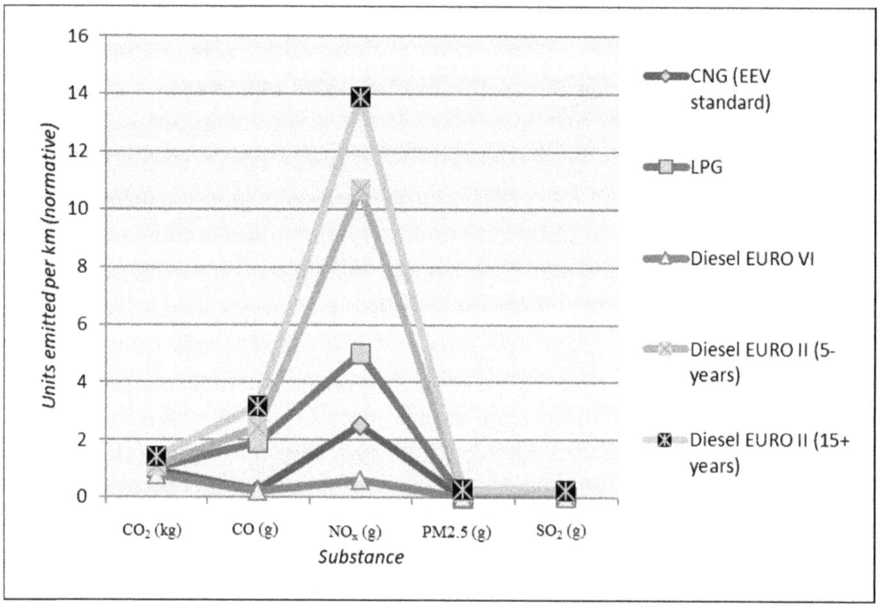

Note: *For a discussion of normative and real pollution factors, see Section 2.3.2 and Annex B.
Source: (DieselNet, 2016[37]), "EU: Heavy-Duty Truck and Bus Engines: Regulatory Framework and Emission Standards", www.dieselnet.com/standards/eu/hd.php (accessed 30 March 2017).

Figure 6.17. Assumed amount of health-damaging substances emitted per distance travelled (real)*

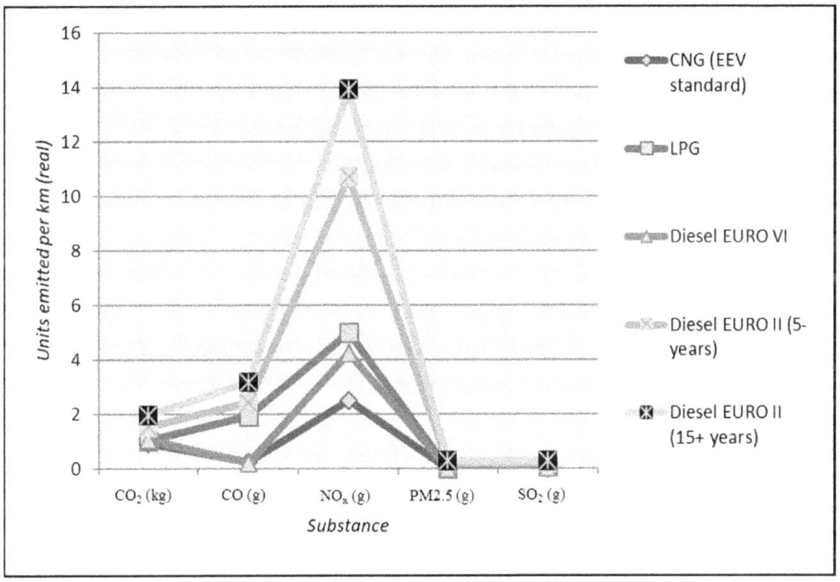

Note: *For a discussion of normative and real pollution factors, see Section 2.3.2 and Annex B.
Source: (DieselNet, 2016[37]), "EU: Heavy-Duty Truck and Bus Engines: Regulatory Framework and Emission Standards", www.dieselnet.com/standards/eu/hd.php (accessed 30 March 2017).

The city of Bishkek experienced an increase in the incidence of respiratory cases, from 136 000 in 2011 to 163 000 in 2015 (Figure 6.18). The increase in Osh was not so rapid, from 67 000 to 78 000 cases, respectively. These figures are not attributable to urban transport alone, although its contribution is expected to be substantial. The WHO statistics also show that diseases of the circulatory system – which air pollutants (especially particulates) are increasingly understood to contribute to – constitute the main causes of death in Kyrgyzstan (50% in 2018) (WHO, 2018[38]).

Figure 6.18. Incidence of respiratory diseases Bishkek, Osh and surrounding regions, 2011-15

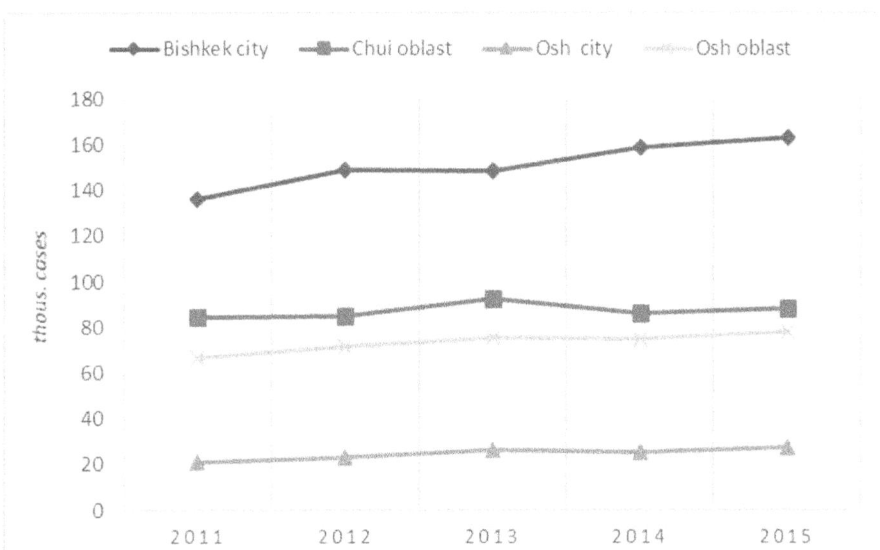

Source: (NSC, 2016[2]), *Environment in the Kyrgyz Republic, Statistical Compilation 2011-2015*, http://stat.kg/media/publicationarchive/8c0e9d22-6bb6-4145-b1d6-8311da33521d.pdf.

The replacement of outdated buses with modern diesel-powered or natural gas-powered buses – or the expansion of trolleybuses networks in place of diesel-powered vehicles – would help reduce the amount of major air pollutants, such as particulates, NO_x and SO_2.

Extending the market share of trolleybuses would improve the situation further as trolleybuses use more than 90% green energy (JICA, 2013[29]). A clean public transport programme can thus be justified from a public health standpoint, considering the huge health cost sums directly carried by the health care system.

6.4. Conclusions for the CPT Programme

Kyrgyzstan's GHG emissions are relatively low. Planned and expected economic development, however, will see these emissions increase unless action is taken to reduce them. This, along with the review of air pollution in Kyrgyz cities, confirms that the CPT Programme can be justified from a public safety and public health standpoint, as well as an environmental standpoint. With road transport contributing the bulk of air pollution, replacing outdated vehicles with modern diesel-powered or natural gas-powered buses and buses with higher capacity would help reduce pollution by particulate matter, as well as NO_x, SO_2 and GHG emissions, in line with the country's emission-reduction objectives.

However, improving the energy intensity of vehicles (megajoule/passenger-km or megajoule/tonne-km) and carbon intenstity of fuels (CO_2e/megajoule) is not enough on its own. In addition to investments to replace vehicle fleets, reducing pollution from urban public transport will require a combination of measures:

- avoiding or reducing the need for travel (either through better urban planning or changing personal behaviour)
- shifting travel from private cars to non-motorised modes (walking, cycling[93]) or public transport
- improving existing forms of transport through technical improvements (especially in energy intensity of vehicles and carbon intensity of fuels and energy carriers).

In this context, road widening would only increase traffic in cities. The combination of mass public transport with non-motorised modes of transport offers the greatest mitigation potential. The first step in this direction would be to increase the capacity and number of public transport vehicles (bus and trolleybuses). The diversification of the fleet structure, increasing energy efficiency and a modal shift from car to public transport would also improve resiliency against future energy price rises (diesel, gas, electricity). Regulations on the operation of ageing vehicles, sufficient maintenance, and technical inspection of vehicles are necessary prerequisites.

However, there also needs to be an increased demand for these services, as the economic and environmental viability of public transport will only be achieved through increased demand. Improving the quality of the public transport to meet passenger expectations, including redesigning the urban transport network, would make it more attractive. It would also help to reduce the social costs of transport – such as time lost due to congestion, air pollution, accidents etc. – which can generally account for several percent of GDP (though this has not been assessed in Kyrgyzstan).

Notes

1. See NSC on land used by farms in the Kyrgyz Republic at: http://stat.kg/en/opendata/category/181.

2. According to the 2009 census, a large majority of Kyrgyz, Dungans and Kalmucks (each 93-95%) aged 15 years and over indicated Russian as their second language, only 10% of the population aged 15 years and over indicated Kyrgyz as a fluently spoken second language (NSC, 2009[39]).

3. The seven *oblasts* are Batken, Jalal-Abad, Issyk-Kul, Naryn, Osh, Talas and Chui.

4. Numbers for both cities as of end of 2018. See NSC on resident population at: http://stat.kg/en/opendata/category/39.

5. See NSC on total population by sex, by main age groups urban and rural areas, at: www.stat.kg/en/statistics/download/dynamic/315.

6. See NSC on total population by nationality at: http://stat.kg/en/opendata/category/312.

7. See UNDP country information on Kyrgyzstan at: www.kg.undp.org/content/kyrgyzstan/en/home/countryinfo.html.

8. See NSC on GDP in national currency at: www.stat.kg/en/opendata/category/26; and in foreign currency at: www.stat.kg/en/opendata/category/2315.

9. Investment Promotion and Protection Agency (www.invest.gov.kg).

10. See the ADB for an overview of Kyrgyzstan's economy: www.adb.org/countries/kyrgyz-republic/economy.

11. Kumtor, the main Kyrgyzstan's gold mine, approaches end of mine life due to advanced resource depletion.

12. See the NSC database on the structure of GDP by types of economic activity in Kyrgyzstan: http://stat.kg/en/opendata/category/2314.

13. See UNDP 2018 statistical update on Kyrgyzstan at: http://hdr.undp.org/sites/all/themes/hdr_theme/country-notes/KGZ.pdf.

14. According to the World Bank, middle-income economies start with a GNI per capita of USD 1 045 and go up to USD 12 746. Lower-middle-income and upper-middle-income are separated with a threshold of USD 4 125 per capita. On the WB classification update for Kyrgyzstan, see: http://www.worldbank.org/en/news/press-release/2014/07/24/kyrgyz-republic-becomes-lower-middle-income-country.

15. See the WB database on GNI per capita for Kyrgyzstan at: https://data.worldbank.org/indicator/NY.GNP.PCAP.PP.CD?locations=KG. Kyrgyzstan's GNI per capita (previously, GNP per capita) has nearly tripled from its 1995 value of 1 210 (current international dollars). Nonetheless, Kyrgyzstan has – along with Tajikistan – the lowest values for the former Soviet states.

16. WB Poverty and Equity Portal (http://povertydata.worldbank.org).

17. See natural gas production, imports and consumption in Kyrgyzstan at: https://www.indexmundi.com/g/g.aspx?v=136&v=137&v=139&c=kg&l=en.

18. See proved natural gas reserves of Kyrgyzstan at: https://www.indexmundi.com/g/g.aspx?v=98&c=kg&l=en.

19. See crude oil production, imports, consumption and reserves at: https://www.indexmundi.com/g/g.aspx?v=88&v=91&v=93&v=97&c=kg&l=en

20. Personal communication with the State Agency for Regulation of the Fuel and Energy Complex.

21. See Gazprom's foreign projects – Kyrgyzstan: www.gazprom.com/about/production/projects/deposits/kyrgyzstan.

22. The actual document can be found in the resolution.

23. See production of electric power on power stations at: www.stat.kg/en/statistics/download/dynamic/344.

24. The reliability of power supply is influenced by frequent outages and occasional breakdowns (these are usually longer than necessary due to limited availability of spare parts for outdated – Soviet-times – technology). Also the quality of the Kyrgyzstan's power system is hit by regular voltage and frequency fluctuations.

25. See WB's Sustainable Energy for All (SE4ALL) database at: https://data.worldbank.org/indicator/EG.ELC.ACCS.ZS?locations=KG.

26. Including pumped storage. Neighbouring Tajikistan, which also produces over 90% of its electricity from hydro resources, but because of larger population, its installed capacity is higher (5 190 MW). On the other hand, much more populated Kazakhstan and Uzbekistan have lower installed capacities (2 554 MW and 1 731 MW, respectively). See (IHA, 2018[11]).

27. Water releases are subject to inter-governmental agreement under which Kyrgyzstan supplies Uzbekistan with water in summer for irrigation in return for gas and electricity in winter.

28. Personal communication with the State Agency for Regulation of the Fuel and Energy Complex.

29. Besides using local coal, about 50% is imported from Kazakhstan (altogether, ca. one million tonnes/year). Apart from coal as the major fuel, the two CHP plants use natural gas and mazut as additional fuels. According to information from the National Energy Holding Company, the modernisation of the two CHPs (e.g. new filters) reduced the emissions CO_2 and polluting substances (these, even by 95%).

30. This includes Bishkek CHP (666 MW) from 1961 and Osh CHP (50 MW).

31. Figures are most probably based on 2012/2013 data.

32. See NSC for structure of GDP by types of economic activity at: www.stat.kg/en/statistics/download/dynamic/935.

33. And personal communication with the State Agency for Regulation of the Fuel and Energy Complex.

34. See NSC for electro-balance of industries economies at: www.stat.kg/en/statistics/download/dynamic/343.

35. The generation company is OJSC Electric Power Plants (6 HPPs and 2 CHPs). Power transmission is done by OJSC National Electric Grid of Kyrgyzstan (comprising six local enterprises) and regional distribution by OJSCs Severelektro, Vostokelektro, Oshelektro and Jalalabatelektro. The National Electric Grid of Kyrgyzstan is allowed to set electricity prices for industrial consumers but not for the general population (UNCTAD, 2013[13]).

36. As a part of Government Order No. 299-p of 24 July 2013. See http://cbd.minjust.gov.kg/act/view/ru-ru/209920.

37. Economic regulation (tariffs, licensing, and dispute resolution) was under the State Department for Regulation of Fuel and Energy Complex, while technical regulation was under the State Inspectorate for Energy and Gas.

38. See www.regulatortek.kg. For general information about the state agency in English, see https://erranet.org/member/kyrgyz-republic.

39. See https://24.kg/archive/en/vlast/180475-news24.html.

40. This, of course, must be offset by lower support for other sectors, such as public infrastructure (e.g. roads) and services (e.g. education). In addition, energy subsidies contribute to the country's indebtedness and jeopardise its macro-economic stability.

41. It is estimated that 45% of available generation capacity is beyond its useful service life, and the similar state of transmission and distribution assets exacerbates the risk of network failures (Gassner et al., 2017[16]).

42. For the main trends in the Kyrgyz banking sector in 2018, see www.nbkr.kg/index1.jsp?item=80&lang=ENG. For a list of commercial banks and number of branches, see www.nbkr.kg/index1.jsp?item=69&lang=ENG.

43. By the Resolution of the Supreme Council of the Kyrgyz Republic No. 873-X11 of 6 March 1992 "On the transformation of the State Bank of the Kyrgyz Republic into the National Bank of the Kyrgyz Republic".

44. See www.econstor.eu/obitstream/10419/54609/1/644131357.pdf.

45. For IMF's Articles of Agreement, see: https://www.imf.org/external/pubs/ft/aa/index.htm.

46. See IMF press release at: www.imf.org/en/News/Articles/2015/09/14/01/49/pr9516.

47. After an unprecedentedly rapid application process.

48. Based on WB inflation data for Kyrgyzstan (http://api.worldbank.org/v2/en/indicator/FP.CPI.TOTL.ZG?downloadformat=excel); and estimated on KGS/USD currency exchange data (https://data.worldbank.org/indicator/PA.NUS.FCRF?locations=KG).

49. See www.econstor.eu/obitstream/10419/54609/1/644131357.pdf.

50. See NBKR's strategic directions for the period at: www.nbkr.kg/index1.jsp?item=3326&lang=ENG.

51. See NSC for assets and liabilities of commercial banks at: www.stat.kg/en/statistics/download/dynamic/470.

52. For non-banking financial institutions, see NBKR at: www.nbkr.kg/DOC/14052019/000000000052254.xls.

53. For GDP statistics, see www.stat.kg/en/statistics/download/dynamic/741.

54. See NBKR for balance of payments of the Kyrgyz Republic at: www.nbkr.kg/DOC/10042019/000000000052023.xls.

55. See NBKR for newly issued credits by commercial banks within the period at: www.nbkr.kg/DOC/30042019/000000000052194.xls.

56. See NBKR for newly issued credits by commercial banks within the period at: www.nbkr.kg/DOC/30042019/000000000052194.xls.

57. See NBKR for credits of commercial banks by the end of the period at: www.nbkr.kg/DOC/25042019/000000000052132.xls.

58. See NBKR for official exchange rates at: www.nbkr.kg/EXCEL/dailyeng.xls.

59. Which volume in 2016 amounted to KGS 982.2 million whereas in 2015 to KGS 689.6 million (NBKR, 2018[18]).

60. See NBKR for deposits in commercial banks by the end of the period at: www.nbkr.kg/DOC/25042019/000000000052135.xls.

61. See banking legislation at: www.nbkr.kg/index1.jsp?item=1200&lang=ENG.

62. As of end of June 2018.

63. Whereas agriculture is credited mainly in local currency (28.9% vs 2.2%) and trade in foreign currency (38.9% vs. 20.6%) of all loans.

64. Not including consumer loans.

65. See NBKR for credits of commercial banks by the end of the period at: www.nbkr.kg/DOC/25042019/000000000052132.xls.

66. The decrease in lending activities of non-bank financial institutions was also connected with their transformation into commercial banks before 2017 (NBKR, 2018[18]).

67. See credits of commercial banks by regions of the Kyrgyz Republic, at the end of period, at: www.nbkr.kg/DOC/29042019/000000000052183.xls.

68. See NBKR for credits of commercial banks at the end of the period at: www.nbkr.kg/DOC/25042019/000000000052132.xls; and deposits in commercial banks at the end of the period at: www.nbkr.kg/DOC/25042019/000000000052135.xls.

69. See NBKR for the main trends in the Kyrgyz banking sector in 2018 at: www.nbkr.kg/index1.jsp?item=80&lang=ENG.

70. For the English version, see www.nbkr.kg/index1.jsp?item=42&lang=ENG.

71. For further information, see the CAREC Program (www.carecprogram.org).

72. Personal communication with the Ministry of Transport and Roads.

73. Personal communication with the Ministry of Transport and Roads.

74. See NSC database on freight by all types of transport in tonnes at: http://stat.kg/en/opendata/category/1975.

75. Personal communication with the National Statistical Committee.

76. See CAIT 2.0 WRI's Climate Data Explorer at: www.climatewatchdata.org/countries/KGZ.

77. See CAIT 2.0 WRI's Climate Data Explorer at: www.climatewatchdata.org/countries/KGZ.

78. For IPCC AR5 reports, see: www.ipcc.ch/assessment-report/ar5.

79. Personal communication.

80. Information about municipal and private carriers' routes is available online at http://bus.kg/ including calculations of the best routes depending on destination.

81. Personal communication with Bishkek City Hall.

82. Personal communication with Bishkek City Hall.

83. Personal communication with Bishkek City Hall.

84. Metro Report International (www.metro-report.com).

85. For EBRD Bishkek Public Transport Project, see www.ebrd.com/work-with-us/projects/psd/bishkek-public-transport-project.html.

86. In 2013, the Japan International Cooperation Agency (JICA) conducted a study on improvement of public transportation in Bishkek. See (JICA, 2013[29]).

87. Personal communication with Osh City Hall.

88. Personal communication with Osh City Hall.

89. National Statistical Committee of the Kyrgyz Republic (http://stat.kg).

90. For EBRD Osh Public Transport Project, see: www.ebrd.com/work-with-us/projects/psd/osh-public-transport-project.html.

91. Personal communication with Osh City Hall.

92. The Group 1 category is used when there is sufficient evidence of carcinogenicity in humans.

93. According to information from NGO Bicycle Kyrgyzstan, there are two bicycle lanes in Bishkek and about 10 000 bicycles in the city. However, only 10% of bicycle owners use them as a mode of transport due to poor infrastructure for non-motorised travel, poor traffic safety and air pollution problems. There is an irreplaceable role for NGOs such as Bicycle Kyrgyzstan and MoveGreen in conducting research and awareness campaigns to alter citizens' preferences and behaviour. Solely financial aspects – such as lower costs for public or non-motorised transport – cannot bring sustainable solutions.

Bibliography

ADB (2012), "Sector Assessment (Summary): Transport", *Country Partnership Strategy: Kyrgyz Republic, 2013-2017,* Asian Development Bank, Manila, http://www.adb.org/sites/default/files/linked-documents/cps-kgz-2013-2017-ssa-03.pdf. [27]

CIS (2014), *Commonwealth of Independent States in 2013 – Statistical Yearbook*, Interstate Statistical Committee of the Commonwealth of Independent States, Moscow. [4]

DieselNet (2016), "EU: Heavy-Duty Truck and Bus Engines: Regulatory Framework and Emission Standards", *DieselNet website*, http://www.dieselnet.com/standards/eu/hd.php (accessed on 30 March 2017). [37]

EEC (2015), *Eurasian Economic Integration: Facts and Figures*, Eurasian Economic Commission, Moscow, http://www.eurasiancommission.org/en/Documents/broshura26_ENGL_2014.pdf. [20]

Gassner et al. (2017), *Analysis of the Kyrgyz Republic's Energy Sector*, Final Report, May 2017, World Bank Group, Washington, D.C, http://documents.worldbank.org/curated/en/370411513356783137/pdf/122080-WP-PUBLIC-TheStateoftheKyrgyzRepublicsEnergySectorFinalMay.pdf. [16]

GoK (2016), *Third National Communication of the Kyrgyz Republic under the UN Framework Convention on Climate Change*, Government of Kyrgyzstan, Bishkek, https://unfccc.int/sites/default/files/resource/NC3_Kyrgyzstan_English_24Jan2017.pdf. [1]

GoK (2015), *Social Security Programme of the the Kyrgyz Republic for 2015-2017 (in Russian)*, Government of Kyrgyzstan, Bishkek, http://cbd.minjust.gov.kg/act/view/ru-ru/97348. [17]

GoK (2013), *Action Plan for the Reform of the Energy Sector 2013-2014 (in Russian)*, Government of Kyrgyzstan, Bishkek, http://cbd.minjust.gov.kg/act/view/ru-ru/209920. [15]

GoK (2013), *Programme of the Government of the Kyrgyz Republic on energy saving and policy planning on energy efficiency in the Kyrgyz Republic for 2015-2017 (in Russian)*, Government of Kyrgyzstan, Bishkek, http://cbd.minjust.gov.kg/act/view/ru-ru/97870. [10]

GoK (2012), *Mid-Term Power Sector Development Strategy of the Kyrgyz Republic for 2012-2017 (in Russian)*, Government of Kyrgyzstan, Bishkek, http://www.energo.gov.kg/uploads/files/6923950867655473d3b4888aeef124f4.doc. [14]

GoK (2012), *Strategy for Development of Road Transport in the Kyrgyz Republic for 2012-2015*, Government of Kyrgyzstan, Bishkek, http://cbd.minjust.gov.kg/act/view/ru-ru/93738?cl=ru-ru. [25]

GoK (2008), *National Energy Programme of the Kyrgyz Republic for 2008-2010 and the Strategy for the Development of the Fuel and Energy Complex up to 2025, in Russian*, Government of Kyrgyzstan, Bishkek, http://cbd.minjust.gov.kg/act/view/ru-ru/58883?ckwds=%25d1%2581%25d1%2582%25%2025d1%2580%25d0%25b0%25d1%2582%25d0%25b5%25d0%25b3%25d0%25b8%25d1%25%20258f%2B%25d1%2580%25d0%25b0%25d0%25b7%25d0%25b2%25d0%25b8%25d1%2582%25d0%25b8%25d1%258f%2B%25d1%2582%25d0%. [9]

Hasanova, S. (2018), *Financial Inclusion, Financial Regulation, Financial Literacy, and Financial Education in the Kyrgyz Republic*, ADBI Working Paper Series, No. 850, July 2018, http://www.adb.org/sites/default/files/publication/432336/adbi-wp850.pdf. [21]

IHA (2018), *Hydropower Status Report, Sector Trends and Insights*, International Hydropower Association, London, http://www.hydropower.org/download/file/nojs/18956. [11]

IMF (2018), *Fourth and Fifth Reviews under the Three-Year Arrangement under the Extended Credit Facility, and Request for Modification of Performance Criteria–Press Release; and Staff Report*, Country Report No. 18/53, February 2018, International Monetary Fund, Washington, D.C., http://www.imf.org/~/media/Files/Publications/CR/2018/cr1853.ashx. [24]

IRU (2013), *Road Transport in Kyrgyzstan – 2013*, International Road Transport Union, Bishkek, http://www.iru.org/sites/default/files/2016-03/en-road-transport-kyrgyzstan-13.pdf. [26]

JICA (2013), *The Study on Improvement of Urban Transportation in Bishkek City of the Kyrgyz Republic, Final Report, October 2013*, Final Report, October 2013, Japan International Cooperation Agency, Tokyo, http://open_jicareport.jica.go.jp/pdf/12127585_01.pdf. [30]

Kadyraliev, A. (2011), "Public transport system in the capital of Kyrgyzstan: current situation and analysis of its performance", *WIT Transactions on the Built Environment,* Vol. 116, Urban Transport XVII, pp. 239-250, http://www.witpress.com/Secure/elibrary/papers/UT11/UT11021FU1.pdf (accessed on 30 August 2019). [29]

Levina, M. (2018), "Smog over Kyrgyzstan capital city: causes, effects, and solutions", *The Times of Central Asia*, Vol. 27 January, http://www.timesca.com/index.php/news/26-opinion-head/19261-smog-over-kyrgyzstan-capital-city-causes-effects-and-solutions (accessed on 30 August 2019). [33]

Lim et al. (2012), "A comparative risk assessment of burden of disease and injury attributable to 67 risk factors and risk factor clusters in 21 regions, 1990-2010: a systematic analysis for the Global Burden of Disease Study 2010", *The Lancet,* Vol. 380, Issue 9859, pp. 2224-2260, https://doi.org/10.1016/S0140-6736(12)61766-8. [35]

Mokrenko, A. (2017), "Air pollution in Bishkek exceeds maximum permissible concentration 2-3 times", *News Agency 24.kg,* 28 December, https://24.kg/english/72240_Air_pollution_in_Bishkek_exceeds_maximum_permissible_concentration_2-3_times (accessed on 30 August 2019). [31]

Moody's (2019), "Rating Action: Moody's affirms the Kyrgyz Republic's B2 issuer rating; maintains stable outlook" Moody's Investors Service, 1 March, http://www.moodys.com/research/Moodys-affirms-the-Kyrgyz-Republics-B2-issuer-rating-maintains-stable--PR_393450 (accessed on 30 August 2019). [6]

MRI (2017), "Bishkek Trolleybus Order Placed", *Metro Report International,* 20 November, http://www.metro-report.com/news/single-view/view/bishkek-trolleybus-order-placed.html. [32]

NBKR (2018), *National Bank of the Kyrgyz Republic: Annual Report 2017*, National Bank of the Kyrgyz Republic, Bishkek, http://www.nbkr.kg/DOC/18072018/000000000050344.pdf. [22]

NBKR (2018), *The Financial Sector Stability Report of the Kyrgyz Republic*, December edition, National Bank of the Kyrgyz Republic, Bishkek, http://www.nbkr.kg/DOC/15012019/000000000051444.pdf. [18]

NSC (2018), *Kyrgyzstan, Brief Statistical Handbook, 2015-2017*, National Statistical Committee of the Kyrgyz Republic, Bishkek, http://www.stat.kg/media/publicationarchive/16db2910-6b8d-48f9-80b9-45b7ac3347bd.pdf. [3]

NSC (2016), *Employment and Unemployment, Results of the Integrated Selective Survey of Household Budgets and Workforce*, National Statistical Committee of the Kyrgyz Republic, Bishkek, http://stat.kg/media/publicationarchive/824fc464-7e56-4b23-a009-f07b5a1a21cb.pdf. [7]

NSC (2016), *Environment in the Kyrgyz Republic, Statistical Compilation 2011-2015*, National Statistical Committee of the Kyrgyz Republic, Bishkek, http://stat.kg/media/publicationarchive/8c0e9d22-6bb6-4145-b1d6-8311da33521d.pdf. [2]

NSC (2009), *Population and Housing Census of the Kyrgyz Republic of 2009. Book I: Main social and demographic characteristics of population and number of housing units*, National Statistical Committee of the Kyrgyz Republic, Bishkek, https://unstats.un.org/unsd/demographic-social/census/documents/Kyrgyzstan/A5-2PopulationAndHousingCensusOfTheKyrgyzRepublicOf2009.pdf. [39]

OECD (2016), *Monitoring competitiveness reforms in Kyrgyzstan*, Peer Review Note, 24 November, OECD, Paris, http://www.oecd.org/eurasia/competitiveness-programme/central-asia/Monitoring-competitiveness-reforms-Kyrgyzstan.pdf. [19]

OECD (2013), *Improving Access to Finance for SMEs in Central Asia through Credit Guarantee Schemes, Private Sector Development Policy Handbook*, OECD, Paris, http://www.oecd.org/global-relations/AccesstoFinanceforSMEs.pdf. [23]

Pope, C. et al. (1995), "Particulate air pollution as a predictor of mortality in a prospective study of U.S. adults", *American Journal of Respiratory Critical Care Medicine*, Vol. 151, pp. 669-674, http://www.atsjournals.org/doi/abs/10.1164/ajrccm/151.3_Pt_1.669?url_ver=Z39.88-2003&rfr_id=ori:rid:crossref.org&rfr_dat=cr_pub%3dpubmed. [34]

UNCTAD (2013), *National Services Policy Review: Kyrgyzstan*, United Nations Conference on Trade and Development, New York and Geneva, https://unctad.org/en/PublicationsLibrary/ditctncd2010d2_en.pdf. [13]

UNISON (2013), *Analysis of Electricity Distribution and Consumption System in Kyrgyzstan*, UNISON Civic Foundation, Bishkek, http://energy.unison.kg/sites/default/files/an_report_eng.pdf. [12]

USAID (2017), *Greenhouse Gas Emissions in Kyrgyzstan*, USAID Factsheet, United States Agency for International Development, Washington, D.C., http://www.climatelinks.org/sites/default/files/asset/document/2017_USAID_GHG%20Emissions%20Factsheet%20Kyrgyzstan.pdf. [28]

WHO (2018), *A service framework and roadmap for the development of care systems for heart attack and stroke in Kyrgyzstan*, World Health Organization, Regional Office for Europe, Copenhagen, http://www.euro.who.int/__data/assets/pdf_file/0019/402922/KGZ-Ro. [38]

WHO (2013), *Health Effects of Particulate Matter Policy Implications for Countries in Eastern Europe, Caucasus and Central Asia*, World Health Organization, Regional Office for Europe, Copenhagen, http://www.Euro.who.int/__data/assets/pdf_file/0006/189051/Health-effects-of-particulate-matter-final-Eng.pdf. [36]

World Bank (2019), *The Kyrgyz Republic Country Snapshot*, April 2019, World Bank Group, Washington, D.C., http://pubdocs.worldbank.org/en/967461554997981958/Kyrgyz-Republic-Snapshot-Apr2019.pdf. [5]

World Bank (2017), *Kyrgyz Republic: A resilient economy... on a slow growth trajectory. With a special focus on Kyrgyzstan's ailing energy sector*, Kyrgyz Republic Economic Update No. 5, World Bank Group, Washington, D.C., http://documents.worldbank.org/curated/en/710331496766602711/pdf/115684-WP-PUBLIC-add-series-SpringKGZBEUFinal.pdf. [8]

Laws and regulations

(listed by most recent publishing date, in Russian)

Law No. 206 of 16 December 2016 "On the National Bank of the Kyrgyz Republic, Banks and Banking Activity", http://cbd.minjust.gov.kg/act/view/ru-ru/111486.

Government Resolution No. 601 of 25 August 2015 "On approval of the Programme of the Government of the Kyrgyz Republic on energy saving and policy planning on energy efficiency in the Kyrgyz Republic for 2015-2017", http://cbd.minjust.gov.kg/act/view/ru-ru/97869.

Government Resolution No. 85 of 27 February 2015 "About the Social Security Programme of the Kyrgyz Republic for 2015-2017", http://cbd.minjust.gov.kg/act/view/ru-ru/97347.

Government Resolution No. 660 of 20 November 2014 "On approval of the medium-term tariff policy of the Kyrgyz Republic on electric and thermal energy for 2014-2017", http://cbd.minjust.gov.kg/act/view/ru-ru/97149.

Government Resolution No. 295 of 15 May 2012 "On draft laws of the Kyrgyz Republic "On introducing amendments and additions to the Law of the Kyrgyz Republic "On energy"", "On introducing amendments and addenda to the Law of the Kyrgyz Republic "On electric power industry"", and "On introducing changes to the Law of the Kyrgyz Republic "On energy saving"", http://cbd.minjust.gov.kg/act/view/ru-ru/93583?cl=ru-ru.

Government Resolution No. 677 of 4 October 2012 "On approval of the Strategy for Development of Road Transport in the Kyrgyz Republic for 2012-2015", http://cbd.minjust.gov.kg/act/view/ru-ru/93738?cl=ru-ru.

Government Resolution No. 330 of 28 May 2012 "About the Mid-Term Power Sector Development Strategy of the Kyrgyz Republic for 2012-2017", http://cbd.minjust.gov.kg/act/view/ru-ru/93854?cl=ru-ru.

Government Resolution No. 47 of 13 February 2008 "On the project of the National Energy Programme of the Kyrgyz Republic for 2008-2010 and the strategy for the development of the fuel and energy complex up to 2025", http://cbd.minjust.gov.kg/act/view/ru-ru/58883?ckwds=%25d1%2581%25d1%2582%%2025d1%2580%25d0%25b0%25d1%2582%25d0%25b5%25d0%25b3%25d0%25b8%25d1%%20258f%2B%25d1%2580%25d0%25b0%25d0%25b7%25d0%25b2%25d0%25b8%25d1%2582%25d0%25b8%25d1%258f%2B%25d1%2582%25d0%25be%25d0%25bf%25d0%25bb%25d0%25b8%25d0%25b2%25d0%25bd%25d0%25be.

Government Resolution No. 239 of 23 April 1997 "About privatisation and privatisation programme of the Kyrgyz state joint-stock holding company "Kyrgyzgosenergoholding"", http://cbd.minjust.gov.kg/act/view/ru-ru/34362?cl=ru-ru.

Law No. 8 of 28 January 1997 "On power industry", *Erkin Too* newspaper No. 8 of 12 February 1997, http://cbd.minjust.gov.kg/act/view/ru-ru/508/30?cl=ru- (unofficial translation available at: https://cis-legislation.com/document.fwx?rgn=411).

7. Policy and regulatory framework for the transport sector

This chapter briefly discusses the main regulatory framework dealing with or having an impact on urban public transport in Kyrgyzstan (including energy efficiency, air pollution, or climate change). All the legislative requirements and set-ups presented here – both technical and administrative – are discussed in the context of the extent to which they create demand for green investment in Kyrgyzstan's public transport sector.

7.1. Regulatory framework affecting urban public transport

The general regulatory framework includes various acts that affect public transport, such as the legal relationships between the transport operators and passengers, and between operators and public administration bodies. Besides technical and road safety regulations, it also includes fiscal (such as customs duties for imported vehicles), social (consumer) and environmental protection (such as emissions or energy efficiency standards).

The Ministry of Transport and Roads is responsible for transport and communications policy, regulation, planning and development.

The Road Safety Secretariat and the Main Road Safety Department of the Kyrgyz Republic collect and analyse road traffic data and co-ordinate accident prevention initiatives, while also contributing to national development strategies in the field of road transport.

7.1.1. The Law on Transport is the primary legal basis for the CPT Programme

The transport system is administered by the Ministry of Transport and Roads of Kyrgyzstan (in 2016, its name was changed from the Ministry of Transport and Communications to reflect its new functions).

In 1998, Law No. 89 (of 8 July) "On transport" was adopted, covering all means of transport in the Kyrgyz Republic. Law No. 121 of 18 July 2016 "On railway transport" and the Air Code of the Kyrgyz Republic No. 281 of 6 August 2015 were adopted separately.

In Bishkek, city transport is regulated by the regulatory document "The rule of the organization of passenger and freight transport traffic to Bishkek" passed by the city council on 8 July 2003. The document defines fundamental regulations for the city's entire transport system, including:

- Regulations for organising passenger and freight transport in Bishkek taking into account minimum requirements for passenger safety, health care, safety of vehicles on roads, environmental and consumer protection, and vehicle registration.
- Responsibilities of the city administration for co-ordinating, managing and monitoring contractual obligations for passenger traffic services. The city administration develops the network of routes and allocates routes among operators on a competitive basis.
- Determining the operators of trolleybus routes through a competitive system.
- Measures to ensure that if tariffs do not ensure profitability for public transport operators, subsidies shall be provided from the city budget.
- Annual testing of the route network according to specific indicators.

Whilst the Law on Transport provides the legal basis for the CPT Programme, the municipal regulations in Bishkek should be modified to provide an incentive to invest in clean transport. For example, the regulations should provide for the possibility of offering investment subsidies to transport providers that switch to less polluting means of transportation.

7.1.2. Regulations for private carriers do not ensure safety

Kyrgyzstan has adopted state regulations for licensing transport activity and services; these include the following laws and regulations:

- Law No. 195 of 19 October 2013 "On license authorisation system in the Kyrgyz Republic".
- Government Order No. 260 of 31 May 2001 "On licensing of separate types of activities".
- Law No. 89 of 8 July 1998 "On transport".

Private individuals can act as private carriers of citizens, provided they have a license/permit from the tax inspection office for their place of residence. No requirements need to be met in order to obtain this license/permit. Any person with a vehicle in use can transport passengers, including over long distances. Therefore, many drivers have insufficient qualifications for ensuring the safe transport of passengers.

Through the licensing mechanism, the state should exercise complete control over this branch, ensuring that the transport legislation of the Kyrgyz Republic is observed and establishing the minimum necessary requirements for the safety and quality of the transport services provided.

However, in practice the system has not resulted in greater safety in automobile transportation or in the quality of the transport services provided. Both local and national officials report road transport safety as a primary concern.

7.1.3. Traffic regulations in the Kyrgyz Republic have not increased road safety

Traffic regulations were approved through Government Resolution No. 421 of 4 August 1999 and entered in force on 1 September 1999. These established traffic rules, the interaction between public transport and other road users, the technical conditions to be adhered to in order for a vehicle to be permitted to operate, as well as the responsibilities for ensuring the safety of all parties involved in transport (GoK, 1999[1]).

However, poor road safety on Kyrgyz roads and the high accident rate led to a policy dialogue on road safety in 2016 involving the Deputy Minister of Health, stakeholders from the government, the police, NGOs and health service providers. A legislative review of the laws on risk factors was also conducted. The dialogue resulted in many initiatives and legislative amendments being proposed (WHO, 2018[2]).

The CPT Programme could serve as a catalyst for increased road safety by increasing the safety of the public transportation fleet.

7.1.4. Regulations for vehicle environmental safety do not meet international standards

The legal framework for state technical inspection is provided for under Law No. 151 of 8 May 2009: "General technical regulation on ensuring environmental safety in the Kyrgyz Republic".

In 2012, obligatory technical inspection was cancelled by regulation. While it was subsequently restored, the legislation does not contain accurate and effective mechanisms for the state regulation and control of motor transport activity. Furthermore, responsibilities and sanctions for failing to fulfil the requirements are not included in the regulations.

The law does not reflect international environmental safety standards for vehicles. It needs to be reformed, in particular to bring legal, normative and technical considerations in line with modern conditions and international standards – not only for passenger and freight transportation, but also for the environment and climate change.

As a consequence, the rolling stock is not appropriate for ensuring safe or high-quality public and freight transport service. The CPT Programme could kick-start new investment in a public transport fleet that meets environmental safety standards, which in turn could provide the blueprint for improving environmental safety standards in other vehicle fleets.

7.1.5. The law on municipal property should be better enforced

Parking in the city of Bishkek remains a high priority for review and reform because of insufficient spaces available and the methods drivers use to park, which often disturbs the flow of traffic.

On-street parking spaces in the city of Bishkek are on public land belonging to the municipality. They are regulated by Law No. 37 of 15 March 2002 "On municipal property ownership", and the Land Code of the Kyrgyz Republic No. 45 of 2 June 1999.

According to these laws, the parking spaces are free for users, but private individuals sometimes occupy public land or roads and declare them as a car park and charge for their use in contravention of law.

In 2014 the city management of Bishkek made an attempt to organise fee-based car parks in the city. A project was begun to plan city infrastructure that would allow land to be designated for parking. However, this reform did not succeed due to restrictions in the Land Code. The national parliament did not support this legislative initiative and the project was halted.

The probability of success of the CPT Programme would be increased by introducing fee-based parking and better regulation of parking in Bishkek.

7.1.6. Investment law provides equal treatment of foreign and national investors

Since investment is a major prerequisite for economic development, the Kyrgyz Republic's investment legislation is quite liberal.[1] The Ministry of Economy is the executive body responsible for developing the national investment policy.

Law No. 66 of 27 March 2003 "On investments in the Kyrgyz Republic" sets out the main principles of the national investment policy, which aims to improve the investment climate in the republic and promote local and foreign investment by guaranteeing investors fair legal treatment and protection of their investments.

Under this legislation, foreign investors enjoy the same treatment as national individuals and legal entities.[2] The legislation provides broad rights and guarantees to foreign investors, including guarantees of export and repatriation of investment (Art. 5), guarantees of protection against investment expropriation (Art. 6), coverage of losses incurred by investors, guarantees of income use (Art. 7), freedom of monetary transactions (Art. 8), and others.[3]

Investors investing in top priority economic and social sectors and in areas of the country that meet national development programme (projects) priorities may be granted investment incentives in accordance with Kyrgyz laws (Art. 4). The law, however, does not specify priority sectors, nor does it specify which law or entity specifies them.

Any form of investment can be made in any object or type of business (as long as they are not prohibited under Kyrgyz law), including state-licensed businesses, pursuant to Law No. 195 of 19 October 2013 "On license authorisation system in the Kyrgyz Republic".

7.1.7. Law on public-private partnerships provides scope for private sector involvement in CPT Programme

Public-private partnerships (PPPs) involve a long-term (up to 50 years) interaction between public and private partners for designing, financing, constructing, rehabilitating and reconstructing assets, as well for managing existing or new assets, including infrastructure.

The PPP legislation in Kyrgyzstan is based on the Constitution of the Kyrgyz Republic and was approved by Law No. 7 of 22 February 2012 "On public-private partnership in the Kyrgyz Republic".

Under this law, PPP applies to (i.e. is allowed for) infrastructure assets and/or infrastructure services, among others, in the following sectors:

- generating, transmitting and distributing electric and thermal power
- processing, storing, transporting, transmitting and distributing oil and natural gas
- automobile, railway, water, air, and urban electric transport
- roads and railways (including bridges and tunnels)
- public utilities and public services.

One of the principles guiding this law is that PPP projects must comply with environmental protection requirements. To assist in the implementation of PPP projects, the public partner may provide or help to provide the following types of government financial support to the private partner and/or project company:

- providing rights to an infrastructure asset, and to other movable or immovable property
- assisting in obtaining licenses, permits and approvals
- providing easements for publicly and/or municipally owned movable or immovable property in order to enable specified uses
- granting the right to collect tariffs and to generate revenues from other types of activities not directly associated with the implementation of the PPP project
- setting discounted rental payments for use of the publicly and/or municipally owned property
- granting exclusive rights to engage in the activity in the framework of the concluded PPP agreement
- providing other kinds of support on the part of the public partner.

This legislation for public-private partnership provides for private sector involvement in the financing and implementation of the CPT Programme.

7.1.8. Local public administration law gives municipalities responsibility for urban public transport

Law No. 101 of 15 July 2011 "On local self-government" (adapted 2017) establishes and regulates the organisation and functioning of local government at the level of administrative and territorial units of the Kyrgyz Republic. Thus, municipalities are appropriate partners for implementing the CPT Programme.

7.1.9. The basic principles of budgetary law allow for financing the CPT Programme

According to Art. 15 of Law No. 78 of 11 June 1998 "On the basic principles of budgetary law in the Kyrgyz Republic", the Ministry of Finance can take the decision to grant credits financed by the republican budget to local budgets if local budgets are experiencing financial difficulties. Following this, the Ministry of Finance could also extend financial support to municipalities to implement the CPT Programme.

7.1.10. The financial and economic basis of local government law allows for debt financing of investment programmes

Law No. 215 of 25 September 2003 "On financial and economic basis of local government" enables local governments to issue short-term, medium-term and long-term loans, with the consent of local parliament and the Ministry of Finance and subject to some restrictions.

For example, according to Art. 11, local governments have no right to incur a loan if their total stock of debt, including estimated new debt obligations, exceeds 20% of their revenue. Thus, the creditworthiness of local governments can be calculated and the financial contributions of local governments in the CPT Programme should be clarified before the programme launch.

7.1.11. The licensing law covers urban public transport

Licensing is regulated by Law No. 195 of 19 October 2013 "On license authorisation system in the Kyrgyz Republic". To carry out foreign trade activity, licenses and permits are issued that meet the requirements of international treaties and acts constituting the law of the Eurasian Economic Union in the field of licensing.

Licenses are only required for activities and operations specified by law and to maintain national security, government monopoly, law and order and to protect the environment, ownership, life and health of citizens. Under Kyrgyz law, licensing is mandatory, among others, for the following activities:

- the production, transmission, distribution, sale, export and import of electricity (except electricity produced from renewable sources or from other sources for personal use with capacity up to 1 000 kWh)
- the production, transmission, distribution, sale, export and import of heat (except heat produced from renewable sources or from any sources for personal use)

- processing of oil and natural gas, except industrial-scale production and the sale of bioethanol produced from vegetable feed
- the production, transfer, distribution and sale of natural gas
- urban planning, research and design of residential, public and production buildings and structures (Category I, II and III facilities)
- passenger transport services by motor vehicle (except taxis)
- international cargo transportation by truck.

Permits are required among others for the following operations:

- importing used automobile tyres as waste for recycling purposes
- the purchase, sale, storage, transportation, carrying, import, and export of special means of transport approved by the Government of the Kyrgyz Republic
- discharging pollutants into the environment.

Licenses are issued by the competent government authorities (licensors) exercising control over licensed activities. Licenses issued in other countries are recognised as valid in Kyrgyzstan if appropriate international treaties are in place.

Licenses are issued within 30 calendar days of filing an application along with all the required documents. Operators of passenger transport must hold licenses that are valid for five years.

The State Department for the Regulation of Fuel and Energy is responsible for granting energy production licences and setting energy tariffs (UNDP, 2014[1]).

7.1.12. Under the Tax Code clean vehicles could be tax-exempt

Taxation is regulated by the Tax Code of the Kyrgyz Republic No. 230 of 17 October 2008 and other regulatory legal acts. The Ministry of Economy determines tax policy in the country, while the State Tax Service exercises control over compliance with tax laws and the full and timely payment of taxes. The current Tax Code entered into force on 1 January 2009.

The following national taxes are paid under the general tax regime:

- profit tax
- income tax
- value added tax
- excise tax
- mining taxes (bonuses and royalties)
- sales tax.

There are also the following local taxes:

- land tax
- property tax.

Value added tax

Value added tax (VAT) is a tax collected and remitted to the government on the value of VAT-taxable supplies in the territory of the Kyrgyz Republic, including taxable import supplies.

Taxable supplies are subject to a standard VAT rate of 12%. Preferential activities and sectors attract a zero VAT rate:[4]

- the export of goods, except gold and silver alloy and refined gold and silver
- the international carriage of passengers, luggage and cargo, except by rail
- catering services on transit flights and related international carriage, except international carriage by rail
- services related to the supply of electricity to pump stations supplying irrigation water to fields and drinking water to the population.

Kyrgyz tax legislation lists supplies that are exempt from VAT, including (Article 246):

- passenger transport in the territory of the Kyrgyz Republic, except by cars with fewer than six passenger seats
- international passenger, luggage and cargo transport by rail
- supplies of goods, works and services by private partners and (or) a project company under a public-private partnership agreement subject to approval by the Kyrgyz Government during the period specified in the public-private partnership agreement.

The Ministry of Economy has started considering the green economy in its mission. In practice, a fiscal policy concept exists for 2015-2020 stipulating that a tool for stimulating the green economy will be developed.[5] The ministry has also launched a working group on green tax in order to find options to stimulate the green economy.

The tax regime means that VAT exemption could be sought for transport means purchased under the CPT Programme – whether from domestic or foreign suppliers.

7.1.13. Customs regulations could exempt clean buses from import duties

Customs relations in Kyrgyzstan are regulated by the Customs Union legislation (including the Customs Code of the Customs Union); the customs legislation of the Kyrgyz Republic, which is based on the Constitution of the Kyrgyz Republic and consists of Law No. 184 of 31 December 2014 "On customs regulation in the Kyrgyz Republic"; other normative legal acts; and international treaties and other international customs law provisions.[6]

The State Customs Service is in charge of customs regulation in the Kyrgyz Republic. Customs regulation concerns, among others:

- release of imported goods for consumption on the domestic market
- exports
- customs transit
- customs warehouses
- processing within the customs territory

- processing outside the customs territory
- processing for internal consumption
- temporary import (admission)
- temporary export
- re-import
- re-export duty-free trade
- free customs zone
- free warehousing
- special customs procedures (customs procedures specifying the requirements and terms of use and/or disposal of individual categories of goods within the customs territory of the Customs Union or outside it.

This means that, if applicable, foreign buses purchased under the CPT Programme should be exempt from import duties.

7.1.14. Competition law and the need to increase public transport fares

The State Agency for Anti-Monopoly Regulation under the Government of the Kyrgyz Republic is in charge of implementing the general state policy for protecting and developing competition; state regulation and supervising natural and permitted monopolies; and preventing, restricting and restraining monopoly activities and bad faith competition, as set out in Law No. 116 of 22 July 2011 "On competition".

The functions of the State Agency for Anti-Monopoly Regulation include:

- assessing the competitive environment in the markets for goods and services (works)
- protecting the rights of business entities and individuals from monopolistic abuses, unfair competition, and acts and actions (omissions) of state government and local self-government bodies directed at limiting competition
- issuing opinions on bills for the protection and development of a competitive environment
- approving prices (tariffs) for services (works)
- reviewing complaints and claims of individuals and legal entities of any type of ownership asserting non-compliance with antimonopoly, consumer protection and unfair advertising laws.

An increase in transport tariffs required after implementing the CPT Programme will require approval from the State Agency for Anti-Monopoly Regulation.

7.1.15. Insurance laws should create the basis for functioning insurance systems

Activities of insurance companies are regulated by the Civil Code (of the Kyrgyz Republic No. 15 of 8 May 1996) and the following laws of the Kyrgyz Republic:

- Law No. 209 of 31 July 2015 "On mandatory insurance of premises from fire and natural disasters"
- Law No. 192 of 24 July 2015 "On obligatory insurance of civil liability of vehicle owners"
- Law No. 31 of 26 January 2009 "On features of insurance in crop production"
- Law No. 202 of 15 August 2008 "On obligatory civil liability insurance of organisations operating hazardous production facilities"
- Law No. 194 of 5 August 2008 "On obligatory civil insurance of employer's liability for causing harm to life and health of an employee in performing their (official) labor duties"
- Law No. 189 of 4 August 2008 "On obligatory civil liability insurance of carrier to passengers"
- Law No. 188 of 4 August 2008 "On obligatory civil liability insurance of of carrier of dangerous goods"
- Law No. 96 of 23 July 1998 "On organisation of insurance in the Kyrgyz Republic"
- and other normative legal acts.

In 2015, there were 17 insurance organisations, including two reinsurance organisations, operating in Kyrgyzstan. The insurance products concern more than 84 types of voluntarily insurance and 5 types of mandatory insurance.

These businesses are mainly concentrated in Bishkek (16 companies) with only one company registered in Jalal-Abad.

However, according to the Centre for Development of Renewable and Energy Efficiency, no insurance for vehicles is available in practice. However, an insurance norm should be soon introduced related to damages.

7.2. Regulatory framework for energy efficiency and fuel standards

The State Committee for Industry, Energy and Subsoil Use of the Kyrgyz Republic is responsible for creating the policy and legislative framework for the energy sector, as well as developing strategies and energy-related legislation.

Several laws in Kyrgyzstan focus on the energy sector, energy efficiency, the use of renewable energy and on energy in buildings. The most important laws are:

- Law No. 77 of 8 June 1998 "On oil and gas", which aims to establish a legal framework in line with international standards to ensure economic efficiency, reliability, and security of operations and activities of organisations in the oil and gas industry; the protection of consumers and producers; and the creation of favourable conditions for attracting investment in the oil and gas industry for the intensive increase of production.
- Law No. 56 of 30 October 1996 "On energy industry", which makes energy generation subject to licencing. The licence is issued by the State Department for Regulation of Fuel and Energy.

- Law No. 88 of 7 July 1998 "On energy saving", which includes a broad variety of instruments covering the whole production chain from mining to energy distribution and consumption. Its secondary legislation, institutional provisions and implementation are very general.
- Law No. 283 of 31 December 2008 "On renewable energy sources", which aims to develop and use renewable energy sources, improve energy structure and diversify energy resources. In this context it exempts imported and exported equipment and material for use in renewable energy power plants from custom duties.
- Law No. 8 of 28 January 1997 "On power industry".

Some of the laws are outdated and were amended by Government Resolution No. 295 of 15 May 2012. However, there is a significant lack of effective implementation.

7.3. Regulatory framework for environmental protection

The State Agency for Environment Protection and Forestry (SAEPF) is in charge of environmental protection, ecological security and nature management policy, while the State Inspection Office for Environmental and Technical Safety (SIETS) is responsible for state supervision and control of environmental and technical safety.

Kyrgyz legislation supports environmental protection and the rational use of natural resources through the following laws:

- Law No. 224 of 29 November 2011 "On Technical regulations "On radiation safety".
- Law No. 18 of 3 May 2011 "On specially protected natural territories".
- Law No. 151 of 8 May 2009 "General technical regulation on ensuring environmental safety in the Kyrgyz Republic", which concerns the special ecological safety requirements for the protection of atmospheric air, water bodies, species of fauna and flora, soil and natural landscapes, as well as for the disposal of production and consumption waste.
- Law No. 67 of 22 May 2004 "On bases of technical regulation in the Kyrgyz Republic".
- Law No. 53 of 16 June 1999 "On environmental protection", which concerns the general legal framework for comprehensive environmental protection and for its use, including environmental standard setting, the legal regime of specially protected areas, and rules and procedures.
- Law No. 54 of 16 June 1999 "On environmental impact assessment".
- Law No. 51 of 12 June 1999 "On protection of atmospheric air" (discussed in detail in Section 7.4).
- Law No. 48 of 9 June 1999 "On biosphere territories in the Kyrgyz Republic".

In February 2018, Law No. 24 "On introducing amendments to the Code of the Kyrgyz Republic on administrative responsibility" was adopted. This law should strengthen administrative responsibility and help to reduce violations of the rules and requirements concerning hydrometeorological, environmental and pollution observations, collection and processing.

Currently, a concept for the low-carbon development of the Kyrgyz Republic until 2020 is under development (Mokrenko, 2017[4]).

7.4. Regulatory framework for air pollution

Law No. 51 of 12 June 1999 "On protection of atmospheric air", subsequently amended several times, regulates the management and protection of atmospheric air and the prevention of negative impacts on it. The law designates the arrangements that shall be carried out, including establishing:

- air quality standards
- maximum emission limits to the atmosphere
- regulations on emissions from stationary and non-stationary sources
- requirements for use of the atmosphere.

The national standards for the quality of atmospheric air in inhabited places in Kyrgyzstan are laid out in a special document.[7] This document was approved by the Resolution of the Chief State Health Officer of the Kyrgyz Republic No. 20 on 28 May 2004 and registered in the Ministry of Justice (No. 64-04 of 10 June 2004). This document establishes quality standards for 656 pollutants.

Table 7.1 presents ambient air quality standards for major pollutants associated with the transport sector.

Table 7.1. Ambient air quality standards (mg/m^3)

Pollutant	Maximum permissible concentration	Average daily concentration	Hazard class
Total suspended particulates (TSP)	0.15	0.05	3
Sulphur dioxide (SO_2)	0.5	0.05	3
Carbon monoxide (CO)	5	3	4
Nitrogen dioxide (NO_2)	0.085	0.04	2
Nitric oxide (NO)	0.4	0.06	3
Tetraethyl lead	0.0001	0.00004	1

Source: (ADB, 2010[3]) *KGZ: CAREC Transport Corridor 1 (Bishkek–Torugart Road) Project 3*, www.adb.org/sites/default/files/project-document/62464/42399-02-kgz-eia-draft-01.pdf.

7.5. International agreements on climate change

Kyrgyzstan's intended nationally determined contribution (INDC) sets out the country's expected contributions to climate change mitigation (GoK, 2015[4]):

- Long-term GHG emissions target: limit per capita GHG emissions to a maximum of 1.23 tCO_2, or 1.58 tCO_2 in 2050, to achieve the below 1.5°C or 2°C objective, with a probability of 66% and 50% respectively
- By 2030 Kyrgyzstan will reduce GHG emissions by between 11.49 and 13.75% below business as usual (BAU) levels.[8] With international support, Kyrgyzstan could implement additional mitigation measures to achieve reductions of between 29.00 and 30.89% below BAU in 2030.
- By 2050 Kyrgyzstan will also reduce GHG emissions by between 12.67 and 15.69% below BAU. With international support it could implement additional mitigation measures to achieve reductions of between 35.06 and 36.75% below BAU in 2050.
- The time frame is 1 January 2020 – 31 December 2030, and 2050.
- Base year: not used to determine the targets as they are indicated in per capita GHG emissions, but 2010 is taken for emissions modelling.

Nationally appropriate mitigation actions (NAMAs) refer to a set of policies and actions that countries undertake as part of their commitment to reduce greenhouse gas emissions. These can be various policies aimed at transformational changes within a single sector or across two or more sectors of the economy. Developed countries can support the implementation of NAMAs in developing countries by financing technologies or capacity-building activities.

The UNFCCC website provides a NAMA Register, a publicly accessible platform where all countries can place their NAMAs. This makes it possible to inform the public of the need for financial or other support for the development or implementation of NAMAs.

The UNFCCC Register contains one NAMA project for the Kyrgyz Republic – the "Modernisation of heat supply of residential and public buildings". Its objective is to support the reorganisation of the local heating sector as part of the institutional reform agenda in Kyrgyzstan. Today, the local heating sector consists of a huge number of small, inefficient boiler houses and a poor distribution system. The project is intended to contribute to institutional reform and the establishment of low-carbon development goals. The project is still under development.[9]

7.6. Conclusions for the CPT Programme

This analysis of the regulatory and legal basis in the fields of transport and environmental protection and management shows that some work in the right direction has been completed. However, operating and inspection procedures inefficiently used in practice, are sometimes inconsistent and do not significantly involve local governments or representatives of the population.

Kyrgyzstan therefore requires several legislative and policy improvements. In particular, it needs to adopt international environmental quality standards, procedures and norms, including international methods of measuring and calculating environmental pollution, passing more stringent emissions and fuel standards, and ensuring their enforcement.

Beyond these normative acts – and also beyond the scope of this chapter/report – are the skill levels of the personnel involved in the transport sector, who are also an important component of traffic safety. The material and technical resources of driving schools and their training programmes do not meet modern requirements for training qualified specialists in public transport.

Notes

1. See IPPA's investor's guide on investment climate at: https://invest.gov.kg/investors-guide/investment-climate.

2. According to Article 4 of Law No. 66 of 27 March 2003 "On investments in the Kyrgyz Republic", foreign investors are subject to the same legal regime as national entities.

3. Law No. 66 of 27 March 2003 "on investments in the Kyrgyz Republic".

4. This means that VAT on inputs can be reclaimed. In contrast, for tax exempt goods, VAT cannot be recovered.

5. Personal communication.

6. See IPPA's investor's guide on customs regulations at: https://invest.gov.kg/investors-guide/customs-regulations.

7. "Hygienic standards of GN 2.1.6.1338-03: The threshold limit values (TLVs) of pollutants in atmospheric air of inhabited places."

8. In the absence of any mitigation activities.

9. See NAMA database: www.nama-database.org/index.php/Kyrgyzstan.

Bibliography

ADB (2010), *KGZ: CAREC Transport Corridor 1 (Bishkek–Torugart Road) Project 3*, Environmental Assessment Report – Draft Environmental Impact Assessment, November 2010, http://www.adb.org/sites/default/files/project-document/62464/42399-02-kgz-eia-draft-01.pdf. [5]

GoK (2015), *Intended Nationally Determined Contribution – Submission of the Kyrgyz Republic*, Government of Kyrgyzstan, Bishkek, https://www4.unfccc.int/sites/submissions/INDC/Published%20Documents/Kyrgyzstan/1/Kyrgyzstan%20INDC%20_ENG_%20final.pdf. [6]

GoK (1999), *Traffic Regulations of the Kyrgyz Republic*, Government of Kyrgyzstan, Bishkek, https://kg.usembassy.gov/wp-content/uploads/sites/190/2016/08/traffic_regulations.pdf. [1]

Mokrenko, A. (2017), "Air pollution in Bishkek exceeds maximum permissible concentration 2-3 times", *News Agency 24.kg*, 28 December, https://24.kg/english/72240_Air_pollution_in_Bishkek_exceeds_maximum_permissible_concentration_2-3_times. [4]

UNDP (2014), *Renewable Energy Snapshot: Kyrgyzstan*, United Nations Development Programme, New York, http://www.eurasia.undp.org/content/dam/rbec/docs/Kyrgyzstan.pdf. [3]

WHO (2018), "Road safety: Kyrgyzstan sees decrease in deaths", *WHO News*, 23 January, World Health Organization, Washington, D.C., http://www.euro.who.int/en/countries/kyrgyzstan/news/news/2018/01/road-safety-kyrgyzstan-sees-decrease-in-deaths. [2]

Laws and regulations

(listed by most recent publishing date, in Russian)

Law No. 24 of 19 February 2018 "On introducing amendments to the Code of the Kyrgyz Republic on administrative responsibility", http://cbd.minjust.gov.kg/act/view/ru-ru/111757.

Law No. 121 of 18 July 2016 "On railway transport", http://cbd.minjust.gov.kg/act/view/ru-ru/111398 (unofficial translation available at: https://cis-legislation.com/document.fwx?rgn=87257).

Air Code of the Kyrgyz Republic No. 281 of 6 August 2015 http://cbd.minjust.gov.kg/act/view/ru-ru/111262 (unofficial translation available at: https://cis-legislation.com/document.fwx?rgn=79187).

Law No. 209 of 31 July 2015 "On mandatory insurance of premises from the fire and natural disasters", http://cbd.minjust.gov.kg/act/view/ru-ru/111253 (unofficial translation available at: https://cis-legislation.com/document.fwx?rgn=78371).

Law No. 192 of 24 July 2015 "On obligatory insurance of civil liability of vehicle owners", *Erkin Too* newspaper No. 72-73 of 7 August 2015, http://cbd.minjust.gov.kg/act/view/ru-ru/111236 (unofficial translation available at: https://cis-legislation.com/document.fwx?rgn=78374).

Law No. 184 of 31 December 2014 "On customs regulation in the Kyrgyz Republic", *Official Journal of Laws of the KR* No. 99 of 6 June 2017, http://cbd.minjust.gov.kg/act/view/ru-ru/205436 (unofficial translation available at: http://cis-legislation.com/document.fwx?rgn=79264).

Law No. 195 of 19 October 2013 "On license authorisation system in the Kyrgyz Republic", *Erkin Too* newspaper No. 87 of 29 October 2013, http://cbd.minjust.gov.kg/act/view/ru-ru/205058 (unofficial translation available at: http://cis-legislation.com/document.fwx?rgn=63232).

Government Resolution No. 295 of 15 May 2012 "On draft laws of the Kyrgyz Republic "On introducing amendments and additions to the Law of the Kyrgyz Republic "On energy"", "On introducing amendments and addenda to the Law of the Kyrgyz Republic "On electric power industry"", and "On introducing changes to the Law of the Kyrgyz Republic "On energy saving"", http://cbd.minjust.gov.kg/act/view/ru-ru/93583?cl=ru-ru.

Law No. 7 of 22 February 2012 "On public-private partnership in the Kyrgyz Republic", *Erkin Too* newspaper No. 17 of 28 February 2012, http://cbd.minjust.gov.kg/act/view/ru-ru/203607 (unofficial translation available at: http://cis-legislation.com/document.fwx?rgn=50238).

Law No. 224 of 29 November 2011 "On Technical regulations "On radiation safety"", *Erkin Too* newspaper No. 104 of 6 December 2011, http://cbd.minjust.gov.kg/act/view/ru-ru/203468 (unofficial translation available at: https://cis-legislation.com/document.fwx?rgn=48390).

Law No. 18 of 3 May 2011 "On specially protected natural territories", *Erkin Too* newspaper No. 35 of 11 May 2011, http://cbd.minjust.gov.kg/act/view/ru-ru/203262 (unofficial translation available at: https://cis-legislation.com/document.fwx?rgn=43145).

Law No. 116 of 22 July 2011 "On competition", *Erkin Too* newspaper No. 60 of 26 July 2011, http://cbd.minjust.gov.kg/act/view/ru-ru/203356 (English version available at: https://wipolex.wipo.int/en/text/343354).

Law No. 101 of 15 July 2011 "On local self-government", *Erkin Too* newspaper No. 59 of 22 July 2011, http://cbd.minjust.gov.kg/act/view/ru-ru/203102 (unofficial translation available at: http://cis-legislation.com/document.fwx?rgn=45734).

Law No. 151 of 8 May 2009 "General technical regulation on ensuring environmental safety in the Kyrgyz Republic", http://cbd.minjust.gov.kg/act/view/ru-ru/202693 (unofficial translation available at: https://cis-legislation.com/document.fwx?rgn=27858).

Law No. 31 of 26 January 2009 "On features of insurance in crop production", *Erkin Too* newspaper No. 9 of 6 February 2009, http://cbd.minjust.gov.kg/act/view/ru-ru/202550/10?cl=ru-ru (unofficial translation available at: https://cis-legislation.com/document.fwx?rgn=26304).

Law No. 283 of 31 December 2008 "On renewable energy sources", *Erkin Too* newspaper No. 4 of 29 January 2009, http://cbd.minjust.gov.kg/act/view/ru-ru/203243 (unofficial translation available at: http://cis-legislation.com/document.fwx?rgn=28654).

Tax Code of the Kyrgyz Republic No. 230 of 17 October 2008, *Official Journal of Laws of the KR* No. 5 of 10 January 2009, http://cbd.minjust.gov.kg/act/view/ru-ru/202445 (unofficial translation available at: http://cis-legislation.com/document.fwx?rgn=24860).

Law No. 202 of 15 August 2008 "On obligatory civil liability insurance of organisations operating hazardous production facilities", *Erkin Too* newspaper No. 62 of 19 August 2008, http://cbd.minjust.gov.kg/act/view/ru-ru/202416 (unofficial translation available at: https://cis-legislation.com/document.fwx?rgn=24057).

Law No. 194 of 5 August 2008 "On obligatory civil insurance of employer's liability for causing harm to life and health of an employee in performing their (official) labor duties", *Erkin Too* newspaper No. 59-60 of 12 August 2008, http://cbd.minjust.gov.kg/act/view/ru-ru/202408/10?cl=ru-r (unofficial translation available at: https://cis-legislation.com/document.fwx?rgn=23956).

Law No. 189 of 4 August 2008 "On obligatory civil liability insurance of carrier to passengers", *Erkin Too* newspaper No. 59-60 of 12 August 2008, http://cbd.minjust.gov.kg/act/view/ru-ru/202403 (unofficial translation available at: https://cis-legislation.com/document.fwx?rgn=23961).

Law No. 188 of 4 August 2008 " On obligatory civil liability insurance of of carrier of dangerous goods", http://cbd.minjust.gov.kg/act/view/ru-ru/202402/10?cl=ru-ru (unofficial translation available at: https://cis-legislation.com/document.fwx?rgn=24059).

Resolution of the Chief State Health Officer of the Kyrgyz Republic No. 20 of 28 May 2004 "On approval of sanitary and hygienic regulations", http://cbd.minjust.gov.kg/act/view/ru-ru/31344.

Law No. 67 of 22 May 2004 "On bases of technical regulation in the Kyrgyz Republic", *Sheets of Jogorku Kenesh of the KR*, 2004, No. 9 (1151), Art. 407, http://cbd.minjust.gov.kg/act/view/ru-ru/1453 (unofficial translation available at: https://cis-legislation.com/document.fwx?rgn=6744).

Law No. 215 of 25 September 2003 "On financial and economic bases of local government", *Erkin Too* newspaper No. 74 of 3 October 2003, http://cbd.minjust.gov.kg/act/view/ru-ru/1341/20?cl=ky-kg.

Law No. 66 of 27 March 2003 "On investments in the Kyrgyz Republic", *Journal of Laws of the KR* No. 76 of 14 June 2004, http://cbd.minjust.gov.kg/act/view/ru-ru/1190 (unofficial translation available at: http://cis-legislation.com/document.fwx?rgn=3560).

Law No. 37 of 15 March 2002 "On municipal property ownership", *Erkin Too* newspaper No. 23 of 27 March 2002, http://cbd.minjust.gov.kg/act/view/ru-ru/992. (unofficial translation available at: https://cis-legislation.com/document.fwx?rgn=226).

Government Order No. 260 of 31 May 2001 "On licensing of separate types of activities", http://cbd.minjust.gov.kg/act/view/ru-ru/6848 (unofficial translation available at: https://cis-legislation.com/document.fwx?rgn=496).

Government Resolution No. 421 of 4 August 1999 "On approval of the traffic regulations and basic provisions for the admission of vehicles to the operation and the duties of officials to ensure road safety", http://cbd.minjust.gov.kg/act/view/ru-ru/33663 (unofficial translation available at: http://cis-legislation.com/document.fwx?rgn=28000).

Law No. 53 of 16 June 1999 "On environmental protection", *Erkin Too* newspaper No. 54-55 of 7 July 1999, http://cbd.minjust.gov.kg/act/view/ru-ru/218. (unofficial translation available at: https://cis-legislation.com/document.fwx?rgn=293).

Law No. 54 of 16 June 1999 "On environmental impact assessment", http://cbd.minjust.gov.kg/act/view/ru-ru/219 (unofficial translation available at: https://cis-legislation.com/document.fwx?rgn=299).

Law No. 51 of 12 June 1999 "On protection of atmospheric air", *Erkin Too* newspaper No. 51 of 25 June 1999, http://cbd.minjust.gov.kg/act/view/ru-ru/216 (unofficial translation available at: http://cis-legislation.com/document.fwx?rgn=290).

Law No. 48 of 9 June 1999 "On biosphere territories in the Kyrgyz Republic", *Erkin Too* newspaper No. 51 of 25 June 1999, http://cbd.minjust.gov.kg/act/view/ru-ru/213. (unofficial translation available at: https://cis-legislation.com/document.fwx?rgn=70).

Land Code of the Kyrgyz Republic No. 45 of 2 June 1999, http://cbd.minjust.gov.kg/act/view/ru-ru/8 (unofficial translation available at: http://cis-legislation.com/document.fwx?rgn=301).

Law No. 96 of 23 July 1998 "On the organisation of insurance in the Kyrgyz Republic", *Erkin Too* newspaper No. 103-104 of 5 August 1998. http://cbd.minjust.gov.kg/act/view/ru-ru/105 (unofficial translation available at: https://cis-legislation.com/document.fwx?rgn=256).

Law No. 89 of 8 July 1998 "On transport", *Erkin Too* newspaper No. 93-94 of 17 July 1997, http://cbd.minjust.gov.kg/act/view/ky-kg/97/30?cl=ky-kg (unofficial translation available at: https://cis-legislation.com/document.fwx?rgn=400).

Law No. 88 of 7 July 1998 "On energy saving", *Erkin Too* newspaper No. 97-98 of 24 July 1998, http://cbd.minjust.gov.kg/act/view/ru-ru/96/10?cl=ru-ru (unofficial translation available at: http://cis-legislation.com/document.fwx?rgn=418).

Law No. 78 of 11 June 1998 "On the basic principles of budgetary law in the Kyrgyz Republic", *Erkin Too* newspaper No. 79-80 of 24 June 1998, http://cbd.minjust.gov.kg/act/view/ru-ru/86.

Law No. 77 of 8 June 1998 "On oil and gas", *Erkin Too* newspaper No. 77-78 of 19 June 1998, http://cbd.minjust.gov.kg/act/view/ru-ru/85/10?cl=ru-ru (unofficial translation available at: http://cis-legislation.com/document.fwx?rgn=361).

Law No. 8 of 28 January 1997 "On power industry", *Erkin Too* newspaper No. 8 of 12 February 1997, http://cbd.minjust.gov.kg/act/view/ru-ru/508/30?cl=ru- (unofficial translation available at: https://cis-legislation.com/document.fwx?rgn=411).

Law No. 56 of 30 October 1996 "On energy industry", *Regulations of the KR*, 1996, No. XI; http://cbd.minjust.gov.kg/act/view/ru-ru/663/10?cl=ky-kg (unofficial translation available at: https://cis-legislation.com/document.fwx?rgn=413).

Civil Code of the Kyrgyz Republic No. 15 of 8 May 1996, *Sheets of Jogorku Kenesh of the KR*, 1996, No. 6, Art. 80, http://cbd.minjust.gov.kg/act/view/ru-ru/4 (unofficial translation available at: https://cis-legislation.com/document.fwx?rgn=51).

Annex A. Overview of clean technologies and fuels in the transport sector

This overview looks at buses that run on four major types of cleaner fossil fuels or other sources of power. These include compressed natural gas (CNG)/liquefied natural gas (LNG), liquefied petroleum gas (LPG), diesel with Euro VI engines and electricity.

For each fuel type we discuss the following:

- the main features of the fuel
- comparative advantages of the technology
- comparative drawbacks of the technology
- worldwide market penetration of the technology.

Table A.3 summarises the main points for each type of fuel.

Compressed natural gas vehicles

Description

Compressed natural gas (CNG) is a natural gas under pressure that remains clear, odourless and non-corrosive. Although vehicles can use natural gas as either a liquid or a gas, most vehicles use the gaseous form, compressed to about 218 kg/cm^2. CNG can be used as an alternative to conventional petrol and diesel fuels. Methane (CH_4) – which is the main component of CNG – is found above oil deposits or may be collected from landfills or wastewater treatment plants, where it is known as biogas.

It is stored and distributed in hard containers at a pressure of 20-25 MPa (Megapascals), usually in cylindrical or spherical shapes. Most natural gas comes from three types of wells: natural gas-and-condensate wells, oil wells and coal bed methane wells. Well-extracted natural gas requires treatment before it can be used in vehicles.

CNG is used in traditional petrol (internal-combustion-engine) automobiles that have been modified or in vehicles especially manufactured for CNG use, either with a dedicated system separate from the petrol system to extend range (dual-fuel), or in conjunction with another fuel, such as diesel (bio-fuel). CNG vehicles have been introduced in a variety of commercial applications, from light-duty trucks and sedans, like taxicabs; to medium-duty trucks, like UPS (United Parcel Service) delivery vans and postal vehicles; and heavy-duty vehicles such as transit buses, street sweepers and school buses.

CNG's volumetric energy density is estimated to be 42% of that of LNG (because it is not liquefied; see Box A.1) and 25% that of diesel fuel.

Box A.1. A comparison of CNG and LNG

CNG and LNG are often confused. However, while both are stored forms of natural gas, the key difference is that CNG is stored as a gas at high pressure, while LNG is stored at a very low temperature, becoming liquid in the process. CNG is cheaper to produce and store than LNG, as it does not require an expensive cooling process or cryogenic tanks. CNG requires the use of very high pressures and a much larger volume of storage for the same mass of petrol. Therefore, natural gas is often transported over large distances in the form of LNG – in ships, trains or pipelines – and then converted into CNG before distribution to the end user.

Advantages

CNG combustion produces fewer undesirable gases than other fuels and is safer in the event of a spill, because natural gas is lighter than air and disperses quickly when released. In 2014, a comparison of Euro VI heavy-duty vehicles on CNG and diesel, conducted by the Danish Technological Institute,[1] showed that CNG had a higher consumption of fuel but that NO_x emissions were lower. The levels of noise, CO_2 (contrary to other findings, see below) and particulate pollution were the same, however.

Natural gas is produced worldwide at a relatively low cost and is cleaner burning than petrol or diesel fuel. Natural gas vehicles emit on average 80% fewer ozone-forming emissions – i.e. carbon dioxide (CO_2) and nitrogen oxide (NO_x) – than petrol-powered vehicles. In addition:

- CNG does not contain any lead, thereby eliminating fouling of spark plugs
- CNG-powered vehicles have lower maintenance costs than other hydrocarbon-fuel-powered vehicles
- CNG fuel systems are sealed, preventing fuel losses from spills or evaporation
- CNG-powered vehicles are considered to be safer than petrol-powered vehicles
- CNG-powered vehicles produce less pollution and are more efficient.

CNG emits significantly fewer direct carbon emissions than petrol or oil when combusted. An engine running on petrol emits 22 kilograms of CO_2 per 100 kilometres, whereas a CNG-powered engine emits 16.3 kilograms of CO_2 per 100 kilometres. Therefore, switching to CNG can help mitigate greenhouse gas (GHG) emissions. However, natural gas leaks increase GHG emissions. The ability of CNG to reduce GHG emissions over the entire fuel lifecycle will depend on the source of the natural gas and the fuel it replaces.

Natural gas emits 30% less CO_2 per British thermal unit (BTU) than oil, 90% fewer particulates than conventional fuels, and fewer pollutants such as sulphur dioxide (SO_2) and nitrogen oxides (NO_x).

Drawbacks

The cost of fuel storage tanks is a major barrier to more widespread and rapid adoption of CNG as a fuel. Municipal governments are the most visible adopters of CNG technology in public transport vehicles, as they can more quickly amortise the money invested in the new (and usually cheaper) fuel. In other parts of the world, as the industry has expanded, the cost of fuel storage tanks has fallen.

CNG-powered vehicles require bigger fuel tanks than conventional petrol-powered vehicles. Since it is a compressed gas rather than a liquid like petrol, CNG takes up more space for each GGE (gasoline gallon equivalent).[2] Usually, CNG tanks take up space in the trunk of cars or bed of pickup trucks modified to run additionally on CNG. This problem is solved in CNG vehicles that have factory-built tanks under the body of the vehicle, leaving the trunk free. Another option is roof installation (typically for buses), which requires attention to structural strength. Besides taking up space, tanks also add to the vehicle weight (especially when full). Rapid refuelling technology also requires expensive infrastructure investment and may lead to gas leaks.

Further, where an insufficient number of alternative fuel vehicles are in use investors may be reluctant to invest in infrastructure, while the manufacturing industry will not offer alternative fuel vehicles at competitive prices when demand is low because consumers are reluctant to buy them given the lack of an alternative fuel infrastructure.

Market penetration worldwide

CNG-powered vehicles are increasingly used in Iran, Pakistan and the Asian-Pacific region. India and China have witnessed rapid growth in recent years, and India, in particular, is forecast to become the world's largest natural gas vehicle market (EC, 2016[1]), with their use especially common in New Delhi, and other large cities like Ahmedabad, Mumbai, Kolkata, Lucknow and Kanpur.

Their use is also increasing in South America, Europe and North America given rising petrol prices.

About 1.2 million vehicles run on CNG in Europe, but these represent only 0.7% of the European Union (EU)-28 and Switzerland's vehicle fleet. Italy alone accounts for 75% of the market. More than 3 000 refuelling points are available, two-thirds of them in Germany and Italy. In total, 18 million CNG vehicles are in operation worldwide, representing 1.2% of the world's vehicle fleet (EC, 2016[2]).

While the number of vehicles using CNG worldwide continues to grow steadily, alternative fuel vehicles in general only represented 3.4% of the European car fleet in 2012, and the use of alternative fuels in heavy-duty vehicles and maritime and aviation modes is negligible (EC, 2016[2]).

By 2025, LNG use in heavy-duty transport is expected to grow to 12 000 vehicles, mainly in Poland and Hungary. This is according to national plans submitted to the European Commission, which also foresee in total 431 refuelling stations and other infrastructure development in the EU – as a part of the Trans-European Transport Network (TEN-T) – to a total value of up to EUR 257 million by 2025 (T&E, 2018[3]).[3]

Liquified petroleum gas vehicles

Description

Also known as propane-butane mixture, liquified petroleum gas (LPG) is a flammable mixture of hydrocarbon gases used as fuel in heating appliances, cooking equipment and vehicles. LPG is prepared by refining petroleum (crude oil) or "wet" natural gas extracted from petroleum or natural gas streams as they emerge from the ground. It currently provides about 3% of all energy consumed worldwide, and burns relatively cleanly, without soot and very few sulphur emissions. As a gas, it does not pose ground or water pollution hazards, but it can contribute to air pollution. Further, its energy density per unit of volume is lower than either that of petrol or fuel oil, as its relative density is lower.

In some countries, LPG has been used since the 1940s as an alternative to petrol for spark ignition engines. In some cases, additives in the liquid extend engine life, and the ratio of butane to propane is kept quite precise in fuel LPG. Two recent studies have examined LPG and fuel oil mixes and found that smoke emissions and fuel consumption are reduced but hydrocarbon emissions are increased. The studies were split on carbon monoxide (CO) emissions, with one finding significant increases, and the other finding slight increases at low engine load but a considerable decrease at high engine load.

LPG has a lower energy density than either petrol or fuel oil, so the equivalent fuel consumption is about 10% higher. Many governments impose lower taxes on LPG than on petrol or fuel oil, which helps offset the greater consumption of LPG. LPG is the third most widely used motor fuel in the world after diesel and petrol. Estimates from 2013 show that over 24.9 million vehicles are fuelled by LPG worldwide. Over 25 million tonnes are used annually as a vehicle fuel.

Advantages

LPG is non-toxic, non-corrosive and free of tetraethyl lead or any additives, and has a high octane rating. It burns more cleanly than petrol or fuel oil and is especially free of the particulates present in the latter.

Commercially available LPG is currently derived mainly from fossil fuels. Burning LPG releases CO_2. The reaction also produces some CO. LPG does, however, release less CO_2 per unit of energy than coal or oil. It emits 81% of the CO_2 per kilowatt hour (kWh) produced by oil, 70% of that of coal, and less than 50% of that emitted by coal-generated electricity distributed via the grid.

Other advantages of LPG include the following:

- LPG burns more cleanly than higher molecular weight hydrocarbons, because it releases fewer particulates.
- The inherent advantage of LPG over CNG is that it requires far less compression (20% of CNG cost), is denser (because it is a liquid at room temperature) and thus requires far cheaper tanks (consumer) and fuel compressors (providers) than CNG.
- Its advantages over petrol and diesel include cleaner emissions and less wear on engines than petrol.

Drawbacks

LPG main disadvantages may be summarised as follows:

- Safety: LPG is heavier than air, which causes it to collect in a low spot in the event of a leak, making it much more hazardous to use than CNG; more care is needed in handling.
- Environment: LPG is not as efficient or environmentally friendly as CNG and electric options for alternative fuels for buses.
- Technology: LPG provides less upper cylinder lubrication than petrol or diesel, so LPG-fuelled engines are more prone to valve wear if they are not appropriately modified.

Market penetration worldwide

LPG is currently the most adopted alternative fuel in road transport in terms of number of vehicles. The LPG market is dominated, in terms of vehicles, by five countries, which together account for almost half of global consumption: Turkey (4 million vehicles), the Russian Federation (3 mln), Poland (2.8 mln), Korea (2.4 mln) and Italy (2 mln) (EC, 2016[1]).

However, LPG is losing momentum in the European Union, United States and Japan, because compared to electric mobility and even CNG, its environmental benefits over conventional fuels are limited. However, LPG is still promising in developing markets in China, India and the Russian Federation.

Diesel vehicles with Euro VI engines

Description

Petrol and diesel remain the most common fuels for all vehicles.

Biodiesel – which is increasingly being used in diesel engines – is brought to the market mainly via blending with conventional diesel. The largest market is the European Union (EU), followed by the United States and Brazil. Biodiesel does not, however, reduce NO_x emissions from vehicles, which is an increasing focus of attention for cities.

US regulations attempting to reduce the impact of these fossil fuels on the environment have mandated the supply of ultra-low sulphur diesel and the use of ethanol (also known as E85) in petrol.

Table A.1 and Table A.2 contain a summary of the EU emission standards that apply to diesel buses. They show two different types of testing requirements: 1) steady state testing (Table A.1), which lists emission standards applicable to diesel (compression ignition – CI) engines only, with steady-state emission testing requirements; and 2) transient testing (Table A.2), which lists standards applicable to both diesel and gas (positive ignition – PI) engines with transient testing requirements.

Table A.1. EU emission standards for heavy-duty diesel engines (steady-state testing)

Tier	Date	Test cycle	CO	HC	NO_x	PM	PN	Smoke
					g/kWh		1/kWh	1/m
Euro I	1992 < 85 kW	Economic Commission for Europe of the United Nations (ECE/UN) Regulation-49	4.5	1.1	8.0	0.612		
	1992 > 85 kW		4.5	1.1	8.0	0.36		
Euro II	October 1996		4.0	1.1	7.0	0.25		
	October 1998		4.0	1.1	7.0	0.15		
Euro III	*October 1999 Enhanced environmentally friendly vehicles (EEVs) only*[b]	European Stationary Cycle (ESC) and European Load Response (ELR)	*1.5*	*0.25*	*2.0*	*0.02*		*0.15*
	October 2000		2.1	0.66	5.0	0.10 - 0.13[a]		0.8
Euro IV	October 2005		1.5	0.46	3.5	0.02		0.5
Euro V	October 2008		1.5	0.46	2.0	0.02		0.5
Euro VI	31 December 2013	World Harmonized Stationary Cycle (WHSC)	1.5	0.13	0.4	0.01	$8.0x10^{11}$	

Note: [a]PM = 0.13 g/kWh for engines < 0.75 dm3 swept volume per cylinder and a rated power speed > 3 000 min-1; [b] EEV is a European emissions standard for buses and trucks (> 3.5t in the category M_2 and M_3). Vehicles equipped with EEV engines exceed the emission quality of the Euro 5 standard applicable to all new vehicle types from 1 September 2009 on trucks and buses.
Source: (DieselNet, 2016[4]), "EU: Heavy-Duty Truck and Bus Engines: Regulatory Framework and Emission Standards", www.dieselnet.com/standards/eu/hd.php (accessed 30 March 2017).

Table A.2. EU emission standards for heavy-duty diesel engines (transient testing)

Tier	Date	Test cycle	CO	MNHC	CH_4[a]	NO_x	PM[b]	PN[c]
					g/kWh			1/kWh
Euro III	October 1999 Enhanced environmentally friendly vehicles (EEVs) only	European Transient Cycle (ETC)	3.0	0.40	0.65	2.0	0.02	
	October 2000		5.45	0.78	1.6	5.0	0.16[d]	
Euro IV	October 2005		4.0	0.55	1.1	3.5	0.03	
Euro V	October 2008		4.0	0.55	1.1	2.0	0.03	
Euro VI	31 December 2013	World Harmonized Transient Cycle (WHTC)	4.0	0.16[e]	0.5	0.46	0.01	$6.0x10^{11}$

Notes: a – for gas engines only (Euro III-V: NG only; Euro VI: NG + LPG).
b – not applicable to gas-fuelled engines at the Euro III-IV stages.
c – for diesel engines; particle number (PN) limit for positive ignition engines to be defined.
d – PM=0.21 g/kWh for engines < 0.75 dm^3 swept volume per cylinder and a rated power speed > 3 000 min^{-1}.
e – total hydrocarbon content (THC) for diesel engines.
Source: (DieselNet, 2016[4]), "EU: Heavy-Duty Truck and Bus Engines: Regulatory Framework and Emission Standards", www.dieselnet.com/standards/eu/hd.php (accessed 30 March 2017).

Advantages

The main advantages of shifting to diesel buses with Euro VI engines include:

- The purchase price of modern diesel-fuelled engines is typically lower than moving to cleaner technologies (such as LPG or CNG).
- The need for additional investments in the vehicle itself or in supporting infrastructure is not as great as for LPG and CNG, which often require vehicle modifications or supporting infrastructure (such as specialised filling stations or maintenance centres).
- A standard diesel city bus delivers lower carbon emissions per passenger than a standard car and CO_2 emissions can be achieved by encouraging more passengers to shift to public transport.

Drawbacks

The main drawbacks of introducing diesel buses with Euro VI engines are:

- The shift from Euro V to Euro VI for heavy-duty vehicles will require considerable investments by manufacturers and public transport operators undertakings and huge outlays from bus manufacturers.
- They cause significant harm to the environment, in the form of particulate matter (PM) from engine exhaust.

Market penetration worldwide

Diesel engines are globally one of the most common choices for combustion engines for buses and other commercial vehicles. For the time being, diesel and biodiesel buses constitute by far the greatest part of the bus fleet (90% of the bus fleets in Europe, according to the results of the 3iBS survey, which surveyed 70 000 buses operated in 63 European cities and regions) (UITP, 2015[5]).

Electricity-powered public transport

Description

The electrification of road transport is expanding in Europe driven by the need for clean public transport, which is encouraging manufacturers to develop new models.

Trams are one of the oldest means of public transport and their popularity has come and gone depending on the country. But recently many cities seeking sustainable urban development are reintroducing tramways into the urban space.

Trolleybuses have followed a similar evolution, and are also experiencing an upsurge in popularity. Their main advantage over trams is that they require no battery or special rail infrastructure (overhead wires are less expensive to construct than rails), and they are also quieter. On the other hand, trolleybuses can be hybridised to run "autonomously" using an on-board battery.

In this context and as the result of technological changes and improvements in vehicle efficiency, all-electric buses are a new strategic means for achieving greenhouse gas mitigation targets (and need even less infrastructure than trams or trolleybuses). The technology is still not as mature as diesel buses, but it is on the way to market maturity. This is confirmed by the increasing number of pilots and plans (Vienna, Berlin, Paris, London, Stockholm, China) that are emerging.

There are several sizes of electric buses to be found on the market, depending on demand and needs. While electric mini and mid-size buses already exist, larger (>10m) buses are still being developed.

With this technology, in addition to transport capacity, it is important to consider vehicle autonomy and charging technologies (i.e. charging at the bus depots or on-board along the bus route).

"Traditional" cable charging takes place at night, after the daily service is complete. It is usually done on normal recharge, so as not to disturb the electricity network. A further possibility is to integrate a fast-charging solution at the end of the line, in order to guarantee continuous operation of the service. This technology has been adopted in Vienna (Austria) – the batteries charge in 10 to 15 minutes and last for 120 to 150 kilometres.

On-board "flash charging" technology allows buses to connect to the charging point on an overhead high-power charging contact when they pull into selected stops, topping up the batteries while passengers get on and off. This very fast charging mode is already used in Geneva (Switzerland) and at the airport of Nice (France).[4]

A similar technology is the pantograph, already used by trains and tramways. For buses, this charging mode can be used at bus stops, at end stops or in depots. A bottom-up pantograph is mounted on the bus roof. The charging procedure starts as the pantograph is raised and comes into contact with the mast pantograph, centred above vehicles' front axle reference position. Several cities – e.g. Gothenburg (Sweden), Namur (Belgium) and Vienna (Austria) – have started adopting this technology.

Induction may become the technology of the future for charging vehicles. When the bus stops at a station equipped with a recharge system buried underground, the on-board charging coil lowers and power transmission can begin. Charging only lasts for the time the passengers get disembark and embark and can restart again at the next station, offering unlimited autonomy. Berlin is the first capital city to adopt this wirelessly charged e-bus line.

Advantages

Electric vehicles offer several advantages over conventional internal combustion engine vehicles:

- Less dependence on oil.
- Lower greenhouse gas emissions and air pollutants when using electricity from "low-carbon" sources of power (Box A.2).
- They are more efficient and better at converting energy from batteries into moving the vehicle than the conventional internal combustion engine. They also recover energy while braking, thus reducing total energy consumption.

- Less noise pollution.
- Significant savings can be made over the lifetime of the vehicle because although investment is higher, the costs of fuel (electricity) and maintenance are lower than for an internal combustion vehicle.
- When the battery has lost some of its capacity it can be used for other purposes, such as for storing renewable electricity that can help regulate the power grid and the development of renewable energy.

Box A.2. How clean is electricity production?

Electricity is an energy carrier that can be converted domestically from a wide variety of primary energy sources. When electricity is produced from renewable energy sources, this can offer a nearly zero-emission well-to-wheel pathway, although this is not always the case (e.g. when a combination of renewable and non-renewable sources is used). Electricity will continue to become increasingly low-carbon as the power sector continues to reduce carbon intensity.

Drawbacks

- The development of electric vehicles depends mostly on the price of the vehicles and their battery (which can be expensive) as well as on the battery performance and energy autonomy.
- Electric buses are more expensive than diesel-powered vehicles, however, over their lifespan the total costs of electric buses are lower.
- Investment in new infrastructure in addition to the bus and battery is needed. The cost varies according to the system chosen and the number of charging points.
- The power grid must be made compatible with the energy requirements of a fleet of vehicles at economically acceptable costs.
- Electric buses can have a negative impact on the environment depending on the battery technologies, resource extraction and cell production processes, as well as the type of electricity production, and how they are disposed of at the end of their lives (e.g. recycling).

Market penetration worldwide

The number of electric buses increased tenfold between 2014 and 2016, reaching a global stock of about 345 000 vehicles in 2016. China leads in the use of electric buses, with more than 343 000 units in operation, followed by Europe with only 1 273 vehicles.

Nevertheless, only 3% of the worldwide bus fleet is currently electric. The increase in the stock does suggest that the market is moving beyond the demonstration phase into commercial development, however.

Table A.3. Comparison of fuels for urban public transport

Parameter	CNG	LPG	Diesel EEV
Purchase cost (diesel = 100 baseline)	120	110	100 (higher than traditional diesel)
Fuel type	Natural gas		Diesel
Range (km)	300	500	750
Consumption per 100 kilometres	60-70 m^3	36 kg	40-50 l
Operating costs	+	+	++
Re-fuelling time	Long; 3-6 hours	Quick (minutes)	Quick (minutes)
Re-fuelling complications	Average (compression)	Very high (liquefaction, storage)	Low
Noise	Low	Low	Low
Pollution	Low emissions of particulates, SO_2, NO_x. Nearly zero contribution to smog	Low emissions of particulates, SO_2, NO_x, nearly zero contribution to smog	Lower emissions than traditional diesel. Higher emissions than CNG and LPG
Use	Small/medium buses	Large buses	All types
Other opportunities and advantages	Fuel can also be made from biomass or landfill gas.	Low temperatures in winter support LNG storage	
Other challenges and disadvantages	Heavy fuel tanks and buses with higher clearance required Dedicated refuelling stations required (for example, at bus depot) Dedicated workshops required Rapid refuelling requires expensive infrastructure investment and may lead to gas leaks	Limited storage time for LPG (buses have to be constantly used, and after five days without use require venting) Fuel is transported and stored at low temperature Requires complicated installations for cleaning and liquefaction at stations	New norms (such as Euro VII or Euro VIII) may impose stringent quality requirements

Notes

1. See Danish Technological Institute on emissions reduction: www.dti.dk/specialists/emission-reduction/37141 (accessed 20 March 2017).

2. GGE is the amount of alternative fuel it takes to equal the energy content of one liquid gallon (ca. 3.785 litres) of petrol. GGE allows consumers to compare the energy content of competing fuels against a commonly known fuel, petrol. GGE also compares petrol to fuels sold as a gas (natural gas, propane or hydrogen) and electricity.

3. According to Directive 2014/94/EU on the deployment of alternative fuels infrastructure, natural gas (CNG and LNG) and liquefied petroleum gas (LPG) are considered as alternative fuels in addition to electricity, hydrogen, biofuels (as defined by Art. 2 of Directive 2009/28/EU), and synthetic and paraffinic fuels (EU, 2014[16]).

4. See new generation of buses: http://new.abb.com/grid/technology/tosa; and autonomous electric buses in France: www.avere-france.org/Site/Article/?article_id=5730 (accessed 26 April 2017).

References

DieselNet (2016), "EU: Heavy-Duty Truck and Bus Engines: Regulatory Framework and Emission Standards", *DieselNet website*, http://www.dieselnet.com/standards/eu/hd.php (accessed on 30 March 2017). [4]

EC (2016), *Alternative Fuels and Infrastructure in Seven Non-EU Markets – Final Report*, European Commission, Brussels, http://ec.Europa.eu/transport/themes/urban/studies/doc/2016-01-21-alternative-fuels-and-infrastructure-in-seven-non-eu-markets.pdf. [1]

EC (2016), *Clean Transport – Support to the Member States for the Implementation of the Directive on the Deployment of Alternative Fuels Infrastructure: Good Practice Examples*, European Commission, Brussels, http://ec.Europa.eu/transport/themes/urban/studies/doc/201. [2]

EU (2014), "Directive 2014/94/EU of the European Parliament and of the Council of 22 October 2014 on the deployment of alternative fuels infrastructure", *Official Journal of the European Union* L 307/1 of 28 October 2014, pp. 1-20, http://data.europa.eu/eli/dir/2014. [16]

T&E (2018), *CNG and LNG for vehicles and ships – the facts*, European Federation for Transport and Environment, Brussels, http://www.transportenvironment.org/sites/te/files/publications/2018_10_TE_CNG_and_LNG_for_vehicles_and_ships_the_facts_EN.pdf. [3]

UITP (2015), *Bus Systems in Europe. Towards a Higher Quality of Urban Life and Reduction of Pollutants and CO2 Emissions*, UITP Position Paper, International Association of Public Transport, Brussels, https://www.uitp.org/sites/default/files/cck-focus-papers-files/UITP_PositionPaper_Bus%20Systems%202015.pdf.pdf. [5]

Annex B. Explanatory guide for using the OPTIC Model

Purpose of the OPTIC Model

The spreadsheet-based Optimising Public Transport Investment Costs (OPTIC) Model is is a simple, easy-to-use decision support tool prepared by the OECD to support the Government of Kyrgyzstan in preparing and estimating the costs and environmental benefits of the Clean Public Transport (CPT) Programme. It was used in particular for costing the replacement of the old bus fleet in urban centres with modern buses equipped with engines that run on:

- compressed natural gas (CNG)
- liquefied petroleum gas (LPG)
- diesel, ideally (imported) Euro 5 fuel
- electricity (trolleybuses and battery-powered trolleybuses).

The OPTIC Model was used to estimate programme costs, and the emission reductions of carbon dioxide (CO_2) and other pollutants from urban public transport – i.e. carbon monoxide (CO), nitrogen oxides (NO_x), particulate matter (PM) and sulphur dioxide (SO_2) – that could potentially be achieved by implementing the proposed project pipelines.

Similar models that exist on the market estimate the greenhouse gas (GHG) emission reductions for a country or for groups of countries. These models mainly focus on GHG emissions from industry and take into account various scenarios for the country's economic development. Such models, however, are not particularly suitable for this investment programme, which focuses on reducing emissions from urban public transport only.

Preparations for using the OPTIC Model

The OPTIC Model consists of seven modules: 1) assumptions; 2) emission factors; 3) transport sector overview with information on current bus fleet and age; 4) determining the subsidy level; 5) cost calculation; 6) emission reductions calculation; and 7) programme costing and environmental effects.

Assumptions

The model has been prepared in Excel and uses macros. Therefore, when starting the model, the macros in Excel should be enabled. This requires setting the security settings to "medium". For earlier versions of Excel (before 2010), security settings can be changed using the following commands: Tools>Macros>Security. For Excel 2010 and 2013, the macro security settings can be set in the "Developer" tab. If the Developer tab is not visible, it can be accessed by going to: File>Options>Customize Ribbon and then selecting "Developer" from the options in the right-hand window.

The user needs to fill in the cells that are highlighted yellow in the Excel sheets. Then these steps should be followed:

1) Complete the information on assumptions and emission factors. Assumptions can be found under the "Assumptions" tab. The following information is essential for the model:

- the average price of a new CNG bus
- the average price of a new LPG bus
- the average price of a new diesel bus equipped with a Euro VI engine
- the average price of a new trolleybus
- the average price of a new CNG minibus
- the average price of a new LPG minibus
- the average price of a new diesel minibus equipped with a Euro VI engine.

For the purpose of this model, the average bus is understood to be a 10-metre-long bus with a total capacity of about 100 passengers.

1) Input the average level of fuel consumption for each type of bus listed above. This information should also be provided for old diesel buses that will be replaced. For the purpose of the model, old diesel buses are divided into several categories: new and more than 5, 10 and 15 years old.

2) Input fuel costs for each type of bus. The information on average kilometres per vehicle per day (kpvpd)[1], which is found in the last column in Table B.1, is essential information to be entered.

Table B.1. Basic assumptions: bus prices and fuel consumption

Type of bus	*Unit price (KGS mln)*	*Fuel consumption*		*Fuel price*		*kpvpd*	*Fuel costs (KGS/vehicle/day)*
New CNG bus	10	38.5 (53.7 m^3/100 km)	kg/100 km	31.7	KGS/kg	200	2 438
New LPG bus	9.09	35.7 (70 kg/100 km)	l/100 km	39.0	KGS/l	200	2 787
New diesel Euro VI bus	8.7	50.0	l/100 km	48.0	KGS/l	200	4 800
New diesel standard bus	2.08	45.0	l/100 km	44.4	KGS/l	200	3 995
Old diesel bus (> 15 years)	n.a.*	56.3	l/100 km	44.4	KGS/l	200	4 994
Old diesel bus (> 10 years)	n.a.*	51.8	l/100 km	44.4	KGS/l	200	4 594
Old diesel bus (> 5 years)	n.a.*	49.5	l/100 km	44.4	KGS/l	200	4 395
Trolleybus	10.5**	100	kWh/100 km	0.03	KGS/kWh	200	5
New CNG minibus	2.30	9.6	kg/100 km	31.7	KGS/l	200	610
New LPG minibus	2.09	8.9	l/100 km	39.0	KGS/l	200	697
New minibus equipped with Euro 6/VI engine	2	11.3	l/100 km	48.0	KGS/l	200	1 080

Note: * The CPT Programme does not foresee purchase of used vehicles; ** average price for trolleybuses and trolleybuses with batteries.
Source: OECD, OPTIC Model.

Emissions factors

After inputting information on the basic assumptions, next the user inputs information on emissions from buses. This can be found under the "Emission factors" tab. The emissions will be identified in kilograms or grams of the emitted pollutant per kilometre of bus operation. The information on emissions is key for calculating emission reductions (Table B.2).

Table B.2. Assumed emission factors according to emission norms (per km)

	CO_2 (kg/km)	CO (g/km)	NO_x (g/km)	PM2.5 (g/km)	SO_2 (g/km)
Diesel Euro 2	1.0812	2.4400	10.7000	0.2200	0.2050
Diesel Euro 2>5 years	1.1893	2.6840	11.7700	0.2420	0.2255
Diesel Euro 2>10 years	1.2974	2.9280	12.8400	0.2640	0.2460
Diesel Euro 2>15 years	1.4056	3.1720	13.9100	0.2860	0.2665
Diesel Euro VI	0.7632	0.2230	0.5970	0.0023	0.0205
CNG (EEV standard)	0.9350	0.2400	2.5000	0.0050	0.0000
LPG	1.0258	1.9200	5.0000	0.0050	0.0652
Trolleybus	0.3384	0	0	0	0
Minibus Euro VI	0.1908	0.0558	0.1493	0.0006	0.0051
Minibus Euro II	0.3514	0.7930	3.4775	0.0715	0.0666
Minibus LPG	0.2564	0.4800	1.2500	0.0013	0.0163

Source: OECD, OPTIC Model.

There are two tables containing emission factors:

- normative emissions according to the standards
- real emissions according to actually measured emissions

The source of information and the reason for providing two different sets of emission factors are discussed at the end of this annex.

Transport sector overview

Next, information on the existing bus fleet in Kyrgyzstan needs to be input into the "Transport" tab (as shown in Table B.3). The fleet is divided by bus type. The last columns contain information on the availability of CNG stations. This information is provided by entering "Yes" or "No" into the respective cells.

Table B.3. Public transport and transport infrastructure in the Kyrgyz Republic

№	Type	City	Existing fleet												
													Fuel		
			Bus	< 5 y.	5-10 y.	10-15 y.	> 15 y.	Mini-bus	< 5 y.	5-10 y.	10-15 y.	> 15 y.	Trolleybus	Diesel	Electricity
1	Urban	Bishkek	468	10	205	253	0	4 000	0	400	800	2 800	130	4 468	130
2	Urban	Osh	86	30	56	0	0	1 166	0	212	661	293	40	1 252	40
3	Suburban	Other cities	150	0	0	0	150	200	0	0	200	0	0	150	0
Total			704	40	261	253	150	5 366	0	612	1 661	3 093	170	5 870	170

Table B.3 (cont.)

№	Type	City	Potential for replacement									
			Pilot phase				Second phase					
			Trolleybus-Trolleybus	Trolleybus-Bus	CNG-Diesel	CNG-Minibus < 15 y.	CNG-Minibus > 15 y.	Trolleybus-Trolleybus	Trolleybus-Bus	CNG-Diesel	CNG-Minibus < 15 y.	CNG-Minibus > 15 y.
1	Urban	Bishkek	78	20	78	0	40	0	0	650	0	80
2	Urban	Osh	17	0	150	0	20	0	0	50	0	30
3	Suburban	Other cities	0	0	0	0	0	0	0	150	0	0
Total			95	20	208	0	60	0	0	850	0	110

Source: OECD, OPTIC Model.

Determining the subsidy level

The module on determining the subsidy level takes into account both the investment costs and savings for public service providers by replacing old buses. New buses using alternative fuels are more efficient because of technological improvements and also due to the lower price of CNG and LPG fuels compared to diesel.

The module takes into account the fact that the investments should generate at least a minimum return for public transport providers; thus, the social discount rate is used to determine the net present value (NPV) of the project. The subsidy is then determined at the level at which NPV is equal to zero (see Box B.1). The economic significance of this calculation is that the subsidy will encourage potential beneficiaries to participate in the CPT Programme without encouraging the beneficiary to make a profit based on the subsidy. The various calculations required to establish the subsidy level for CNG buses are presented in Table B.4 and Table B.5.

Box B.1. Determining the optimal subsidy level

The subsidy should be sufficient to attract potential investors/beneficiaries to apply for support from the CPT Programme, but without making the projects too profitable. This approach to calculating the subsidy will enable the government to avoid over-investing, while at the same time providing an investment incentive for potential beneficiaries without making it too profitable for them as investors. Essentially, the subsidy level should provide just the necessary leverage for individual potential beneficiaries to invest in clean transport.

In order to evaluate a given project, the net present value (NPV) is calculated by totalling the expected net cash flows (cash inflows, or receipts, minus cash outflows, or expenses) over the project operating period and discounting them using a rate that reflects the costs of a loan of equivalent risk on the capital market. An investment will yield a profit if the NPV is positive. All measures that yield a positive NPV using a discount rate that corresponds to the applied rate of return can be deemed beneficial.

The NPV is calculated as in the following formula:

$$NPV = \sum_{i=1}^{n} (NCF_i \times \frac{1}{(1+r)^i})$$

where:

- NCF_i is the net cash flow in the i-th year
- r is the discount rate.

Using discounting considers two factors: the investor's expectations with respect to the measure and the fact that the NPV can be greater than zero during the operating period.

The calculation of the subsidy level should be based on economic principles. If the project is socially significant rather than profitable for the beneficiary, the subsidy should make a small amount of profit. In simple terms, the financial NPV including the subsidy should be approximately at the level of zero KGS, which means that the project yields an acceptable rate of return for the investor/project promoter (revenues from fares combined with lower operating costs).

The "determination of the subsidy level" module uses this principle by making a simple financial analysis of the cash inflows and outflows in each year of the analysis. Cash inflows (receipts) generated by the project include fuel savings expressed in terms of the money saved by customers (public transport providers). In terms of cash outflows (expenses), the simple financial analysis totals the difference between the investment costs of a clean and a traditional bus calculated in the other modules. In the subsidy module, the subsidy is included on the cash outflow side as a negative value.

It was assumed that the investments will be made during the first year of the project and the savings averaged over the nine years of operation. The period of analysis is 10 years, a typical lifetime for this type of project. The subsidy is calculated so that the result of the NPV calculation is equal to zero KGS.

First, the savings on fuel costs were calculated, given the lower price of CNG. The parameters used to calculate fuel savings are presented in Table B.4.

Table B.4. Assumptions for calculating the level of public support for CNG buses

	Fuel consumption	Fuel price	Annual distance	Fuel costs per year
CNG bus	38.5 kg/100 km	31.7 KGS/kg	46 000 km	KGS 561 000
Old diesel bus (>15 years)	56.3 l/100 km	44.4 KGS/l	46 000 km	KGS 1 149 000
Annual difference				KGS 588 000

Source: OECD, OPTIC Model.

The cost of a new CNG bus (KGS 10 million; USD 145 000) was compared with the average cost of a standard diesel bus (KGS 2.08 million; USD 31 000), which beneficiaries would have been likely to purchase in the absence of public support (Table B.5).

Table B.5. Calculation of the level of public support for CNG buses

(KGS)

Year	0	1	2	3	4	5	6	7	9
Investment cost for a new bus	10 million								
Difference in price compared to a standard bus	7.9 million								
Required public support	3.74 million								
Annual fuel cost savings		588 000	588 000	588 000	588 000	588 000	588 000	588 000	588 000
NPV	0								

Source: OECD, OPTIC Model.

Similar calculations are shown for LPG buses (Table B.6 and Table B.7) and for modern diesel buses (Table B.8 and Table B.9).

Table B.6. Assumptions for calculating the level of public support for LPG buses

	Fuel consumption	Fuel price	Annual distance	Fuel costs per year
LPG bus	35.7 l/km	39.0 KGS/l	46 000 km	KGS 641 000
Old diesel bus (> 15 years)	56.3 l/100 km	44.4 KGS/l	46 000 km	KGS 1 1149 000
Annual difference				KGS 507 000

Source: OECD, OPTIC Model.

Table B.7. Calculation of the level of public support for LPG buses

(KGS)

Year	0	1	2	3	4	5	6	7	9
Investment costs for a new bus	9.09 million								
Difference in price compared to a standard bus	7.01 million								
Required public support	3.4 million								
Annual fuel cost savings		507 000	507 000	507 000	507 000	507 000	507 000	507 000	507 000
NPV	0								

Source: OECD, OPTIC Model.

Table B.8. Assumptions for calculating the level of public support for modern diesel buses

	Fuel consumption	Fuel price	Annual distance	Fuel costs per year
Diesel Euro VI bus	50.0 l/100 km	48 KGS/l	46 000 km	KGS 1 104
Old diesel bus (>15 years)	56.3 l/100 km	44.4 KGS/l	46 000 km	KGS 1 149
Annual difference				KGS 45

Source: OECD, OPTIC Model.

Table B.9. Calculation of the level of public support for modern diesel buses

(KGS)

Year	0	1	2	3	4	5	6	7	9
Investment costs for a new bus	8.7 million								
Difference in price compared to a standard bus	6.62 million								
Required public support	6.3 million								
Annual fuel cost savings		45 000	45 000	45 000	45 000	45 000	45 000	45 000	45 000
NPV	0								

Source: OECD, OPTIC Model.

The above calculations do not take into account possible reduced maintenance costs, as old buses tend to require more maintenance over time. However, the maintenance of modern technologies is more expensive, especially when security is of concern when using CNG or LPG, so it is assumed that bus replacement will be neutral in terms of maintenance costs.

The results of the calculation are presented in the tab "Subsidy" (Table B.10).

Table B.10. Calculation of public subsidy for replacement buses

	Costs per bus	Difference in price to standard bus	Annual distance	Annual fuel costs	Annual reference fuel costs*	Subsidy required per bus	Net cost to beneficiary per bus
	KGS mln	KGS mln	km	KGS mln	KGS mln	KGS mln	KGS mln
CNG	10.00	7.92	46 000	561	1 149	3.74	6.26
LPG	9.09	7.01	46 000	641	1 149	3.40	5.69
Diesel Euro V	8.70	6.62	46 000	1 104	1 149	6.30	2.40

Note: *Reference fuel costs refer to old diesel bus.
Source: OECD, OPTIC Model.

Cost calculation

The cost calculation module under the tab "Costs" shows the estimated investment costs and the subsidy required by the CPT Programme. This information is provided in a table format (Table B.11) that contains data on public transport in Kyrgyzstan, the number of buses to be replaced, the type of new buses, total investment costs, the level of subsidy and the net costs to beneficiaries. In this module, users simply input factual information without making any decisions on the programme.

Table B.11. Investment costs, subsidies and net costs for beneficiaries

№	Type	City	Buses to be replaced			New buses						Need for CNG station	Investment costs							
						bus			mini-bus		trolleybus		bus			mini-bus		CNG stations	Trolley buses	Total
			Buses	mini-buses	Trolley buses	Diesel	CNG	LPG	Diesel	LPG	Electricity		Diesel	CNG	LPG	Diesel	LPG			
1	Urban	Bishkok	846	600	78	0	848	0	0	0	98	0	0	8 480	0	0	0	0	1 029	9 509
2	Urban	Osh	350	250	17	0	250	0	0	0	17	0	0	2 500	0	0	0	0	179	2 679
3	Suburban	Other cities	150	0	0	90	60	0	0	0	0	1	783	600	0	0	0	120	0	1 503
Total			1 346	850	95	90	1 158	0	0	0	115	1	783	11 580	0	0	0	120	1 208	13 691

Table B.11. (cont.)

№	Type	City	Subsidy								Net costs for beneficiary							
			bus			mini-bus		CNG stations	Trolley buses	Total	bus			mini-bus		CNG stations	Trolley buses	Total
			Diesel	CNG	LPG	Diesel	LPG				Diesel	CNG	LPG	Diesel	LPG			
1	Urban	Bishkok	0	1 037	0	0	0	0	825	1 862	0	7 443	0	0	0	0	204	7 647
2	Urban	Osh	0	306	0	0	0	0	143	449	0	2 194	0	0	0	0	35	2 230
3	Suburban	Other cities	509	73	0	0	0	24	0	606	274	527	0	0	0	96	0	897
Total			509	1 417	0	0	0	24	968	2 917	274	10 163	0	0	0	96	239	10 773

Source: OECD, OPTIC Model.

Emission reductions calculation

The emission reductions calculation module, under the tab "Emissions", shows the estimated annual emission reduction by type of pollutant. This information is provided in an Excel table (Table B.12) that contains data on transport sector in Kyrgyzstan, the number of buses to be replaced, the type of new buses, the emissions from old buses, emissions from new buses, and emission reduction. In this module, users simply input the factual information without making decisions on the CPT Programme.

Table B.12. Emission reduction based on the purchase of new buses

№	Type	City	Buses to be replaced			New buses						Buses to be replaced				
			Type			Bus			Mini-bus		Trolley-bus	Emissions				
			Buses	Mini-buses	Trolley buses	Diesel	CNG	LPG	Diesel	LPG	Electricity	CO_2 (t)	CO (kg)	NO_x (kg)	PM 2.5 (kg)	SO_2 (kg)
1	Urban	Bishkek	806	600	78	0	848	0	0	0	98	194 486	312 772	1 371 582	28 201	26 278
2	Urban	Osh	350	250	17	0	250	0	0	0	17	80 459	129 537	568 050	11 680	10 883
3	Sub-urban	Other cities	150	0	0	90	60	0	0	0	0	29 222	47 104	206 564	4 247	3 958
Total			1 346	850	95	90	1 158	0	0	0	115	304 166	489 413	2 146 195	44 127	41 119

Table B.12. (cont.)

№	Type	City	New buses Emissions					Emission reduction				
			CO_2 (t)	CO (kg)	NO_x (kg)	PM 2.5 (kg)	SO_2 (kg)	CO_2 (t)	CO (kg)	NO_x (kg)	PM 2.5 (kg)	SO_2 (kg)
1	Urban	Bishkek	79 067	20 148	209 880	420	0	115 420	292 623	1 161 702	27 781	26 278
2	Urban	Osh	23 240	5 940	61 875	124	0	57 218	123 597	506 175	11 556	10 883
3	Sub-urban	Other cities	15 074	3 413	52 617	50	183	14 148	43 692	153 947	4 197	3 775
Total			117 381	29 501	324 372	594	183	186 785	459 912	1 821 823	43 534	40 936

Source: OECD, OPTIC Model.

Programme costing and environmental effects

The CPT Programme costing and environmental effects module is under the tab "Decision". This is the main module for supporting decision making. It can be used for the automatic calculation of the programme costs as well as for manual adjustments.

The upper part of the screen contains the information on the programme target. Users may define one of the following programme targets:

- investment costs
- subsidy budget (amount of funding available for subsidies)
- CO_2 emission reduction
- CO emission reduction
- NO_x emission reduction
- PM2.5 emission reduction
- SO_2 emission reduction.

By clicking on the "Go" button to the right of the respective target (Table B.13), the model calculates the programme financial envelope necessary to achieve the target, for that target only, excluding the other targets.

Table B.13. Adjusting programme costs and environmental effects

Programme target	Costs				Emissions								
	Investment costs	100,000	Go		CO2 (t/a)	10,500	Go	NOx (kg/a)	150,000	Go	SO2 (kg/a)	5,000	Go
	Subsidy budget	100	Go		CO (kg/a)	60,000	Go	PM2.5 (kg/a)	45,000	Go			

Source: OECD, OPTIC Model.

The algorithm for the programme cost calculation is as follows:

- The model reviews the information on public transport for each city, in the order provided in the table in the "Transport" tab. The review is done in three iterations, starting from the urban centres and then respectively for suburban and inter-city connections.
- First, the model determines whether the city has any potential for CNG buses; if so, the model proposes the replacement of an old bus by a CNG bus.
- Then, the previous step is repeated until the target is reached or all old buses in a given iteration are replaced.
- If the city does not have the potential for CNG buses, the model completes the same steps with Euro VI diesel buses.
- If the city lacks the potential for either CNG or Euro VI diesel buses, the model proceeds through the same steps with LPG buses.
- The costs of CNG stations are also taken into account. If the number of buses replaced is higher than 100, it is assumed that a CNG station is a commercial project and a subsidy is not required. Existing CNG stations in Bishkek and Osh are taken into account.

The results are presented in an Excel table (Table B.14) that contains basic information on the number of new buses, investment costs, subsidies and emission reductions per year. If users want to see details, the "Emissions" or "Costs" tabs should be used (described earlier).

Table B.14. Relationship between programme costs and environmental effects

№	Type	City	New buses						Investment costs	Public support	Emission reduction per year				
			Bus			Mini-bus		Trolley bus							
			Diesel	CNG	LPG	Diesel	LPG		million KGS	million KGS	CO_2 (t)	CO (kg)	NO_x (kg)	PM 2.5 (kg)	SO_2 (kg)
1	Urban	Bishkek	0	848	0	0	0	98	9 509	3 972	39 988	195 082	774 468	18 521	17 519
2	Urban	Osh	0	250	0	0	0	17	2 679	1 071	22 839	82 398	337 450	7 704	7 255
3	Sub-urban	Other cities	90	60	0	0	0	0	1 503	755	5 679	29 128	124 263	2 798	2 517
Total			**90**	**1 158**	**0**	**0**	**0**	**115**	**13 691**	**5 799**	**68 506**	**306 608**	**1 236 180**	**29 022**	**27 291**

Source: OECD, OPTIC Model.

Users may change the project pipelines by providing their own information on the number of new buses. The calculations are then updated accordingly.

Programme costing for Phase 1 (pilot phase) and Phase 2 (scaling-up phase)

In the spreadsheet titled "Programme targets" (Table B.15) users may define whether the calculation is being done for the pilot phase (Phase 1), which covers only two cities, or for Phase 1 and 2. The user may also define whether normative or real emission factors are used in the calculation.

Table B.15. Adjusting programme targets

Phase	1 & 2	Emissions	real	Scenario	1	Go

Source: OECD, OPTIC Model.

By clicking on the "Go" button to the right of the defined phase (scenario), the model calculates the programme costs and emission reductions. The targets are thus ignored.

Sources of information used in the assumptions

The current version of the model uses information from different sources, both Kyrgyz and international. This section describes the sources of information for each assumption used:

- **Data on urban public transport** (number of buses, fuel type and age) were provided by the cities of Bishkek and Osh and the National Statistical Committee (NSC).

- The **average prices of buses** were obtained from estimates from the European Bank for Reconstruction and Development (EBRD) tenders, municipal tenders, statements of bus and minibus operators in questionnaires, and market research on the internet.
- The **fuel prices** were obtained from market research on the main distribution companies on the internet, and in particular the national regulator (ANRE).
- **Fuel consumption** was calculated by reviewing technical information from bus producers and several bus utilities introducing new buses (*Der Betrieb mit Flüssiggas als Alternative zum Dieselantrieb (Operation with LPG as an alternative to diesel propulsion)*;[2] *Cost and Benefits of Clean Technologies for Bus Rapid Transit (BRT): Summary of Results for Kampala* (ICCT, 2012[6]); *Comparison of Modern CNG, Diesel and Diesel Hybrid-Electric Transit Buses: Efficiency and Environmental Performance* (MJB&A, 2013[7]); *CNG vs. Diesel Bus Comparison*; *Infrastructure for Alternative Fuels* (European Expert Group on Future Transport Fuels, 2011[8])[3] and *A Realistic View of CNG Vehicles in the US* (Nath et al., 2014[9]).

Emission factors

The emission factors were taken from:

- The section on "Exhaust Emissions of European Monitoring and Evaluation Programme" in the European Environment Agency (EEA) *Air Pollution Emission Inventory Guidebook 2013; Technical Guidance to Prepare National Emission Inventories* (EEA, 2016[10]).
- Euro II-VI emission standards.
- Euro II-V fuel standards (for SO_2).
- The revised 1996 Intergovernmental Panel on Climate Change (IPCC) *Guidelines for National Greenhouse Gas Inventories, Vol. 3: The Reference Manual* (IPCC, 1996[11]).
- The Emissions Factors Toolkit (EFT) published by Defra and the Devolved Administrations (Defra and the Devolved Administrations, 2017[12]).
- For electricity, the CO_2 Emission factor & transmission and distribution loss factor provided in the U4E Country report: http://united4efficiency.org/wp-content/uploads/2017/05/MDA_U4E-Country-Assessment-Report.pdf

The various emission standards used in the calculations are provided in Table B.16. They are practically entirely based on the European emission regulations for new heavy-duty diesel engines, commonly referred to as Euro I-VI.

Table B.16. EU emissions standards for heavy-duty diesel engines

(g/kWh)

Tier	Date	Test cycle	CO	HC	NO_x	PM
Euro I	1992 < 85 kW	Economic Commission for Europe of the United Nations (ECE/UN) Regulation-49	4.5	1.1	8.0	0.612
	1992 > 85 kW		4.5	1.1	8.0	0.36
Euro II	October 1996		4.0	1.1	7.0	0.25
	October 1998		4.0	1.1	7.0	0.15
Euro III	*October 1999 Enhanced Environmentally friendly Vehicles (EEVs) only*	European Stationary Cycle (ESC) and European Load Response (ELR)	*1.0*	*0.25*	*2.0*	*0.02*
	October 2000	ESC & ELR	2.1	0.66	5.0	0.10 - 0.13
Euro IV	October 2005		1.5	0.46	3.5	0.02
Euro V	October 2008		1.5	0.46	2.0	0.02
Euro VI	31 December 2013		1.5	0.13	0.4	0.01

Source: (EC, 2017[13]), *Transport Emissions: Air Pollutant from Road Transport*, http://ec.Europa.eu/environment/air/transport/road.htm (accessed 16 February 2017). Similarly, the EU fuel standards for sulphur content for Euro 2-5, used in the calculations, are provided in Table B.17.

Table B.17. EU fuel standards for sulphur content

Name	EU Directive	European Committee for Standardisation (CEN) Standard	Implementation date	Sulphur limit (ppm)
n/a	-	EN 590:1993 (d) EN 228:1993 (g)	October 1994	2 000
Euro 2	93/12/EEC	-	October 1996	500 (diesel)
Euro 3	93/12/EEC	EN 590:1999 (d) EN 228:1999 (g)	January 2000	350 (diesel); 150 (petrol)
Euro 4	98/70/EC	EN 590:2004 (d) EN 228:2004 (g)	January 2005	50*
Euro 5	2003/17/EC	EN 590:2009	January 2009	10, 10**

Note: * "Sulphur-free" 10ppm fuel must be available; ** non-road fuels limit
Source: (EC, 2017[13]), *Transport Emissions: Air Pollutant from Road Transport*, http://ec.Europa.eu/environment/air/transport/road.htm (accessed 16 February 2017).

On the other hand, the estimated CO_2 emission factors for a number of pollutants emitted by European heavy-duty diesel vehicles come from the *Revised 1996 IPCC Guidelines for National Greenhouse Gas Inventories* and its *Reference Manual* (IPCC, 1996[11]) (Table B.18).

Table B.18. Estimated CO_2 emission factors for European heavy-duty diesel vehicles

	CO_2
Total g/km	770
g/kg fuel	3 140
g/MJ	74

Source: (IPCC, 1996[11]), *Revised 1996 IPCC Guidelines for National Greenhouse Gas Inventories, Volume 3: The Reference Manual*, Intergovernmental Panel on Climate Change, Mexico City, www.ipcc-nggip.iges.or.jp/public/gl/invs6.html.

The current norms for air pollution and CO_2 emissions can be taken from the *EMEP/EEA Air Pollution Emission Inventory Guidebook 2016* (EEA, 2016[10]). Table B.19 presents the Tier 1 approach to measuring exhaust emissions (and is explained in the source document for the table).

Table B.19. Tier 1 air pollution emission of heavy-duty diesel vehicles

(g/kg fuel)

	CO	NMVOC	NO_x	PM	N_2O
Diesel	7.58	1.92	33.37	0.94	0.051
CNG (buses)	5.70	0.26	13.00	0.02	n.a.

Source: (EEA, 2016[14]), *EMEP/EEA Air Pollution Emission Inventory Guidebook 2016. Technical Guidance to Prepare National Emission Inventories. Part B: Sectoral Guidance Chapters – Road Transport 2018*, https://www.eea.europa.eu/publications/emep-eea-guidebook-2016/part-b-sectoral-guidance-chapters/1-energy/1-a-combustion/1-a-3-b-i/view.

The *EME/EEA Air Pollution Emission Inventory Guidebook 2016* is also used as a source for estimating the CO_2 emission factors for different fuels used in operating heavy-duty vehicles (Table B.20).

Table B.20. Tier 1 CO_2 emission factors for different road transport fossil fuels, all vehicle types

Fuel type	gCO_2 / kg of fuel*
Petrol	3 169
Diesel	3 169
LPG**	3 024
CNG (or LNG)***	2 743

Note: *CO_2 emission factors are based on an assumed 100% oxidation of the fuel carbon (ultimate CO_2); ** LPG assumed to be 50% propane + 50% butane; *** CNG and LNG assumed to be 100% methane.
Source: (EEA, 2016[14]), *EMEP/EEA Air Pollution Emission Inventory Guidebook 2016. Technical Guidance to Prepare National Emission Inventories. Part B: Sectoral Guidance Chapters – Road Transport 2018*, https://www.eea.europa.eu/publications/emep-eea-guidebook-2016/part-b-sectoral-guidance-chapters/1-energy/1-a-combustion/1-a-3-b-i/view.

A couple of sources were used for fuel consumption values used in the model, combined with the authors' own assumptions, particularly for LPG consumption volumes (Table B.21).

Table B.21. Assumed fuel energy content and consumption of heavy-duty vehicles

Fuel type	Energy (unit)	Consumption (g/km)
Petrol	8.77 (kWh/l)	300*
Diesel	9.86 (kWh/l)	240
CNG	13.16 (kWh/kg)	500
LPG	6.6 (kWh/l)	340*

Note: * Own assumptions.

Source: (EEA, 2016[14]), *EMEP/EEA Air Pollution Emission Inventory Guidebook 2016. Technical Guidance to Prepare National Emission Inventories. Part B: Sectoral Guidance Chapters – Road Transport 2018*, https://www.eea.europa.eu/publications/emep-eea-guidebook-2016/part-b-sectoral-guidance-chapters/1-energy/1-a-combustion/1-a-3-b-i/view; www.erdgasauto.at (in German, accessed 14 March 2019).

It was assumed that the emission factors for old engines are the same as for a new one. However, in new engines energy efficiency is higher and fuel consumption 10% lower than in buses more than 5 years old, 15% lower than buses of more than 10 years old, and 25% lower than buses of more than 15 years old.

The specific emission factors used in the model are provided in Table B.2 above. The emission factors presented in Table B.2, however, are based on maximum levels, according to specific norms. The real emissions may vary, mainly because normative emissions are tested in laboratory conditions and not in actual traffic. This is a concern primarily in the case of diesel engines, where emission reduction depends on the installed emission reduction equipment. In the case of CNG and LPG, emissions are less problematic, because lower emissions are mainly the result of using cleaner fuels.

In 2014, the ICCT issued a report on real-world exhaust emissions from modern diesel cars presenting measurements of real emissions. The analysis showed that real-world emissions of CO_2 and NO_x are higher than the limits (respective Euro norms) by an average of 40% and 70%, respectively (Franco et al., 2014[15]).

Figure B.1. Percentage of tested vehicles that exceed Euro limits in urban cycle

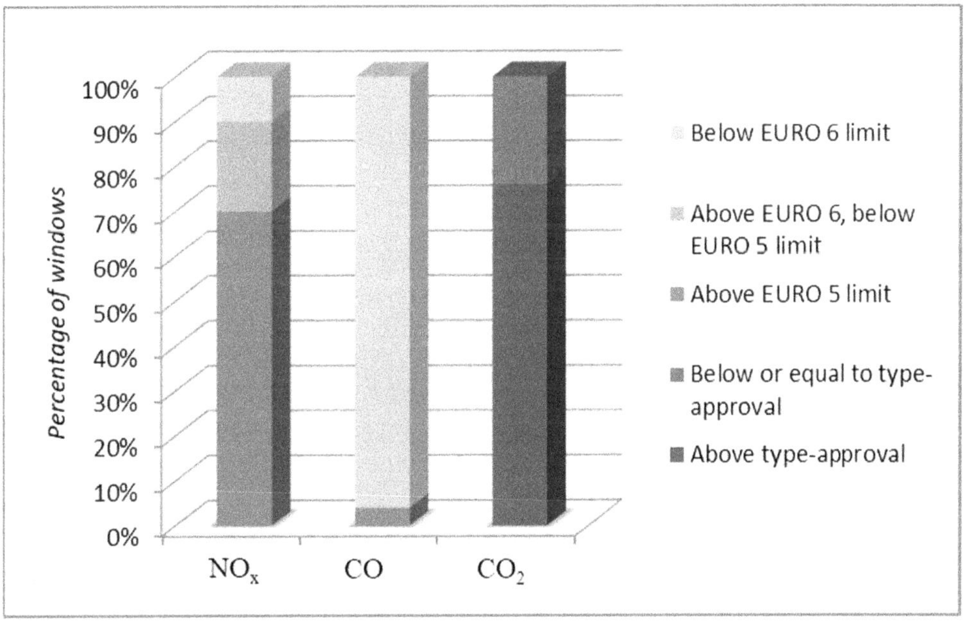

Note: The "window" represents a sample.
Source: (Franco et al., 2014[15]).

Thus, the model also offers an alternative set of emission factors taking into account the fact that real emissions may exceed normative ones. Table B.22 presents the real emission factors used in the model.

Table B.22. Assumed emissions factors adjusted to real values (per km)

Engine and fuel type	CO_2 (kg/km)	CO (g/km)	NO_x (g/km)	PM2.5 (g/km)	SO_2 (g/km)
Diesel Euro II	1.5137	2.4400	10.7000	0.2200	0.2050
Diesel Euro II > 5 y.	1.6650	2.6840	11.7700	0.2420	0.2255
Diesel Euro II > 10 y.	1.8164	2.9280	12.8400	0.2640	0.2460
Diesel Euro II > 15 y.	1.9678	3.1720	13.9100	0.2860	0.2665
Diesel Euro VI	1.0685	0.2230	4.2387	0.0023	0.0205
CNG (EEV standard)	0.9350	0.2400	2.5000	0.0050	0.0000
LPG	1.0258	1.9200	5.0000	0.0050	0.0652

Source: OECD, OPTIC Model.

The user can change both normative and real emission factors according to modelling needs.

Notes

1. The model assumes that an average bus operates 330 days per year.
2. For information on CNG vehicles, see www.erdgasauto.at (in German).
3. For a fuel costs comparison between CNG and diesel, see: www.bus.man.eu/cng_optimizer/index.html.

References

Defra and the Devolved Administrations (2017), *The Emissions Factors Toolkit (EFT)*, UK Department of Environment, Food and Rural Affairs, https://laqm.defra.gov.uk/review-and-assessment/tools/emissions-factors-toolkit.html (accessed on 15 February 2017). [12]

EC (2017), *Transport Emissions: Air Pollutant from Road Transport*, European Commission, Brussels, http://ec.Europa.eu/environment/air/transport/road.htm (accessed on 16 February 2017). [13]

EEA (2016), *EMEP/EEA Air Pollution Emission Inventory Guidebook 2016. Technical Guidance to Prepare National Emission Inventories*, EEA Report No. 21/2016, EMEP European Environment Agency, Copenhagen, http://www.eea.europa.eu/publications/emep-eea-guidebook-2016/at_download. [10]

EEA (2016), *EMEP/EEA Air Pollution Emission Inventory Guidebook 2016. Technical Guidance to Prepare National Emission Inventories. Part B: Sectoral Guidance Chapters – Road Transport 2018*, EEA Report No. 21/2016, EMEP European Environment Agency, Copenhagen, https://www.eea.europa.eu/publications/emep-eea-guidebook-2016/part-b-sectoral-guidance-chapters/1-energy/1-a-combustion/1-a-3-b-i/view. [14]

European Expert Group on Future Transport Fuels (2011), *Infrastructure for Alternative Fuels*, European Expert Group on Future Transport Fuels, Brussels, http://ec.Europa.eu/transport/themes/urban/cts/doc/2011-12-2nd-future-transport-fuels-report.pdf. [8]

Franco, V. et al. (2014), *Real-World Exhaust Emissions from Modern Diesel Cars. A Meta-Analysis of Pems Emissions Data from EU (Euro 6) and US (Tier 2 Bin 5/Ulev II) Diesel Passenger Cars*, International Council on Clean Transportation, Berlin, http://www.theicct.org/sites/default/files/p. [15]

ICCT (2012), *Cost and Benefits of Clean Technologies for Bus Rapid Transit (BRT). Summary of Results for Kampala*, International Council on Clean Transportation, Kampala, http://mirror.unhabitat.org/pmss/listItemDetails.aspx?publicationID=3484. [6]

IPCC (1996), *Revised 1996 IPCC Guidelines for National Greenhouse Gas Inventories, Volume 3: The Reference Manual*, Intergovernmental Panel on Climate Change, Mexico City, http://www.ipcc-nggip.iges.or.jp/public/gl/invs6.html. [11]

MJB&A (2013), *Comparison of Modern CNG, Diesel and Diesel Hybrid-Electric Transit Buses: Efficiency and Environmental Performance*, M.J. Bradley and Associates, Concord, Massachusetts and Washington, D.C, http://mjbradley.com/sites/default/files/CNG%20Diesel%20Hybrid%20. [7]

Nath et al. (2014), "A Realistic View of CNG Vehicles in the US", *BCG Perspectives* 16 June, Boston Consulting Group, Boston, https://www.bcg.com/de-de/publications/2014/energy-environment-automotive-realistic-view-cng-vehicles-us.aspx (accessed on 30 August 2019). [9]

Annex C. Example of a project application form

Bus/minibus/trolleybus replacement

<table>
<tr><td>Project Name</td><td colspan="5"></td></tr>
<tr><td>Name of the project applicant</td><td colspan="5"></td></tr>
<tr><td>Address</td><td colspan="5"></td></tr>
<tr><td>Contact details</td><td colspan="5"></td></tr>
<tr><td>Legal status</td><td colspan="5"></td></tr>
<tr><td>Bank account number, bank, branch and address</td><td colspan="5"></td></tr>
<tr><td>Location of the project (city)</td><td colspan="5"></td></tr>
<tr><td>Description of the project:</td><td colspan="5"></td></tr>
<tr><td>Number of buses used for regular services in the city</td><td colspan="5"></td></tr>
<tr><td>Number of minibuses used for regular services in the city</td><td colspan="5"></td></tr>
<tr><td>Number of bus lines operated by the company in the city</td><td colspan="5"></td></tr>
<tr><td>Number of minibus lines operated by the company in the city</td><td colspan="5"></td></tr>
<tr><td rowspan="2">Planned bus replacement</td><td colspan="2">Buses that will be replaced</td><td colspan="3">New buses</td></tr>
<tr><td>Older than 15 years</td><td>10- to 15 years old</td><td>CNG</td><td>LPG</td><td>Diesel</td></tr>
<tr><td>Number of buses (#)</td><td></td><td></td><td></td><td></td><td></td></tr>
<tr><td>Costs (KGS 1 000)</td><td>X</td><td>X</td><td></td><td></td><td></td></tr>
<tr><td>Total costs (KGS 1 000)</td><td>X</td><td>X</td><td colspan="3"></td></tr>
<tr><td rowspan="2">Planned minibus replacement</td><td colspan="2">Buses that will be replaced</td><td colspan="3">New buses</td></tr>
<tr><td>Older than 15 years</td><td>10- to 15 years old</td><td>CNG</td><td>LPG</td><td>Diesel</td></tr>
<tr><td>Number of minibuses (#)</td><td></td><td></td><td></td><td></td><td></td></tr>
<tr><td>Costs (KGS 1 000)</td><td>X</td><td>X</td><td></td><td></td><td></td></tr>
<tr><td>Total costs (KGS 1 000)</td><td>X</td><td>X</td><td colspan="3"></td></tr>
<tr><td>Planned trolleybus replacement</td><td colspan="5"></td></tr>
<tr><td>Number of trolleybuses (#)</td><td colspan="5"></td></tr>
<tr><td>Costs (KGS 1 000)</td><td colspan="5"></td></tr>
<tr><td>If CNG buses are proposed:
Does a CNG filling station exist in the city?</td><td colspan="5"></td></tr>
</table>

Annex D. Example of a project pre-appraisal form

Bus replacement

Criteria	Yes/No
Criteria related to the location of the project	
Is the project located in the urban centre of the city listed in the list of eligible costs?	
Criteria related to the type of eligible projects	
Is the project type on the list of eligible projects?	
Are all the proposed project costs found in the list of eligible costs?	
Is the number of older buses (of between 10 and 15 and more than 15 years old) equal to new buses (using the factor 1 bus = 5 minibuses)?	
Criteria related to the type of eligible beneficiaries	
Is the type of beneficiary found on the list of eligible beneficiaries?	
Other eligibility criteria	
Are there existing plans for the city to implement additional investments that improve the urban public transport system in the city?	
Total: "Yes" if all answers are checked yes, "No" if at least one answer is no	

Annex E. Example of a project appraisal form

Measuring the environmental efficiency of an investment implies calculating the unit cost of decreasing, for example, PM2.5 emissions. The unit cost should be calculated as the difference between PM2.5 emissions from old diesel buses and from new buses. The calculation should use real emission factors from the model.

The best project receives 10 points, the worst 0 points; other projects receive points proportional to their position.

	Criteria	Weight	Max No. of points	Points
A	**Project preparation**	0.1		
1	Prepared business plan or strategic for project implementation in the city		0-1	
B	**Project location**	0.2		
1	Buses that will be replaced in polluted districts of cities		5	
2	Buses that will be replaced are used only in the centre of the eligible city		5	
3	Buses that will be replaced are used in the city centre and on the outskirts/suburbs of the eligible city		3	
4	Buses that will be replaced are used in the city and connecting the rural area outside the eligible city		0	
C	**Project type**	0.2		
1	CNG-powered buses		10	
2	Trolleybuses		5	
3	LPG-powered buses		1	
4	Modern diesel buses			
D	**Project size**	0.2		
1	More than 20 buses to be replaced		10	
2	Between 10 and 20 buses to be replaced		5	
3	Fewer than 10 buses to be replaced		1	
E	**Proposed system of improvements of urban public transport in the city:**	0.1		
1	Length of the new bus lanes (0 points < 2km, 1 p.– up to 2km, 2p. > 2km)		2	
2	Number of traffic lights with priority for public transport (0 points < 2, 1 p.– up to 4, 2p. > 5)		2	
3	Number of bus stops newly equipped with online information for passengers (0 points < 2, 1 p.– up to 4, 2p. > 5)		2	
4	Number of new bus stops (0 points < 2, 1 p.– up to 4, 2p. > 5)		2	
5	Other measures (points according to expert opinion)		2	
F	**Environmental efficiency**	0.2		
1	Unit efficiency	(F2-F3) /F4		
2	Calculated annual PM2.5 emissions from old buses [PM2.5 kg]			
3	Calculated annual PM2.5 emissions from new buses [PM2.5 kg]			
4	Project costs			
5	Points for environmental efficiency – the best project with unit efficiency U_{best} receives 10, the worst with unit efficiency U_{worst} receives 0, others with unit efficiency U receive $10*(U-U_{worst})/(U_{best}-U_{worst})$		10	
G	**Total: (weights x points)**			

Annex F. List of public transport routes in Bishkek (in Russian)

Route No.	Name of final stops	Plan of an exit	Route length (km)	Name of carrier
100	ж/м Арча-Бешик (кольцевой)	30	31	ОАО «Акжолтой»
101	ж/м Ынтымак – мкр.Джал (кольцевой)	30	35	ОАО «Акжолтой»
102	ж/м Кыргызстан – Ошский р/к	29	25	БАТП «Лига»
103	Рабочий городок - ВДНХ	20	38	ОсОО «КейДжи Транскомпани»
104	ж/м Эне-Сай – 10 мкр.	20	39	ОсОО «Ай-Эл транс»
105	с.Ново-Покровка – 12 мкр.	22	52	ОсОО «Галоп»
106	12 мкр. – ж/м Ак-Ордо	35	46	ОсОО «Элек»
107	«ж/м Арча Бешик -ж/м.Ак-Босого»	15	34	ОАО «Акжолтой»
108	ж/м 28 Га-РТС	8	56	ОсОО «Жазада тр»
110	ул.Интергельпо-ул. Баялинова	18	26	ОАО «Акжолтой»
111	ж/м Аска-Таш –с-о Новопокровка	15	42	ОАО «Акжолтой»
115	ж/м Ак-Ордо-ж/м Кырман	10	21	ОсОО Прокси- Сервис :не работает
116	Вост.автовокзал (кольцевой)	40	17,1	ОАО «Акжолтой»: не работает
114	Зап.автовокзал (кольцевой)	40	17,2	ОАО «Акжолтой»
117	12 мкр.(Набер.) – ж/м Ак-Бата	36	50	ОсОО «Дордой-Транс»
118	ф.Барат. Авто - ж/м Бакай-Ата	30	34,6	ОсОО «Куюн»
121	ж/м Ак-Босого – Аламед. райбольн.	18	27	ОсОО «Ай-Эл транс»
122	с-о Кок- Жар– Кызыл -Аскер	18	38	ОсОО «Ника-Плюс»
123	Аламедин 1 – р/к Дордой	11	34	ОсОО «Элек»
127	Ош р-к. – Киркомстром	9	21	ОАО «Акжолтой»
128	ж/м Рухий-Мурас – ж/м Ак Бата	26	52	ОАО «Акжолтой»
129	«БЧК – 1-я СТО»	21	27	БАТП «Лига»
130	ж/м Арча-бешик – ж/м Ак-Жар	27	44	ОсОО «Трансгруппкомм.»
131	Аламедин 1 – 8 мкр.	22	29	ОАО «Акжолтой»
132	12 мкр. – Зап.автовокзал	32	34,7	ОсОО «Батыр Хан Мурагер
133	ж/м Сон Көл-ж/м Колмо – с.Чон-Арык	22	34	БАТП «Лига»
134	«ж/м.Арча-Бешик-Н.Покровка»	31	44,4	ОсОО «Спейсталс»
135	ж/м Бакай-Ата – ж/м Арча-Бешик	27	40	ОсОО «Трансгруппкомм.»
136	ж/м Кок-Жар – .-ж/м Арча-Бешик.	25	42	ОсОО «Трансгруппкомм.»
137	«Воен.часть -мкр.Тунгуч-ул Исакеева»	31	44	ОсОО «Элек»
138	ст. Сокулук – ж/м Кок-Жар	30	50	ОсОО «БайШамТранс»
139	ж/м Ак-Ордо – ЦУМ	23	20	БАТП «Лига»
144	Кирпичный з-д – ж/м Кок Жар	18	38	ОсОО «Батыр Хан Мурагер»
143	ж/м Ак-Босого - ж/м Кыргызстан	21	28	БГАТП «Лига»
145	12 мкр.наб. – с.Маевка	20	40	ОсОО «Узар -Вест»
146	«ж/м Бакай-Ата –ж/м Арча-Бешик»	24	34,5	ОсОО «Бек-Тоо»
147	«ж/м Арча-Бешик – Аламедин -1»	27	37	ОАО «Акжолтой»

148	ж/м Арча-Бешик – ж/м.Ала-Тоо	30	43,7	ОсОО «Байзак-Аска»
150	«мкр.Асанбай» (кольцевой)	15	22,5	БАТП «Лига»
152	«ж/м Арча Бешик – гор.Энергетиков»	26	29,5	ОсОО «Юрам»
154	мкр.Тунгуч (кольцевой)	15	28	ОсОО «Батыр Хан Мурагер»
155	мкр.Асанбай – с.Маевка	16	36	БАТП «Лига»
157	ж/м Ак-Ордо – ж/м Алтын-Ордо	7	34	ОсОО «Трансгруппкомм.»
159	ж/м Арча-Бешик –р/к Элитстрой	12	18	БАТП «Лига»
161	ДЭУ – р/к Дордой	26	48	БАТП «Лига»
162	с.Н.Покровка – 12 мкр.	28	52	ОсОО «Восточный Экспр.»
163	«с.Ново-Покровка – 10 мкр.»	20	52	ОАО «Акжолтой»
164	ж/м Кок-Жар – ж/м Баетова	30	34	ОАО «Акжолтой»
166	Аю грант- комфорт-Кызыл-Аскер»	33	37	ОсОО «Ак Ниет-Транс»
167	«мкр.№12-Жилгородок»	20	43,5	ОсОО «Экспресспрофитранс»
169	«ж/м Ак-Ордо – ф.Шоро»	25	46	ОАО «Акжолтой»
170	12 мкр. – с. Чон-Арык	20	44	БАТП «Лига»
171	ж/д Вокзал – с.Садовое	7	23,5	ОсОО «АО Каниет»
172	12 мкр. – мкр.Учкун-2	30	40	ОсОО «Элек»
173	«ж/м.Ала-Тоо-ж/м Калыс-Ордо»	22	49	ОАО «Акжолтой»
174	ж/м Балбан – 12 мкр.(Набер.)	8	28	БАТП «Лига»
175	10 мкр. – ул.Пригородная	34	42	ОсОО «Яглахар»
176	Арча-Бешик –ж/м Ак-Босого	22	40	БАТП «Лига»
177	«р/к Сары-Өзөн -р-к.Дордой»	20	29,9	ОАО БГАТП
179	ж/м Кара- Жыгач мкр. Достук	29	37	БАТП «Лига»
180	с-о Кок-Жар –с. Маевка	19	48	ОАО «Акжолтой»
184	ж/м Алтын-Казык– ж\мАлтын Ордо	12	34	ОсОО «БайШамТранс»
185	ж/м Ак-Ордо – ж/м Ак-Бата	25	48	ОсОО «Трансгруппкомм.»
186	ж/м Келечек-Ген. Прокуратура-с.Орто-сай	9	38	ОсОО «Кулан Бек»
188	ж/м Ынтымак – ж/м Тунгуч	24	44	ОсОО «БайШамТранс»
191	«ж/м Полицейский городок – р/к Дордой»	8	24	ОсОО «Дордой-Транс»
192	«ж/м Ак-Ордо-ж/м Дордой-2»	36	44	ОсОО «Совет Бригады»
193	«мкр.№12 – ж/м Калыс -Ордо»	36	57	ОсОО «Совет Бригады»
195	«мкр.Асанбай - ж/м.Колмо»	35	38	ОсОО «Ника-Плюс»
196	ТЧЧК-Киркомстром	10	27	БАТП «Лига»
199	12 мкр.– ж/м Алтын-Ордо	34	35,9	ОсОО «БайШамТранс.»
200	ж/мАк- Орго – с.Беш-Кунгей	42	60	БАТП «Лига»
202	ф.Шоро – ж/м Арча-Бешик	30	37	ОсОО «Восточный Экспр.»
203	ЭПОВС - р-к.Дордой	30	41	ОсОО «Ата-Жол»
204	«мкр.№12 – ж/м Ак- Ордо.»	29	35	ОсОО «Восточный Экспр.»
206	ж/м Мурас-Ордо- Ош р/к	20	24	ОсОО «Жазада-Транс»
210	с.Орто-Сай – з/д Фрунзе	16	32	ОсОО «Ай-Эл Транс»
211	ж/м Тынчтык – АЗС МТФ	26	45	ОсОО «Восточный Экспр.»

212	12 мкр.(набер.)- Военная часть	34	44	БАТП «Лига»
213	Вост.автовокзал (кольцевой)	24	16	ОсОО «Кут-Консун»
214	Зап.автовокзал (кольцевой)	39	17,4	ОсОО «Спейсталс»
215	Юракедемия. – ж/м Ак-Ордо	37	42,6	ОсОО «Куюн»
216	ж/м Ак-Орго – Аламедин 1	35	50	ОсОО «Ника-Плюс»
218	«р/к Додой-Моторс - р-к.Дордой»	33	28	ОсОО «КейДжиТрасКомпани»
219	мкр.Учкун – ж/м Баетова	16	32	ОсОО «АрДар и Ко»
220	мкр.Аламедин 1 – ж/м Ала-Тоо	34	48	ОсОО «БайШамТранс»
222	ж/м Ак-Ордо – ж/м Алтын -Ордо	23	42	ОсОО «Ника-Плюс»
223	12 мкр.Наб. – В.Антонвока-Авторынок	27	41	ОсОО «Кут-Консун»
224	ж/м Жениш -ж/м.Келечек	25	40,7	ОсОО «Кулан-Бек»
225	10 мкр. - Теплица (с.Маевка)	21	40	ОсОО «Ника-Плюс»
226	«мкр.№6 – р-к.Дордой»	13	32	ОсОО «Дордой-Транс»
227	ж/м Кок-Жар – ул.Луговая	25	34	ОсОО «Юрам»
228	«Горводоканал – ж/м.Бакай-Ата»	10	24,7	ОсОО «Улма-Транс»
229	ж/м «Рухи-Мурас -ул. Мир»	7	45	ОсОО «КаунтиТрансСервис»: не работает
230	«ЦУМ-Плаза - р-к Дордой»	12	14	ОсОО «Транском Юнити»
231	519 контр-Ошский р-к	10	28	ОсОО Дордой тр.
233	Аламединский р/к – р/к Дордой	16	20,5	ОсОО «Дордой-Бис»
236	ж/м Ак-Ордо-Ошский рынок	10	27	ОсОО «Экспресспрофитранс»
234	ТЦ Мадина – р/к Дордой	16	21,5	ОсОО «Дордой-Бис»
238	«г.Энергетиков-авторынок Азамат»	23	48	ОсОО «Бэсто»
240	«110 квартал – ж/м.Эне Сай»	21	40	ОсОО «Бек-Тоо»
243	мкр Асанбай – ж/м Жениш	32	42	ОсОО «Академтранссервис»
248	ж/м Ала-Тоо – 3- Стеклозавод	8	48	ОсОО «Байзак Аска»
251	«Кара-Жыгач - Жилгородок»	26	54,2	ОсОО «Куюн»
252	«мкр.Асанбай-р-к.Дордой»	16	34	ОсОО «Дордой-Транс»
254	«с.Восток-ж/м Ала-Тоо-3»	23	52	ОсОО «Жазада-Транс»
257	«Мед.училище – Калыс-Ордо»	13	22,6	ОсОО «Уланбек-Транс»
258	«Авторынок – ж/м Учкун»	40	56	ОсОО «Байзак-Аска»
260	ж/м Салкын-Төр – ж/м Бакай-Ата	27	36,1	ОсОО «Толкут»
262	540 контур – ж/м Кырман	20	31	ОсОО «Спейсталс»
264	ж/м Поле Чудес –ж/ м Арча-Бешик	15	29,7	ОсОО «Куюн»
265	с.Кашка-Суу – ж/м Умут	16	54	Сапар транс-Ассоциация
266	БЧК – с.Арчалы	18	54	ОсОО «Академтранссервис»
269	«Военное училище (кольцевой)»	24	29,8	ОсОО «Куюн»
270	«р-к.Дордой-ж/м.Ак-Орго»	15	44	ОсОО «Аргымак транс KG»
275	ж/м Ак –Орго-Западный А/Вокзал	10	38	ОсОО «Батыр Хан»
277	Ул. Токтогула- р-к Дордой	5	42	ОсОО «Аба Ирис»
281	«ул.Муромская АЗС-р-к.Оберон»	12	48	ОсОО «Герон»
285	с.Ленинское – ул. Шопокова	40	44	ОсОО «Кара-Суу Арго»

286	ул.Карсакова БЧК – ж/м Ак-Жар	30	52	ОсОО «Спейсталс»
290	ж/м Тынчтык – р/к Кербен	28	38	ОсОО «Ак- Жол тр. »
295	«с.Аршан – Ошский р/к»	15	44	Сапар транс-Ассоциация

ORGANISATION FOR ECONOMIC CO-OPERATION AND DEVELOPMENT

The OECD is a unique forum where governments work together to address the economic, social and environmental challenges of globalisation. The OECD is also at the forefront of efforts to understand and to help governments respond to new developments and concerns, such as corporate governance, the information economy and the challenges of an ageing population. The Organisation provides a setting where governments can compare policy experiences, seek answers to common problems, identify good practice and work to co-ordinate domestic and international policies.

The OECD member countries are: Australia, Austria, Belgium, Canada, Chile, the Czech Republic, Denmark, Estonia, Finland, France, Germany, Greece, Hungary, Iceland, Ireland, Israel, Italy, Japan, Korea, Latvia, Lithuania, Luxembourg, Mexico, the Netherlands, New Zealand, Norway, Poland, Portugal, the Slovak Republic, Slovenia, Spain, Sweden, Switzerland, Turkey, the United Kingdom and the United States. The European Union takes part in the work of the OECD.

OECD Publishing disseminates widely the results of the Organisation's statistics gathering and research on economic, social and environmental issues, as well as the conventions, guidelines and standards agreed by its members.

OECD PUBLISHING, 2, rue André-Pascal, 75775 PARIS CEDEX 16
ISBN 978-92-64-39276-2 – 2019

www.ingramcontent.com/pod-product-compliance
Ingram Content Group UK Ltd.
Pitfield, Milton Keynes, MK11 3LW, UK
UKHW051501290926
15471UKWH00008B/1348

9 789264 392762